Sale truck

D0043809

ENERGY LAW

IN A NUTSHELL

By

JOSEPH P. TOMAIN
Dean and
Nippert Professor of Law
University of Cincinnati
College of Law

HON. RICHARD D. CUDAHY
Judge, United States Court of Appeals
for the Seventh Circuit

THOMSON

WEST

Mat #40191639

COPYRIGHT © 1992 By WEST PUBLISHING CO.
COPYRIGHT © 2004 By West, a Thomson business
                    610 Opperman Drive
                    P.O. Box 64526
                    St. Paul, MN 55164–0526
                    1–800–328–9352

ISBN 0–314–15058–7

TEXT IS PRINTED ON 10% POST
CONSUMER RECYCLED PAPER

To Kathy, Joe, and John
J.P.T.

*To my wife, Janet, and children, Rick, Kit,
Tia, Dan, Michaela, Molly, and Patrick*
R.D.C.

*

OUTLINE

————————

V

Page

CHAPTER 2. ENERGY POLICY

CHAPTER 5. OIL

CHAPTER 6. NATURAL GAS

CHAPTER 7. COAL

OUTLINE

TABLE OF CASES

References are to Pages

XIII

*

ENERGY LAW
IN A NUTSHELL

*

INTRODUCTION

We have two goals for *Energy Law*. First, the book serves as a primer for the fundamental legal rules and institutions in the field of energy law. We will familiarize you with the principal cases and statutes as well as with the important federal agencies that affect the regulation of energy produced from various natural resources. Energy law became a term of art in the late 1970's with the passage of President Carter's National Energy Act. Nevertheless, energy law has its predecessors most notably public utility law and oil and gas law. Public utility law, with no less of a contributing scholar than Felix Frankfurter, addressed the public regulation of the natural gas and electric industries together with water industry regulation (and, of course, telecommunications and many aspects of transportation). Until the 1930's, as we will develop in more detail, public utility regulation was a matter of state law. During the New Deal, federal utility regulation of natural gas and electric utilities gained in importance and continues to do so to this day. Oil and gas law is a different matter entirely concentrating as it does on state common law and statutory law concerning the exploration and production of energy resources and the leasing of lands containing them.

Our second goal addresses lawyering skills. We have no illusion that most of you will actually find careers as energy law practitioners (although many of you may). Nevertheless, no one among you who practices law can avoid contact with administrative agencies. Administrative or regulatory law practice touches virtually every aspect of law from tax and patents to education and zoning. *Energy Law* then is an example of applied administrative law. As such, this book serves as an introduction to government regulation as a lawyering skill, which addresses the interaction of law, policy, and politics. Another way of stating our thesis is to say that all lawyers must understand the history and market and environment in which their client operates. Legal rules do not operate in a vacuum. Indeed, law in the books only comes alive in the world in a context of facts and circumstances as they pertain to a specific client. The lawyering skills, then, involve applying legal rules and using legal institutions in the service of a particular client, and doing so effectively requires an understanding of the world in which the client operates.

In the case of *Energy Law*, we approach the development of these skills in two ways and the book is divided into two parts accordingly. The first part of the book consists of four overview chapters entitled *Energy Economics*, *Energy Policy*, *Energy Administration*, and *Energy Decisionmaking*. The titles of the first three chapters are self-explanatory. The fourth chapter, *Energy Decisionmaking*, is not as self-explanatory as the others. In *Energy Decisionmaking* we discuss two methods used by administrative agencies to make hard choices among energy policies and particular rules. In that chapter we specifically examine cost-benefit analysis and ratemaking.

The second part of the book introduces you to lawyering skills by examining individual energy resources such as oil or coal, describing the relevant industry, and providing a regulatory overview of that particular resource. In this way, we hope to familiarize you with the interaction of law, markets, and regulation.

This version of *Energy Law* is really a third edition and is a revision of *Energy Law in a Nutshell* published in 1981 and also a revision of the energy law portion of *Energy and Natural Resources Law* published in 1992. Over those two decades, history has witnessed the creation of a great deal of energy and environmental law. From one perspective, energy law has changed little during the last two decades. Oil, natural gas, and electricity continue to dominate our country's energy economy in terms of supply and consumption, with little contribution made by renewable or alternative resources. Similarly, large-scale fossil fuel and nuclear plants dominate over smaller dispersed sources of energy. In the text we call this the dominant model of energy law and policy and it continues to depict processes currently.

From another perspective, however, much has changed. World policymakers increasingly discuss energy and the environment as constituting a single system, largely because energy production has major consequences in environmental protection. In doing so, international and domestic politicians and policymakers are developing a common language with which to discuss the relationship between energy and the environment in terms of a concept called sustainable development. It is also the case that some of the industries we discuss, most notably natural gas and electricity, are undergoing dramatic restructurings as our country attempts to move from command-and-control regulation at the federal level to deregulation and to more market-based regulations. The movement toward restructuring and decontrol continues and will presumably do so in the future.

Our work benefits from the first generation of energy law texts which include: Joseph P. Tomain & James E. Hickey with Sheila S. Hollis, ENERGY LAW AND POLICY (1989); Alfred C. Aman, Jr., ENERGY AND NATURAL RESOURCES LAW: THE REGULATORY DIALOGUE (1983); Donald N. Zillman & Laurence H. Lattman, ENERGY LAW (1982); Richard J. Pierce, Jr., Gary D. Allison & Patrick H. Martin, ECONOMIC REGULATION: ENERGY, TRANSPORTATION, AND UTILITIES (1980). Additional and more recent valuable resources include: Fred Bosselman, Jim Rossi, & Jacqueline Lang Weaver, ENERGY, ECONOMICS, AND THE ENVIRONMENT (2000); Energy Law Group, ENERGY LAW AND POLICY FOR THE 21ST CENTURY (2000); a multivolume treatise David J. Muchow & William A. Mogel, ENERGY LAW AND TRANSACTIONS

(2003); Marla E. Mansfield, ENERGY POLICY: THE REEL WORLD (2001); Richard J. Pierce, Jr., *Economic Regulation* (1994).

Finally, you will note that many of the following chapters contain many charts, all of which can be found in the United States Department of Energy Energy Information Agency's annual Energy Review published in October 2003 which can be found at http://www.eia.doe.gov/emeu/aer.

CHAPTER 1

ENERGY ECONOMICS

A. INTRODUCTION

Government regulation, at its most basic level, is a two-step process. First, policymakers assume that the market is functioning efficiently and fairly. If it is not, then a market imperfection is recognized. Second, policymakers can then choose to correct the imperfection through regulation. Not surprisingly, the regulatory process is more complex, involving as it does policy, politics, and law. Before we more fully develop the intricacies of the regulatory process, it is necessary to understand basic concepts in economics. In this chapter we describe the virtues of the market and its basic operations. We also identify market failures, those times when market operations fail to achieve the stated virtues. In subsequent chapters we explain in detail the regulatory responses to those market failures using examples from energy industries.

Economics has been defined as:

[T]he study of how society use scarce resources to produce valuable commodities and distribute them among different people. Paul A. Samuelson & William D. Nordhaus, *Economics* 4 (16th ed. 1998).

Energy law and policies are particularly susceptible to economic analysis because economics helps explain the distribution and allocation of scarce natural resources. The study of energy laws and policies begins with the exploration, recovery, and development of natural resources. Although these resources have alternative uses, moving water can be used for

5

recreation or for electricity production, for example, our study traces their conversion into usable energy. Next, we examine the distribution of those natural resources along the energy fuel cycle from exploration to the distribution of resources to energy producers then to various groups of consumers. Finally, we address economic aspects of our country's energy laws and policies. Before we discuss in detail how markets operate and when they fail to operate, we need to explain some background principles about the discipline of economics.

1. Behavioral Assumptions

In addition to the Samuelson & Nordhaus definition of economics, we can say more simply that economics is the study of how people act in the circumstance of limited resources and unlimited wants. As such, economics is a social or behavioral science because we are exploring human behavior. We find that students often come to the study of economics with some aversion. In part, we suspect, students are afraid of the subject because there is not supposed to be any math in law school. At a deeper level, aversion to economics is based on a suspicion or even dislike of *Homo Economicus*—Economic Man.

In *The Wealth of Nations*, Adam Smith describes Economic Man thus:

It is not from the benevolence of the butcher, the brewer, or the baker, that we expect our dinner, but from their regard to their own interest. We address ourselves, not to their humanity but to their self-love, and never talk to them of our own necessities but of their advantages. Nobody but a beggar chooses to depend chiefly upon the benevolence of his fellow-citizens.[1]

This description of human behavior is unappealing, stressing as it does individual, selfish material gain rather than other

1. As quoted in Jerry Z. Muller, *The Mind and the Market: Capitalism in Modern European Thought* 62 (2002).

perhaps more appealing values such as cooperation or charity. *Homo Economicus* is used for the limited purpose of constructing a heuristic, or model, for economic theory. In other words, economic analysis, like analysis in other disciplines, begins with certain assumptions about the world. In this case, economists make assumptions about human behavior in the marketplace.

Suspicions about the behavioral assumptions behind economics are both right and wrong. The suspicion is correct insofar as *Homo Economicus* is a caricature and not a full description of all human behavior. The suspicion is wrong in assuming too much about the economic model. In other words, the economic model works best when it is based on observations of behavior in the realm of markets. The model is more controversial and works less well when describing other facets of human behavior such as family life. Therefore, economists do not claim too much for their subject, although some economists, like Nobel Laureate Gary Becker, do make broader claims for the discipline. See for example Gary S. Becker, *Accounting for Tastes* (1996).

The behavioral assumptions underlying *Homo Economicus* are simply stated: man is a rational maximizer of individual self-interest. Each of these terms is subject to challenge. Nevertheless, as we will see, the assumptions hold up pretty well.

One might be put off by what seems to be the selfishness and greed of the wealth *maximizing* motivations attributed to people. Yet, economic analysis does not deal with the behavior of every individual all of the time. Rather, the economist speaks generally. All people are not solely motivated by a desire to *maximize* wealth all of the time. Nevertheless, ask yourself: Do you prefer more of something, money, pizza, whatever, rather than less? In short, the maximizing assumption seems to hold.

Another objection is that people do not act *rationally* all of the time. While this may be true, at times, for individuals, the alternative assumption of irrational behavior over the whole range of human conduct makes any analysis unworkable and does not conform with experience. Economists thus assume rationality rather than irrationality. Again, the rationalization assumption appears generally to hold. After all, in much of law reasonableness is the applicable legal standard.

A third objection is that these assumptions take little or no account of altruistic behavior. People certainly act in their *self-interest*; they also act in the interest of others despite adverse economic consequences. The objection that economic analysis disregards altruistic behavior seems right, unless one defines altruism as one person's acting for the benefit of someone else because it makes the actor feel good. Such an expansive definition is tautological and does not advance discussion. Altruism may pose a problem in defining self-interest. Altruism is also problematic for economic analysis.

Finally, the idea of market actors as rational maximizers of their *individual* self-interests leaves little room for collective action. If collective action is defined as action by a group of individuals whose end product is the sum of the end products of the individual actors, then there is no conflict with the economic concept of individual wealth maximization. If, however, collective action is defined as having an end product that is greater than the sum of the end products of the individual actors (synergy) then an economic model based on individual wealth maximization has nothing to say about such collective action. See, Lester Thurow, *Dangerous Currents* (1983).

Therefore economic analysis assumes that voluntary exchanges take place between rational self-interested actors for the purpose of maximizing wealth. There are two general classes of actors on the market stage—consumers and producers. Economists assume that both consumers and producers are rational maximizers of their individual self-interest. Broadly put, producers will produce goods from the least costly resources available in order to maximize their profits and consumers will pay less for an item rather than more in order to maximize the use of their money. From an economic perspective, both producers and consumers attempt to maximize their respective economic positions. These transactions take place in *orderly* markets—another assumption in the economic model. Below we describe in detail how markets operate when functioning well, and when functioning not so well.

In discussing the behavioral assumptions, we said that *Homo Economicus* was a caricature. As such, the caricature limits the ambit of how far the social science of economics can go. Indeed, the new disciplines of behavioral economics, experimental economics, and socio-economics all explore the limitations of the assumptions discussed above. You should also be aware of another limitation of economics which follows.

2. Positive and Normative Economics

It is important to understand the distinction between positive and normative economic analysis. Positive economic analysis is simply a descriptive statement of the economy. For example, it is accurate to describe the fact that as the cost of a gallon of gasoline at the pump rises people will consume less gasoline. Similarly, it is a descriptive statement to say that as the price of oil rises so will the revenue of oil producers. Positive analysis describes the world as it is.

Normative economic analysis describes how the world ought to be. For example, increased revenue for oil producers enables them to search for more oil which may or may not be *good* for the economy and for society. Comments about the *good* economy or the *good* society are normative statements. To say that economics is the study of efficiency is a positive statement. To say that efficiency is *good* is normative. Such normative statements are made regularly by economists, politicians, policy analysts, lawyers, and law students alike. The important point to note is that economists are specially trained to make technical positive statements about the economy and market operations. Economists are no better suited to make normative statements about what constitutes a good economy or a good society than any other persons trained in other disciplines, including the law.

Thus, while economic analysis is a useful tool for understanding the production, distribution, and consumption of scarce natural resources, illuminating questions about energy goals or policies; economic analysis alone is not better suited to make normative statements about how our energy policies, or our society for that matter, should be structured. Questions about whether or not to drill for offshore oil or to develop solar technology have both positive and normative dimensions. It is a positive matter to say how much investment in either project will cost. It is a normative matter to say whether society should invest in one project or the other or both.

Energy laws and policies are discussed positively and normatively. A particular law or policy can be measured against whether or not it maximizes wealth. In other words, whether the law or policy is efficient. Such is a positive economic analysis. Another way of evaluating an energy law or policy is to ask whether or not it results in a fair distribution of wealth or resources or, in other words, is equitable. This form of analysis is normative and is a question often raised by the discipline of welfare economics. These categories of efficiency (positive) and equity (normative) permeate discussions of energy laws and policies.

3. Understanding Property

For any market to operate, enforceable property rights are necessary. In fact, the common law baseline of property, contract, and torts rules essentially provide that necessary protection. Property law establishes the set of legal relationships that *define* property. Contract law enables the *exchange* of property. Tort law *protects*, as best it can, property from injury or damage. Together, property, contract, and tort laws create and maintain economic markets. Hopefully, you will find that last statement fairly straightforward and non-controversial. Matters are only slightly complicated by the fact that in the field of energy law and policy, there are three types of property interests to note—private goods, common goods, and public goods.

a. Private Goods

Private goods easily fit the usual understanding of property. A ton of coal, a cord of wood, even a thousand cubic feet of natural gas (stored within some container) can each be considered a private good. Such goods can be owned, used, and transferred in the ordinary and legal senses of those terms. The traditional concept of private goods means that property rights and duties can be defined *completely*; that owners of property can *exclude* others from using that specified property; and that property can be *transferred* easily from one owner to another. Private goods, then, are characterized by completeness, exclusivity, and transferability.

The coal, wood, and containerized natural gas referred to above have these three attributes. The owner knows the limits and extent of ownership, can exclude others from using these goods, and can transfer these goods for another person's use or ownership. Such goods can be relatively easily priced and exchanged in either a private transaction or in a larger market exchange. Such exchange transactions are relatively easy because both the nature of the good and the attendant legal rights and duties incident to the goods are openly known and understood.

All natural resources do not share these characteristics. Recall that the natural gas example above was qualified in that the natural gas was containerized. Absent containerization, natural gas does not share all of these private property attributes. The inability of a particular natural resource to be owned completely, or the inability to exclude others from it, or the inability to easily transfer ownership, requires economic analysts to talk and think differently about some natural resources—such as natural gas.

b.   Common Goods

Common goods refer to a separate category of resources that are frequently migratory. Natural resources such as oil, natural gas, and water do not stay in one place; rather, they migrate in light of geophysical constraints. Common goods, again natural gas is a good example, must be captured before an owner can exercise dominion or control over it. The problem is that surface owners are uncertain about the placement, even about the existence, of natural gas under the surface. Consequently, common, migrating goods require a different set of property rules in order to define, transfer, or exclude others from their use.

It should be recognized that two attributes, the need for capture and the inability to exclude others, combine to produce what is known as "the tragedy of the commons." To understand this phenomenon, consider an underground reservoir of oil. From the surface, the dimensions of the reservoir are not known and, not surprisingly, the reservoir does not honor any legal boundaries established on the surface. In order to obtain economic benefits from the oil, the surface owner must drill into the reservoir.

The legal (and economic) incentive to drill is known as the rule of capture, which holds that whoever captures the resource keeps it. The reward goes not to the frugal interest holder who keeps the oil in the ground for the future, but to the person who drills and captures it. A landowner is encouraged by the rule of capture to bring the resource to the surface before a neighboring landowner or lessee does. The tragedy is that such common natural resources are overconsumed rather than produced in response to market demand. When there is overconsumption of a resource, the free market in that resource is in disequilibrium and government regulation is usually necessary to correct the defect. State oil and gas conservation laws, for example, are the regulatory response to the tragedy of the commons created by the rule of capture. These laws attempt to limit overconsumption by reducing production and conserving supply.

c. Public Goods

Air, sunlight, and wind cannot be owned in the same ways that a ton of coal, an acre of timber, or even migratory oil or natural gas, can be owned. Because ownership, a person's legal rights and duties relative to a particular good, cannot be completely defined, such goods have different economic consequences.

First, dominion (control) over these resources is difficult, and in many instances, impossible to assess. No one can capture the sun or control the wind, even though energy from these resources can be harnessed. "Rights" to air, sunlight, and wind cannot be defined completely. Because dominion or control is difficult or impossible to maintain, so too is transfer. No one can sell you the wind, even though someone can sell you a kilowatt of electricity generated by a windmill. Nor can anyone sell your sunlight, but they can sell you a solar battery, and in the proper circumstances the law can protect your view of the sun. Compare *Fontainebleau Hotel Corp. v. Forty–Five Twenty–Five, Inc.* (Fla. Dist. Ct. App. 1959) (claim to a right to sunlight not protected) with *Prah v. Maretti* (Wis. 1982) (claim to a right to sunlight protected). Finally, and most perplexing for economic analysis, one person cannot exclude another person from also using some resources. Everyone can sit in the warmth of the sun or emit discharges into the air as examples.

Because ownership cannot be completely defined or easily transferred, and because persons cannot be excluded, the products created by public goods are very difficult to price accurately. In fact, public goods are too often undervalued and, consistent with economic theory, overconsumed. You are familiar with this phenomenon in your study of nuisance law especially in the case of environmental pollution. If a manufacturer pollutes a stream rather than installing pollution control equipment, the goods it produces will cost less than if the cost of the installed equipment was included in the price of the product.

Undervaluation and overconsumption have two interrelated effects—waste and externalities. Waste occurs because apart from capital costs, public goods do not cost anything; they will therefore be consumed disproportionately to their "real" value. Externalities occur because, even though wind and sunlight have zero costs, the users who construct windmills and solar collectors may obstruct views or use land in ways that generate social costs. These costs are not included in the price of the energy generated from the windmill or solar collector. Social costs are the result of overconsumption of low or zero cost resources. These social costs are called externalities precisely because they are not included in, and are external to, the price of the product.

Although we use the terms natural resources, property, and goods interchangeably, please remember that different resources have distinct property attributes that affect economic, policy, and legal analyses.

B. MARKET VIRTUES

Our discussion of economics concentrates on microeconomic analysis which is the operation of a firm within a market as distinct from macroeconomics which examines the overall economy in such matters as rates of unemployment, the amount of money in the economy, interest rates, and the like—the types of things in the domain of Federal Reserve Chairman Alan Greenspan.

The microeconomic market has several virtues, including efficiency, which are classically and wisely described also by Adam Smith in *The Wealth of Nations*:

> Every individual is continually exerting himself to find out the most advantageous employment for whatever capital he can command. It is his own advantage, indeed, and not that of the society, which he has in view. But the study of his own advantage naturally, or rather necessarily leads him to prefer that employment which is the most advantageous to the society. . . .

> He generally, indeed, neither intends to promote the public interest, nor knows how much he is promoting it. By preferring the support of domestic to that of foreign industry, he intends only his own security; and by directing that industry in such a manner as its produce may be of the greatest value, he intends only his own gain, and he is in this, as in many other cases, led by an invisible hand to promote an end which was no part of his intention. Nor is it always the worse for the society that it was no part of it. By pursuing his own interest he frequently promotes that of the society more effectually than when he really intends to promote it."[2]

Through Smith's "invisible hand," market transactions take place as buyers and sellers haggle over goods and prices. In a competitive market, this haggling causes the highest amount of surplus to consumers and producers alike. In other words, through bargaining, consumers are able to get the goods that they most want at the prices they most desire. Similarly, producers are able to respond to consumer demand through new products, innovations, and the like. In short, market transactions advance the economy to its most efficient state, which is to say that resources are put to their most

2. *Id.* at 65–66.

highly valued uses as determined by free bargaining among consumers and producers.

In this way, wealth is maximized, innovation encouraged, consumer and producer surplus maximized, and people's desires are satisfied. It is also the case that liberty and equality are maximized insofar as all consumers are free and equal in the marketplace where all votes are equally counted, votes being dollars. Market advocates therefore claim that the market virtues have both desirable economic and political consequences.

Before those virtues are attained there must be a perfectly competitive market (PCM). A PCM can be realized if a market has the following attributes:

1.   Numerous buyers and sellers.

2.   Product homogeneity.

3.   Large enough quantity of goods so that no single buyer or seller has market power.

4.   Perfect product information.

5.   Freedom of entry and exit from the marketplace.

In most cities, pizza is a good example of a PCM. There are numerous pizzerias such that no single pizzeria controls the market. While consumers have preferences for one pizza over another, pizza is pizza, i.e. the product is homogeneous. Consumers can easily obtain good information (toppings, price, delivery, etc.) about the product. And it does not take a huge investment to open a pizzeria (market entry) or convert one to a sandwich shop (market exit).

Experience tells us that these attributes are not always present and we will discuss the absence of particular attributes when we discuss market failures. A notable example of a market without one of these attributes would be the Standard Oil Company at the turn of the 20th century which dominated the oil market in this country and was judicially determined to be a monopoly. *Standard Oil Co. of New Jersey v. United*

States (S.Ct.1911). It is also the case that market actors do what they can to prevent competition. Actors try to eliminate other actors; differentiate the products from others; capture markets; control product information; and, restrict entry. Think about Microsoft for a moment. Does Bill Gates prefer to compete with Apple or Linux, or would he prefer to be the only game in town?

C. MARKET OPERATIONS

Assuming that the market has the necessary characteristics to be competitive, then the market achieves its virtues by the following operations.

1. Demand

The law of demand is the fundamental economic principle driving the market. The law means that a person will be less willing to pay for another unit of a good if the price rises. If unleaded gas can be purchased for $1.20 per gallon, and if the price rose to $1.50 per gallon, the law of demand says that less gasoline will be purchased. The law is graphically shown by a downward sloping demand curve (D):

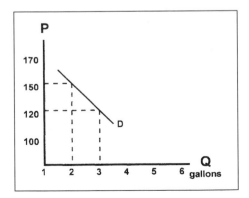

Quite simply, as prices increase, demand decreases. According to the slope of the graph, at a price of $1.20, three Quantities (here gallons) of gasoline will be purchased, whereas only two gallons will be purchased at $1.50. Ask yourself if the law of demand makes sense. Would you buy more or fewer audio CDs if the price rose from $15 to $25?

2. Supply

The law of supply is a corollary to the law of demand. As prices increase, producers are encouraged to place more goods on the market. The classic supply curve is upward sloping. The higher the price of a cord of wood, the greater the quantity of timber that will be produced for the market. The graph below demonstrates that four cords of wood (Q) will be placed on the market at $50 per cord (P), whereas only three cords of wood will be placed on the market at $40 per cord. Again, imagine yourself as a producer of oil, will you place more or less oil on the market if the price of a barrel of oil rises to $40 from $20?

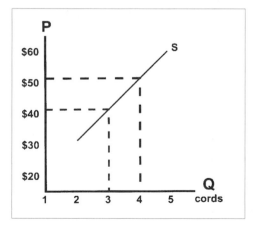

These simple, perhaps obvious, laws of supply and demand are significant for natural resources economics. As the price of a barrel of oil rises on the global oil market, there will be an increase in oil drilling in order to profit from the more lucrative market. Likewise, when the price of interstate natural gas drops below that of intrastate gas, then natural gas producers will try to put their product on the more profitable intrastate market.

The laws of supply and demand determine which goods are produced and, in turn, which resources are used in production. When the price of oil is higher than the price of natural gas, then producers, following the supply curve, are encouraged to produce oil, just as consumers, following the demand curve, are encouraged to purchase natural gas. It would seem, then, that producers' desire for higher prices and consumers' desire for lower prices produce an unresolvable conflict. Not so. Rather, the give and take between producers and consumers push the market toward equilibrium as consumers' demand has an upward effect on prices and as producers' supply has a downward effect to the point of equilibrium.

3. Equilibrium

Imagine a market for coal in which the equilibrium price **E** is $23 per ton. The graphic depiction of that market would have the demand and the supply curves intersect at $23 per ton:

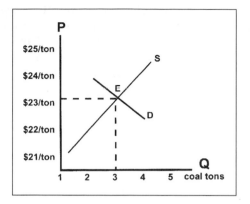

At the equilibrium point **E**, three tons of coal will be sold at $23. Given a competitive market, i.e., buyers and sellers so numerous that no single buyer or seller can affect price, no producer will supply coal at $24 per ton because there will be no buyers because consumers can purchase all they want at $23. Likewise, no consumer *can* purchase at $22 because no producer can afford to supply at that price; otherwise they will go out of business. However, these consequences follow only from a perfectly competitive market. In the absence of such a highly sensitive degree of competition, producers and consumers will experiment with prices, some offering and buying at $24, and others at $22, until the optimum allocation of goods reaches an equilibrium of $23.

Price equilibrium has another effect, particularly as it relates to government price regulation. Imagine a government subsidy to a coal producer which raises the price to $24 for the purpose of protecting producers. That subsidy will have the following effects. The subsidy will increase price and quantity because producers will put more product on the market. Because price increases, however, demand will decline. The consequence is a *surplus* because S > D. Similarly, imagine the government imposing a price ceiling on coal at $22 to protect consumers. In this case, the price ceiling will reduce price and supply and increase demand. Consequently, a *short-age* results because D > S. In both instances, the market is in disequilibrium as a result of government policy choices.

4. Costs

Producers place goods on the market when it is profitable for them to do so. Profit is comprised of revenue minus costs. When the costs of drilling for oil exceed the revenue gained, then it is no longer profitable to drill and no oil will be produced.

Costs follow a pattern. In the beginning of the production cycle, costs start high because of initial investment. However, costs decline as more units are produced. The initial costs of producing the first barrel of oil are extremely high, but fall for the next several thousand barrels. Costs will decline until there are diminishing returns, i.e., until it becomes necessary to invest capital to drill deeper, or to use enhanced recovery techniques, or to drill another well. Each of these latter events adds costs which diminishes profits. In other words, as output increases, costs for the production of a single unit will decline until they reach the point of diminishing returns; then costs will increase. Consequently, cost curves are U-shaped.

It is also important to distinguish between marginal and average costs. Average costs are determined by dividing all costs (C) by the quantity of units produced (Q), C/Q, as the cost curve in the next figure demonstrates.

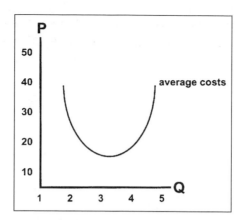

Costs are also defined as marginal costs—the costs associated with the production of the next unit of a good. The marginal cost curve is different than the average cost curve and shifts slightly to reflect the costs associated with the law of diminishing returns. During the production cycle, costs per unit first decline, costs then rise as more investment in production is required. The marginal cost curve compares with the average cost curve as follows:

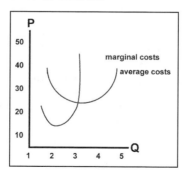

The distinction between average cost and marginal cost is important. If a single oil well, for example, produces 1,000 barrels of oil for a total cost of $20,000, then the *average cost*

is $20 per barrel. If the next barrel of oil costs $25 to produce because of higher drilling costs, then the *average cost* is approximately $20.005 ($20,025 divided by 1001 barrels) even though the *marginal cost* is $25 (the cost of producing the 1,001st unit). A producer should charge $25 for the 1001st barrel rather than $20.005, because $25 accurately represents production costs for that particular barrel of oil.

The distinction between average and marginal costs is also important because average costs will underestimate current costs in an inflationary market. Marginal costs give better information about current production costs and profitability. The marginal cost curve is the individual firm's supply curve because it is the better indicator of current costs and profitability.

5. Marginal Revenue

A discussion of marginal revenue demonstrates why the marginal cost of producing the next unit is the more accurate indicator of cost (and of profit). Optimum price and profit are based on marginal revenue not on total revenue. Producers want to maximize profits. However, profit maximization does not depend on selling the most units. Rather, profit is maximized when marginal cost equals marginal revenue. The following chart shows the relationship between revenue and profits:

Q	P	TR	TC	TP	MC	MR
1	10	10	8	2		
2	9	18	10	8	2	8
3	8	24	14	10	4	6
4	7	28	16	12	2	4
5	**6**	**30**	**18**	**12**	**2**	**2**
6	5	30	20	10	2	0
7	4	28	22	6	2	−2
8	3	24	24	0	2	−4
9	2	18	26	−8	2	−6
10	1	10	28	−18	2	−8

Q = Quantity   TP = Total Profit
P = Price   MC = Marginal Cost
TR = Total Revenue   MR = Marginal Revenue
TC = Total Cost

Notice that total revenue (TR) is maximized at 30, when either 5 or 6 units (Q) are sold. Contrast this level of revenue with the TR of 10, when 10(Q) is the maximum level of units sold. The price must decline as the quantity sold increases in a competitive market where the laws of supply and demand function. To sell more quantity, the producer must lower price, thus running the risk of reducing total revenue. Even in a "gas war" the local gas station cannot lower prices indefinitely. Notice, then, how TR declines as more units are sold after 6(Q). At some point in the production cycle, increasing the number of units sold does not increase total revenue.

From a total revenue standpoint, it makes no difference whether 5 or 6 units are sold because TR is the same at 30. However, if one considers total profitability (TP), then at 5 units TP is 12, and at 6 units TP is 10. TP is the result of deducting total cost (TC) from total revenue (TR). Therefore, a greater profit is made by selling 5 units rather than by selling 6 or more units. Notice that profit is maximized when marginal cost (MC) is equal to marginal revenue (MR), i.e., MC = MR = 2.

6. Price Elasticity of Demand

The law of demand requires that for every change in price there will be change in demand. For every price rise, there will be a decline in demand. The more refined question is: What is the rate of change? If for every 1% price rise there is a 1% decrease in demand, then the price elasticity is said to be unitary. Elastic prices are those prices that respond with a greater percentage decrease in demand for a corresponding increase in price. If audio CDs rise $5, will you buy less or stop buying altogether?

Some goods, however, are so highly valued that there will be less of a percentage decline in demand for every corresponding percentage price increase. Such a situation is said to be inelastic. When prices are inelastic, producers can raise prices without a proportionate corresponding decrease in demand. Products such as water or blood are examples of inelasticity—people will continue to buy as prices rise. Inelastic demand has the effect of increasing producers' revenues and effecting a greater transfer of resources from consumers to producers. For many years, electricity prices were thought to be so inelastic that electric utilities could raise prices to increase profits (absent close public utility commission oversight). However, as electricity (and all energy) prices escalated at a rate greater than inflation, consumers did respond to rising electricity prices by reducing consumption. This reduction in demand had the result of forcing electricity prices down.

These six market operations allow the PCM to achieve the virtues earlier noted. Markets for ball point pens, handheld computers, and hamburgers are examples of at least workably competitive markets. These markets have numerous buyers and sellers, and a great variety of alternatives. Consequently, prices are competitively set as buyers and sellers move into and out of these markets. Natural resources, particularly those used in the production of energy, often do not achieve a state of workable competition because of the existence of market failures. Some resources like oil and natural gas may have property characteristics (notably their migratory nature) that prevent proper supplies from reaching the market without some government oversight. Other industries, e.g., electricity and natural gas transportation, are structured in such a way that firms can exercise market power over consumers. And, other resources, such as the use of air and water, entail costs that are not included in the price of the product. When markets are not competing, government may intervene in order to remedy a market failure and move that market toward competition.

D. MARKET FAILURES

In our political economy, there are two effects of recognizing a market failure. The first effect is descriptive. The identification of the failure points out the inefficiency or unfairness of the market. The second effect is prescriptive. Once a market failure is identified, then this identified defect becomes a justification for government intervention, and helps indicate what sort of regulatory tool is appropriate. The following list of market failures or imperfections is derived from Justice Stephen Breyer's scholarly work, *Regulation and Its Reform* (1982).

1. Monopoly

Some industries, e.g., public utilities and railroads, are so structured that only a small number of firms or only one firm may enter the market. The entry costs are high and viable alternatives are not available. These industries tend towards exercising monopoly or oligopoly power. Because there is an absence of competition, firms need not set prices according to the laws of supply and demand, or according to their costs.

Rather, firms in a monopoly position can restrict output, increase profits, and consequently, impose a social welfare loss by charging higher than competitive prices. Monopoly is the opposite of the PCM and monopoly (and its defects) can be graphically described.

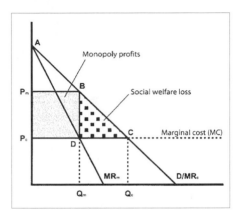

The figure above indicates how a monopolist sets its prices. The monopolists' marginal revenue curve (MR_m) intersects the marginal cost curve (MC) in a different place than it intersects the demand (D) curve which can also be described as the competitive marginal revenue curve (MR_C). In a competitive market, goods are priced at P_c, and quantity Q_c is produced because P_c and Q_c are derived from the intersection of the MC and D/M R_c curves. (Here, the MC curve is flat, assuming a competitive firm in an industry).

The monopolist, however, derives its price and quantity from the intersection of the MC curve and the *monopolist's* marginal revenue curve MR_m. Thus, the monopolist prices at P_m and he produces at Q_m. Notice that the result of the monopoly pricing is a price *increase* from P_c to P_m and a quantity *decrease* from Q_c to Q_m. There are other anticompetitive effects caused by monopolist pricing.

This lower output and higher price results in monopoly profits represented by the darkened rectangle ($P_c P_m BD$). The shaded triangle (BCD) indicates a loss of consumer surplus or a social welfare loss. This loss occurs because to raise prices, the monopolist cuts production below the level that would have been reached in a competitive market, and consumers are forced to forego consumption of the monopolized good for which their marginal benefit, represented by their willingness to pay, exceeds the marginal cost of production. In other words, there are consumers that would have been willing to buy goods along a price range from P_c to P_m. However, these consumers are denied this opportunity because output has been reduced and those goods are not available for consumption. Thus, in a monopoly market, consumers pay higher prices than a competitive market would dictate, and they must forego some consumption opportunities.

Another way of graphically demonstrating this loss is to compare the consumer surplus in a competitive market, represented by the large triangle (ACP_c), with the consumer surplus in the monopoly market, represented by the small triangle (ABP_m). The difference in consumer surplus between these two triangles is allocated to the monopolist's profits and to a social, or deadweight, loss.

The exercise of such monopoly power has been found to be inconsistent with the public interest because prices are higher, quantity is lower, and consumer surplus is less than in the PCM. Regulation is therefore needed to set prices at competitive levels.

It is often said that the transmission systems for electricity and natural gas utilities are "natural monopolies." According to theory, because of large capital costs of entry (e.g. costs of land acquisition and capital construction), it would be economically wasteful to have two or more utilities attempt to serve the same area. Society can be better served with a single electricity transmission line than several because it is wasteful to build more when one will satisfy demand. To avoid waste and monopoly profits, rates (prices) are set by government.

2. Rent Control

Another justification for regulation is to control or capture windfall profits. These are also referred to as economic rents. Economic rents occur when there are sudden increases in the price of a resource without a corresponding increase in costs. In the regulation of the oil industry in the late 1970s, the rationale behind imposition of the Crude Oil Windfall Profits Tax was that if oil prices were allowed to rise to world levels (levels that were artificially high because of the OPEC cartel), then existing domestic oil stocks, which cost less to produce, would also rise to the world price level. The result would be higher profits from domestic reserves unrelated to domestic producers' costs. These profits were seen as excessive and as a "windfall" to domestic oil companies. These producers' windfall profits were taxed, and the revenues raised from these taxes were transferred for other public purposes in the belief that the profits were not "earned" by producers. Iraq's invasion of Kuwait and its threats to Saudi Arabia also caused the world price of oil to rise to the economic benefit of domestic reserves.

3. Externalities

Externalities are costs that are not borne by the actors in a particular transaction. If a manufacturing plant is allowed to pollute and the property of neighboring homeowners is devalued because of the pollution, that devaluation is an externality or spillover cost of the decision to allow the plant to operate. Because polluting firms do not voluntarily incur social costs, regulation appears needed to compensate for the fact that the price of the product does not reflect the costs of production. Environmental laws protecting air and water and land through standard setting are the most pervasive examples of the way government regulation deals with externalities.

4. Information Costs

Regulation is also designed to provide consumers with information that may not be made readily available by private industry because of the high cost of acquiring and distributing that information. Further, information itself has value. Frequently, a firm will not voluntarily incur the costs involved with acquiring or distributing information. Nor will firms give away valuable information. Therefore, in order to make information available so that consumers can make informed market decisions, government will intervene.

Health warnings on cigarettes, mileage ratings on cars, and ingredients labeling are all examples of government mandated distribution of information. Because the market does not supply this information voluntarily, government intervention serves to provide information with which consumers can make choices. Although consumers as a class may have the interest and wherewithal, economically and politically, to seek this information, individual consumers do not. It is often impractical to aggregate large groups of consumers, because the costs of doing so are prohibitively high.

5. Excessive Competition

Excessive competition is another market defect, occurring when prices are set so low that rival companies go out of business. After enough companies leave the market, the remaining few can then engage in monopolistic or oligopolistic pricing. The regulatory response is to set prices at a level where firms can stay competitive. The airline and trucking industries are often cited as examples of excessive competition. These industries petitioned government for relief from that competition, and for price setting at levels sufficient to maintain reasonable profitability. These industries have been deregulated and questions occur concerning whether or not deregulation has resulted in more competition or less. Deregulation in the airline industry, for example, has increased flights, raised and lowered prices in various markets, reduced amenities, eliminated many new entrants, and has given rise to occasional calls for re-regulation, some even by industry actors.

6.   Scarce Resource Allocation

Regulation may also be imposed on an industry to alleviate scarcity. In a time of a natural gas shortage, for example, producers could find it more profitable to service one class of consumers over another. Scarcity is consonant with a market dominated by a profit principle, but it does not necessarily bring about a fair distribution of resources. In the face of a shortage in the natural gas market, government intervened to allocate resources where they are needed most, such as to hospitals, schools, and critical manufacturing facilities.

7.   Rationalization

Another word for rationalization is standardization. Efficiencies are realized when light bulbs, even when made by different manufacturers, are a uniform size, and when electricity service is of a uniform power. If one firm, or a small group of firms, control a particular market, then there is less incentive to move to widespread uniformity. Government regulation, however, can facilitate that uniformity by rationalizing an industry.

8.   Paternalism

Just as the word implies, there are times when government will step into a market because policymakers either want to correct or to preempt behavior. Speed limits, pesticide labeling requirements, and fuel standards each can be seen as a form of paternalist government regulation.

9. Moral Hazard

A moral hazard is a situation in which the probability of a loss, as well as the size of the loss, may be increased because a person has less of an incentive to take precautions. Another way of conceptualizing moral hazard is thinking of it as a situation when someone else pays. Expense accounts, insurance, and medical benefits have the effect of encouraging consumers to consume more than they would if the expenses were internalized (paid directly by the consumer). In the energy and natural resources area, historic cost ratemaking for natural gas and electric utilities is an example of a form of moral hazard, because a utility can build more plants with the knowledge that its customers will pay for the plant through higher rates. This form of ratemaking led to historic excess capacity in the 1970s.

E.   ECONOMICS AND REGULATION

Let's return to the beginning of the chapter where we said that government regulation is a two-step process. Policymakers would prefer that markets work fairly and efficiently and yet there are times when that is not the case and market imperfections are found. These market imperfections, then, become the justifications for government regulation. There is a wide scope of regulation at every level of government in the country. Federal government regulation affects the labels on our food, state property taxes affect public school financing, and local zoning laws determine property uses. As broad as government regulation is, however, there are only a handful of reasons why government enters a market, as Justice Breyer's list of market failures demonstrates. The corollary is also true that there are only a handful of regulatory responses to those market failures and it is this learning we hope you find valuable. We would like you to recognize the fact that there are specific forms of regulation that are used in a variety of circumstances. Ratesetting, for example, has been used to set rates for electricity, natural gas, telephone, and cable television at one time or another in our history. It is also the case that we use a licensing process for nuclear power plants, pharmaceuticals, and radio stations as another example of the flexibility of a particular form of regulation.

How is it, then, that if there are only a handful of reasons for government intervention and only a handful of regulatory responses that the scope and breadth of government regulation is as wide and broad as it is? It is our intent to answer that question by discussing a variety of energy laws and policies. The story that we are about to tell you has its historical dimensions and it also involves the interaction of law, policy, and politics in their many guises. Government regulation has existed since the founding of our country and we have no doubt that it will continue to exist. Still, there seems to be a pattern to regulation to which we now turn.

F. THE REGULATORY LIFE CYCLE

In the United States, as well as other capitalist democracies, government policymakers (executives, legislators, administrators, and judges) begin thinking about society from the *laissez-faire* premise that the free market is preferred over government regulation because of the market virtues discussed above. However, *laissez-faire* is more an ideal than a reality. The reality is that when the market fails, government regulation is often used to correct the defect and stabilize the market. Government regulation, however, may itself fail to achieve its objectives and the system then experiences regulatory failure. Consequently, the process of government regulation can be seen as a "life cycle," falling into six more or less identifiable stages:

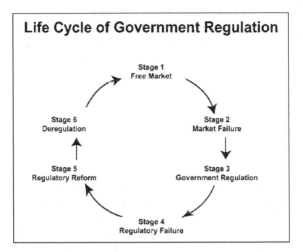

Stage 1, the Free Market, is the period when there is no government intervention in an industry or market. Consistent with our political system of democratic capitalism, this stage adopts a version of *laissez-faire*, limited government. If the market is functioning properly or reasonably well, and if the market is efficient and fair, then government intrusion cannot improve the situation. In the face of a well-working (efficient and fair) market, government regulation will, at a minimum, add unnecessary administrative costs, thus reducing allocative efficiency and causing inequitable distributions. Such a market will not improve with government price or quality controls. Rather, these regulations will likely raise prices, reduce supply, and drive some producers from the market, thus reducing competition.

Achieving or maintaining an ideal free market is difficult. Frequently, a market is in disequilibrium because of the existence of a market failure as earlier described. The existence and identification of market failures become the justification for government intervention into private enterprise that moves regulation from Stage 2 into Stage 3.

A justification for government intervention, Stage 3, is a necessary but insufficient condition for government regulation, because government must respond with the correct regulatory tool to the perceived market failure. The consequence of using the wrong regulatory tool, for example, using price supports to correct inadequate information, may worsen the economy rather than improve it. The goal of a government regulation is to improve a particular market situation by making it more efficient, more fair, or both.

The wrong regulatory tool may make government intervention into the private market more costly, or impose the costs more unfairly, or both. The use of inadequate or incorrect regulation results in regulatory failure, or Stage 4. Questions about the 1990 Amendments to the Clean Air Act, estimated to cost tens of billions of dollars, emerged because the regulatory costs could outweigh the benefits. Such analysis of costs and benefits raises myriad technical, social, and economic questions which ultimately must be resolved through the political process. The question, however, is always the same— do the costs of regulation outweigh the benefits? If clean air regulation costs more than the benefits, then there will be regulatory failure.

There are two reactions to regulatory failure. In the last two stages of the regulatory life cycle, either government can respond by correcting the failure through regulatory reform Stage 5, or government can extract itself from the market altogether by deregulation Stage 6, i.e., by eliminating regulations, thus reverting back to Stage 1—the free market.

Not every regulatory effort goes through each of these stages. A program caught in the stage of government failures, for example, need not entertain a package of regulatory reforms, and may instead proceed to deregulation. Still, the life cycle, and its underlying aspirations for efficiency and fairness, highlight the role that the political process plays in our system of government regulation. The underlying ideology of government regulation is to correct inequities in markets in response to the reality that markets do not always run smoothly. As you continue to study energy law and policy you will continue to engage questions about the amount and sufficiency of the government regulation of the economy.

CHAPTER 2

ENERGY POLICY

Introduction

As this book goes to publication, the first session of the 108th Congress has debated and ultimately failed to pass the Energy Security Act of 2003. The failure to pass this Act is emblematic of energy policy in the United States. The bill was introduced and passed by the House before moving on to the Senate where it was blocked by what it is fair to call a Democratic filibuster. We say that it is fair to call it a Democratic filibuster even though some Senate Republicans such as John McCain vigorously opposed the legislation, calling it a "cookie jar" of goodies for the taking by private interests. We can also say this even though it was supported by Senate Democratic leadership such as Tom Daschle because the proposed legislation brought energy projects into his state of South Dakota.

What is emblematic about the energy legislation is that, while it purports to take a comprehensive look at the energy needs of our country, quite the opposite is the case. Instead, the 1200 page bill addresses a wide variety of specific issues, rather than coordinating any national energy policy or strategy. This lack of coordination in fact has been the history of energy policy in the United States.

To some extent, the word "policy" is a misnomer. At one level, the United States has no full scale, comprehensive or coordinated national energy policy. At another level of generality, however, we can say that the United States has developed an energy policy affecting a set of policies in industries that has continued for over 100 years. This chapter will explain the evolution of what is more or less a dominant model of policy as long as you are aware that we use the term policy loosely and we do not use it to mean a well-coordinated, thought-out plan for the future.

A. ENERGY FACTS

We should acquaint you with some energy terminology. First, the standard definition of energy is the capacity to do work. Most energy in the United States comes from natural resources such as petroleum which, when converted to gasoline, is the major fuel used throughout the transportation industry. Other natural resources, predominantly coal, are burned to create heat, which, in turn, boils water to create steam which turns turbines to generate electricity. Indeed, as you will learn, our energy economy can be divided roughly in half between petroleum and electricity. As individual consumers who drive and use computers, we are not only familiar with these resources, we are dependent upon them.

These two examples of conversion of natural resources into useable energy involve the first two laws of thermodynamics which play important roles in energy policy. The first law of thermodynamics is *conservation*—energy changes form but does not dissipate. In the above example of electricity, *potential* energy in coal, was converted into *heat* energy in steam, which in turn was converted to *work* energy in the form of electricity. If we were to measure all of the potential energy, heat energy, and work energy we would find that they were equal to the amount of energy before and after the conversion. The second law of thermodynamics is *entropy*—energy moves from a localized to dispersed space. Examples are that ice melts and hot pans cool down into the air around them.

Both laws have direct importance for energy policy. Think for a moment about generating electricity from coal. The (1) coal was burned, (2) to heat water, (3) to turn turbines, (4) to generate electricity, (5) to be distributed along high voltage lines, (6) to power your home computer. If we were to measure all of the energy at each of these six steps they would be equal to the energy available (potential energy) contained in the coal to be burned. However, at each step, some of the potential energy in the coal is dispersed either into the air or throughout the distribution system. Consequently, 100% of potential energy is *not* converted into 100% work energy; some is released into the surrounding environment. We casually, and imprecisely say that energy is "lost" in the conversion process. In fact, all of the potential energy is not fully utilized. Thus, one aspect of energy policy is to conserve energy by reducing waste.

B.   ENERGY OVERVIEW

Below we have reprinted several graphs depicting energy in the United States from Energy Information Administration, *Annual Energy Review 2002* (November 2003). Some of the graphs describe U.S. Energy over a fifty-year period. This energy history reveals three significant points about energy policy.

First, as demonstrated by Figure I, *Energy Overview, 1949–2002*, until the late 1950s, the United States was energy self-sufficient; then domestic consumption outgrew domestic production, particularly in oil, and the country became a net importer of energy.

Figure 1

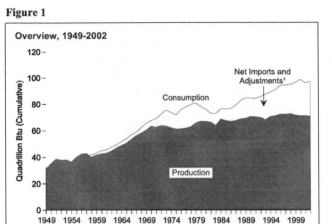

The next three graphs depict the trend of imports and exports over the last 50 years.

Figure 2

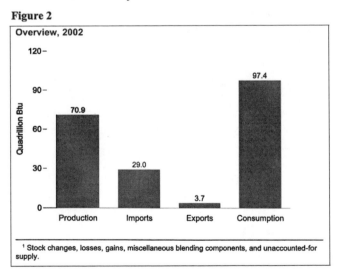

[1] Stock changes, losses, gains, miscellaneous blending components, and unaccounted-for supply.

Figure 3

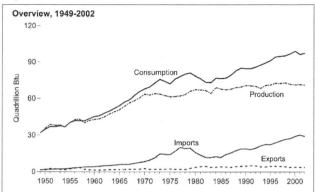

Figure 4

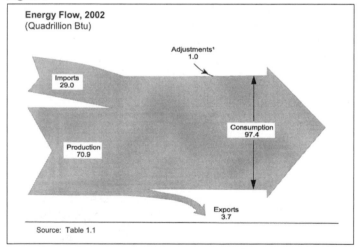

Continuing our look at imports and exports, the following graph shows that the United States is a net exporter of coal and a net importer of petroleum.

Figure 5. Energy Imports and Exports

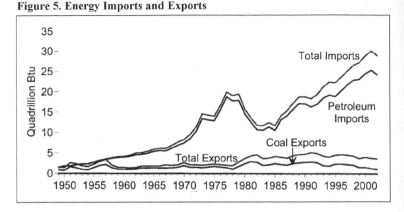

In 2001, the United States imported 27% of all energy consumed, again mostly oil.

The second significant fact, not surprisingly, is that energy consumption continues to increase. As you will see, in Figure 6 *Energy Consumption History and Outlook 1949–2025*, the lines on the graphs continue to rise over time.

Figure 6. Energy Consumption History and Outlook, 1949-2025

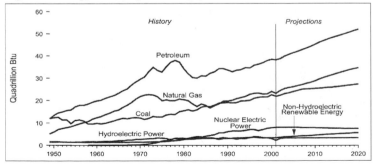

Increased energy consumption has significant policy implications as the story of energy policy will show. Briefly, however, we raise an initial point: What is the correlation between energy and the economy? In other words, if there is a direct relationship, then the more energy that we consume, the better the economy. For most of the 20th Century, this correlation was both assumed and non-controversial. However, as citizens and policymakers became more aware of the negative environmental consequences of energy production, the assumption of a direct correlation between energy consumption and the economy has been questioned. See e.g. Amory Lovins, *Soft Energy Paths: Toward a Durable Peace* (1977).

The third fact that the graphs reveal is that, for over the last fifty years, the mix of resources used to produce energy has remained largely unchanged. In short, for the most part, our energy economy and dominant model of energy policy favors fossil fuels, i.e. oil, natural gas, and coal, as distinguished from alternative natural resources like methane or geothermal power or from renewable resources such as wind power or solar power. While it is the case that alternative resources and renewable resources play an increasing role in our energy policy, their overall role remains small as shown in Figure 7 *Energy Production By Fossil Fuels, Nuclear Electric Power, and Renewable Energy, 1949–2001* and in Figure 8 *Energy Production by Source, 2002.*

Figure 7. Energy Production by Source

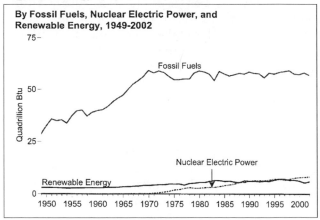

Figure 8. Energy Production by Source

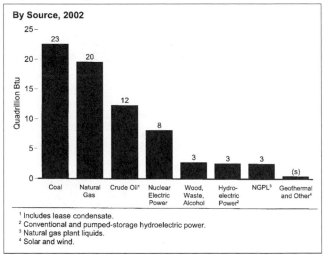

Finally, we should mention energy consumption by sector. Figures 9 and 10 show four consumption sectors. We are all familiar with residential consumption which relies, as does the commercial sector, mostly on electricity and less on heating oil and natural gas. The transportation sector relies almost exclusively on petroleum products. The industrial sector uses all sources for manufacturing processes.

Figure 9. Energy Consumption by Sector Overview

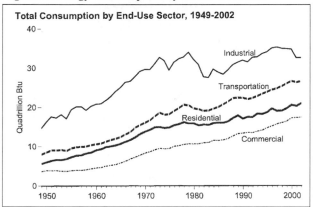

Figure 10. Energy Consumption by Sector Overview

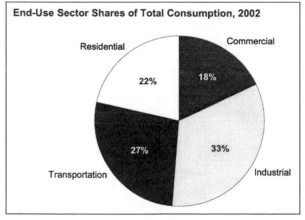

In summation, Figure 11 *Energy Flow, 2002* graphically portrays the current production and consumption pattern in the United States.

Figure 11. Energy Flow, 2002

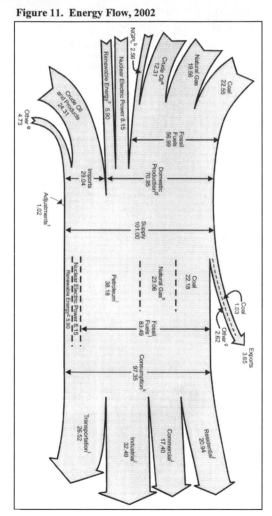

This last diagram equates all forms of energy in terms of quadrillion British Thermal Units (BTUs). This measurement can be used across resources and we can then compare the energy available in a ton of coal or a barrel of oil or a kilowatt of electricity. A BTU is defined as the amount of heat required to raise one pound of water one degree Fahrenheit (F) at 59.5 degrees F. Other energy equations include 1 barrel of oil = 42 gallons; 1 kilowatt hour (kwh) = 3,413 BTUs; 1 kwh = 104 cubic feet of natural gas, and 1 cubic foot of natural gas = 1,035 BTUs.

These equations translate into the following equivalencies:

1 barrel of oil	=	1,700 kwh
	=	5.6 mcf (thousand cubic feet of natural gas)
1 short ton coal	=	3.8 barrels of oil
	=	6,500 kwh of electricity
	=	21 mcf of natural gas
1 mcf natural gas	=	300 kwh of electricity
	=	.18 barrels of oil
	=	.047 short tons of coal
1000kwh	=	59 barrels of oil
	=	.15 short tons of coal
	=	33 mcf of natural gas

Figure 11 shows that in 2002 the United States consumed over 97 quads of energy. One quad equals one quadrillion BTUs, and is the equivalent of 45 million short tons of coal;

170 million barrels of oil; or, 1 trillion cubic feet of natural gas (tcf). Of the 97 quads of energy, coal accounted for 23%, natural gas 24%, petroleum 40%, and nuclear power 8%, renewables about 6%, according to the Energy Information Administration Annual Report.

C. NATIONAL ENERGY POLICY[1]

Energy law as a specific field of study and as an area of law practice is a relatively recent development. The flurry of legislative activity that resulted as a reaction to the Arab Oil Embargo in 1973 and the Iranian Revolution in 1979 is generally considered to constitute the primary body of what is now referred to as energy law. This corpus of law generally involves the federal regulation of the energy fuel cycle. It affects the industrial structures used to extract, transmit, convert, and distribute energy products, and the sectors of the economy that consume that energy.

The United States, and most countries in the world, are currently entrenched in what is known as the second phase of the production and use of energy. Prior to the mid–19th century, energy was generated from renewable natural re- sources—mostly wood. In addition to harnessing the occasion- al stream to grind grain or a windmill to do the same, wood, together with animal and human labor was the primary ener- gy resources. During that period, the country's population was small, and land and resources were plentiful. Any significant official policy of environmental protection was a century away. With Colonel Drake's discovery of petroleum in Titusville, Pennsylvania on August 27, 1859 and Thomas Edison's gener- ation and distribution of electricity in New York City in 1882, the United States experienced a transition from wood and

1. See, Joseph P. Tomain, *The Dominant Model of United States Energy Policy*, 61 U. Col. L. Rev. 355 (1990); Energy Law Group, Energy Law and Policy for the 21st Century, Ch. 6 (2000). Both of these sources contain numerous supporting references.

other renewable resources to our present pattern of energy use that relies principally on fossil fuels and electricity.

Although Congress requires the President to submit to it a biennial national energy plan, it is fair to say that the United States has no coherent and comprehensive plan. Still, as a general proposition, since the late 19th Century the United States has developed an identifiable pattern of energy decisionmaking. This pattern forms what can be properly termed the dominant model of the United States energy policy. The dominant model is not richly detailed nor does is coordinate the nation's several energy markets and industries. Nevertheless, the dominant model contains recognizable variables and themes to be explored in this chapter.

Over the last 100 years, the United States government has fairly consistently implemented energy policies that support private ordering by markets, and that corrects market defects through industry-specific government regulation. Regulators, for example, will correct a dislocation in the nuclear power market without necessarily also addressing the coal market although both are necessary for electricity production. The dominant model relies on fossil fuels (oil, natural gas, and coal) for over three-fourths of the nation's energy production and consumption. Occasionally, particularly during the Carter Administration, the federal government has promoted alternative energy resources. However, alternative sources, play a relatively small role in energy policy.

Although energy law has emerged only in recent years, it has identifiable antecedents. These antecedents help us to recognize the dominant model of federal energy policy, to appreciate recent events, and to understand the implications of both on future energy planning. Since the Industrial Revolution, government regulation has been used to control the production and distribution of the social necessity called energy. Government regulation has paralleled—and supported—the growth and development of energy industries and markets. Perhaps the single most trenchant observation about the history of energy regulation is to note the symbiotic relationship between private energy industries and public energy regulation.

1. 1887–1900

Modern energy regulation began near the end of the nineteenth century with the Supreme Court's opinion in *Munn v. Illinois* (S.Ct.1876). Although *Munn* involved grain elevators, its holding helped to create a major precedent for regulated industries generally, which later had a bearing on energy law. The Court recognized the existence of "natural monopolies" and ruled that states could regulate such industries in the public interest. The Court's message was that government would not tolerate the private exercise of market power and that such an exercise could be restrained by the heavy hand of government price-setting. *Munn* was the first in a series of opinions allocating ratemaking power and establishing government authority for energy decision-making and policymaking. See also, *Federal Power Comm'n v. Hope Natural Gas Co.* (S.Ct.1944). Both of these cases and their implications are discussed in more detail in subsequent chapters.

In 1887, ratemaking became an active part of our political economy through the creation of the Interstate Commerce Commission (ICC), the first modern administrative agency. Although the ICC regulated the rail industry, its ratemaking authority established the pattern for price setting for natural monopolies such as public utilities.

At the end of the nineteenth century, energy was produced on local or regional bases. Consequently, decisions were made and policies developed first at the local and then at the state levels, tracking the structure of the energy industries themselves. At the turn of the 19th Century, there was no over-arching energy policy coordinating the development and use of natural resources. Instead, specific energy resources like oil, coal, and natural gas were regulated independently of one another.

Modern energy industries and markets began to take shape during the last quarter of the nineteenth century. During this period, the country found itself in two significant energy transitions: the transition from wood to coal was completed, and the transition from coal to oil and natural gas was beginning. The second transition was from local and state, to regional and national markets, again mirroring industry development. Even in this initial phase of energy regulation, the dominant policy model can be discerned in its embryonic form. The model defined energy law and policy as a series of rules and regulations promoting the development of individual natural resources industries. Energy regulation emanated from a fundamental tension between an energy delivery system based on private ownership and the need for public regulation. The consequence of this tension was a series of government policies promoting energy businesses.

As the production and distribution of energy moved from local to state, and then to regional, national, and international markets, individual natural resources industries grew accordingly. Firms became larger and more integrated to capture economies of scale. Government regulation followed the pattern of these changes.

2. 1900–1920

During the first two decades of the twentieth century, modern energy industries, energy markets, and federal energy regulation assumed the shape they have today. The country was no longer a low energy society, but was becoming a high energy one dependent on large-scale, capital-intensive, centralized, interstate energy production and distribution. This transition occurred first in oil, then in electricity. The general intent of federal energy regulation was to promote production and industrial stability and, occasionally, to smooth out gross social and economic distortions caused by the exercise of market power by some energy firms.

Coal reigned as king during the Industrial Revolution and well into the 20th Century. Even today the nation depends on coal for about half of its electricity production. Throughout this period, however, oil and natural gas markets also expanded, signaling a transition from coal to the other fossil fuels. The oil and natural gas markets were expanding as new end uses, such as refined petroleum products and automobiles, increased demand. Because of coal's reputation as a dirty burning fuel, the cleaner alternatives of oil and natural gas were preferable. By 1926, oil constituted almost one-fifth of the energy market. Despite the transition from the solid to the liquid and gaseous fossil fuels, the federal government never abandoned coal. Instead of allowing an unimpeded transition to occur in the market, the federal government intentionally supported the use of coal to buoy the industry. See e.g. John G. Clark, ENERGY AND THE FEDERAL GOVERNMENT: FOSSIL FUEL POLICIES, 1900–1946 (1987).

Structurally, the coal, oil, and natural gas industries had similarities and differences which affected government regulation. The basic difference concerns the degree of competition within each industry and the demand for each resource. Coal production was, and continues to be, the most competitive of the three industries. The basic similarity is that each industry has a transportation bottleneck. In the oil and natural gas industries, pipelines are the bottleneck, and in the coal industry railroads are the bottleneck.

During the first two decades of the twentieth century, oil became the paradigm of big industry. After 1911, Standard Oil and related entities controlled 65% of the market, down from 90% in 1900 due to the federal government's successful antitrust litigation. See, *Standard Oil Co. of N.J. v. United States* (S.Ct.1911). Still, in 1919, thirty-two firms controlled 60% of production, and, in 1920, the thirty largest oil firms controlled 72% of the country's refining capacity.

The natural gas industry was less concentrated during these early years because natural gas was seen as a nuisance by-product of oil exploration and was wasted rather than used. Before the turn of the century, small, local natural gas companies were the rule. Municipal manufactured gas companies controlled local gas primarily for street lights. By the end of the first third of the century, however, natural gas was seen as a valuable commodity and the gas transportation network became dominated by a few interstate pipeline companies. This development, paralleling the market power of the oil companies, ultimately led to the passage of the Natural Gas Act in 1938, and the federal regulation of the gas industry.

During this formative period, energy markets moved from local and state, to regional and national levels. Federal intervention into private energy industries was episodic, allowing interindustry and interfuel competition to develop and later flourish. Whenever there were serious blips in energy markets, primarily when production was not flowing smoothly or when distribution was congested, the government would intervene in an attempt to smooth out the blip. In general, pre-World War I government intervention was motivated by a sense of progressivism assisted by antitrust laws. Government would protect consumers from the exercise of monopoly power by large energy firms. The Hepburn Act, 34 Stat. 584 (1906), (which curtailed big oil's control of interstate pipelines), the Interstate Commerce Commission (which regulated the coal-hauling rail industry), the Federal Trade Commission (which protected against economic abuses by monopolies like the domestic oil industry), and the rise of state public utility commissions (which controlled utility rates for gas and electricity) were all aimed at curtailing market power.

World War I only slightly shook the country out of its Golden Age complacency. Professor John Clark has argued in his book, ENERGY AND THE FEDERAL GOVERNMENT FOSSIL FUEL POLICIES, 1900–1946 (1987), that the war solidified the position of private energy industries. He states, "For business, the war in Europe opened great opportunities for profit through an expanding foreign trade. As many businessmen viewed it, America's entrance into the conflict provided no compelling reasons for a swollen federal economic role." At 49. Although the federal government did establish the United States Fuel Administration (USFA), the first energy agency with the power to regulate prices, transportation, and distribution, the USFA did not exercise these powers. The agency enforced actions locally, and its principal goal was to mobilize natural resources for the war, not to coordinate energy industries.

The USFA relied on decentralized administration and on the rhetoric of volunteerism, patriotism, and industry-government cooperation, rather than on the heavy hand of federal intervention. As a consequence, coal production did not appreciably increase during the war, pricing policies were a failure, rail carriers moved coal to the highest bidders first, and coal allocation regulations were conducted on an uncoordinated regional zone basis. The coal industry paid a price for exercising its grip on the nation's energy markets. At the height of World War I, coal was being replaced by oil and natural gas. Nevertheless, the federal government continued to support the coal industry.

Not surprisingly, federal oil and natural gas policies followed a pattern similar to coal regulation, also garnering federal favor. During World War I, several restrictions on oil and natural gas were implemented, including fuel-switching, licensing, price and production controls, and rationing. However, these controls were not integrated into an overall energy policy and they ended with the Armistice.

The regulatory experience from 1900–1920 firmly established cooperative industry-government relations. In the initial two decades of the twentieth century, energy markets were structured by:

(1) Seemingly inexhaustible supplies of oil, natural gas, and coal;

(2) A shift from local to regional and interstate resource production and distribution;

(3) Continuous growth in markets and in energy efficiency;

(4) Increasing industrial concentration, integration, and large-scale production; and,

(5) Transportation bottlenecks in each industry.

These aspects and trends generated a pattern of federal energy regulation that persists to this day. Federal energy regulations reacted to market conditions and mirrored the specific industries being regulated. Regulators did not treat energy industries either in a coordinated fashion or comprehensively. Instead, the coal, oil, natural gas (and electricity) industries have been regulated separately, by tracking each resource through its fuel cycle. Regulation occurs at each of the production, processing, distribution, and marketing stages. Federal regulation has focused on separate markets and industries, rather than on energy production and distribution as a whole system.

3. 1920–1933

During the Roaring Twenties, coal reached the end of its prominence as the nation's energy supplier, yielding this position to oil. This shift did not come without stark socioeconomic difficulties, most notably those suffered by coal miners. Mine operators, naturally, were interested in maintaining their market shares. However, since the coal market was shrinking, the most logical and simple way for the industry to maintain profitability was to reduce wages. With the industry in decline due to excess capacity and reduced demand, cutthroat competition, pressure for wage reduction, and miner's strikes all occurred. Coal's shrinking market and consumers' growing preference for oil and natural gas underscored the significance of fuel substitution, that is, the ability of individuals or firms to switch from one energy resource, such as coal, to another, such as oil.

Promoting fuel substitution is consistent with the country's political economy because it fosters competition. Active fuel substitution also stimulates efficiency as consumers alter their energy demands based on price. Consequently, one theme of government energy regulation has been to encourage several private markets, rather than only a favored few or a single large government energy market.

To encourage the development of oil, the common law developed the rule of capture: oil belongs to the person who captures it. The rule of capture promotes production, but it also results in waste, as producers will capture as much as they can before their neighbors do. In order to reduce such waste, the states enacted gas and oil conservation statutes.

At the federal level, the Federal Oil Conservation Board (FOCB) was created in 1924 to look into the perceived weaknesses of the oil industry. The primary weaknesses were waste, declining reserve estimates, and price instability due in part to the occasional flush field. Instead of curbing production, the FOCB promoted the oil depletion allowance and opened up the public domain under the Mineral Lands Leasing Act of 1920, 30 U.S.C.A. §§ 49, 50, 181, 351 et seq. Both responses favored industry. In short, the FOCB pressed for government controls in order to stop waste and stabilize prices as a form of oil industry protectionism. The FOCB also allowed large firms to control production and reduce the amount of oil on the market, which permitted these firms to capture economic rents. In these ways the FOCB regulatory efforts worked to the great benefit of the major oil companies.

By the end of the 1920s, the fossil fuel industries (oil, natural gas, and coal) were well entrenched. Energy markets, with the exception of coal, were expanding. In addition, interfuel competition and industry concentration were increasing.

The 1930s brought with them a peculiar test of the nation's energy policies. Not only did the country experience a national economic depression that put a downward pressure on prices, but rich oil fields were discovered in the oil producing states, most notably in eastern Texas. These discoveries flooded the market with remarkably cheap oil, with prices dropping below ten cents per barrel. As a result, the major oil companies pushed for firm production controls to insure higher prices. In addition, global oil markets were developing, giving the east coast refineries the option to buy cheap foreign oil. Here again, the majors sought government intervention in the form of import tariffs to protect their markets.

On the eve of the New Deal, the nation's energy industries, markets, and regulations had developed a pattern which continues to dominate energy planning. Oil replaced coal as the dominant fuel, and large, integrated domestic firms continued to prosper. The New Deal did little to alter this pattern, with the notable exception of federalizing the regulatory structure. Federalization came predominantly in the form of regulation of interstate energy sales. It was not, however, an alternative form of energy planning. Rather, it was an adaptation to the nationalization of energy markets.

4. The New Deal Era to World War II

The New Deal experiment introduced federal regulation into nearly every sector of the national economy. Roosevelt's economic philosophy was industrial revitalization through market stabilization and business support. Although energy industries were looked upon with some skepticism, their prior development ensured their survival and growth.

Big oil was the big winner of New Deal regulation. In 1937, twenty companies controlled 70% of the proven reserves and 76% of the refining capacity. In 1941, the Temporary National Economic Committee reported the findings of its investigation into the oil industry and concluded that the "major integrated oil companies markedly increased their pre-depression control of reserves and crude production and maintained a great supremacy in refining capacity, refining output, pipeline ownership, and marketing." Id. at 246.

Coal's troubles continued during the New Deal. The bituminous industry was plagued by productive overcapacity, underemployment of miners, poor working conditions, and chaotic pricing. Instead of recognizing and accepting the declining fortunes of the coal industry, New Deal coal policies attempted to increase wages and promote job security. The result was a labor-sensitive coal policy that did not address either the real capital problems facing the industry or the need to reduce production to reflect market demand. The coal codes of the National Industrial Recovery Administration, like the oil codes before them, were administered by the industry in the coal fields. They were not centralized. In a declining industry, government could not keep mines open and increase miners' wages, even though these were the goals of the New Deal. Nevertheless, the government attempted to pull off the impossible by trying to coordinate prices to the satisfaction of mine operators, mine workers, and consumers. To this end, two National Bituminous Coal Commissions were created to promulgate minimum prices and enforce codes of unfair trade practices.

Coal slightly improved its position during World War II. Production increased, and, more importantly, coal found the market that would serve as its largest customer—electric public utilities. Although the utilities' consumption of coal did not completely offset coal's losses in the railroad, commercial, and residential sectors, electric utilities maintained a long-term, reliable market for coal.

The two most significant and lasting pieces of the New Deal energy legislation are Part II of the Federal Power Act, 16 U.S.C.A.§§ 824a–825r, passed in 1933, and the Natural Gas Act, 15 U.S.C.A. § 717 et seq., passed in 1938. These two statutes focus on regulating the interstate sales of electricity and natural gas, respectively, due to market power in the transportation sectors of those industries. The intent of the two laws was to regulate the electricity and natural gas industries separately, in part because interstate electricity and natural gas markets developed in dramatically different ways (as described in Chapters 6 and 8).

If the New Deal was not up to the challenge of coordinating energy policy in the 1930s, would World War II stimulate such a movement? Not really. The basic regulatory agencies, the Petroleum Administration for War, and the Solid Fuels Administration for War, were divided between oil and coal and continued the old pattern of addressing these energy resources separately. Obviously, energy resources, particularly oil, needed to be mobilized, and, as during World War I, energy policies were greatly influenced by the industries themselves. Worse, industrial concentration continued and war policies favored large firms such as major oil companies, which received the bulk of federal largess being dispensed to build $1 billion of new refineries.

The basic New Deal response to economic problems was to encourage and support industry by stimulating the national market. Regulatory objectives consisted of encouraging production, promoting growth, and providing economic stability for energy industries as a means of supporting the economy as a whole. By limiting objectives to energy production and industrial stability—both in the name of efficiency—there was little room for either energy planning or redistribution of wealth from producers to consumers.

5.   Post–World War II to 1973

There are four notable energy developments between World War II and the energy cataclysm of the 1970s. First, although the coal industry had long lost its prominence, it found a new stable market in the electricity industry. Second, the natural gas industry was destabilized and, beginning in 1954, entered a period of confusion from which it has yet to emerge. Third, the oil industry went from surplus to shortage as the government attempted to rationalize domestic production and foreign imports. Fourth, the entire country jumped headlong into the commercial nuclear market, a market that today is stagnant.

Despite fits and starts in these several industries, the country's energy program emerged relatively unharmed during this period. The energy market generally was transformed from a market of cheap abundant resources to one of more costly energy and to conservation efforts. However, brownouts, gas lines, and curtailments were short-lived. The ability of the country to recover from significant market changes attests to the stability of the dominant model of energy policy.

a. Coal

While the volume of coal production remained relatively even, production shifted from eastern coal which was mined in deep pits to western coal which was surface mined. Although coal prices were not directly set by government, government health and safety regulations made the coal business more expensive. Regulations protecting miner health and safety, and the environment, also raised the cost of doing business. These increased costs raised industry concerns about the ability to maintain market share when nuclear generated electricity was being touted as "too cheap to meter."

b. Natural Gas

The natural gas story is a favorite of pro-market advocates because government intervention has been judged to be a gross failure. There is fairly straightforward language in the Natural Gas Act exempting gas producers from federal regulation, while regulating the interstate pipelines that transported the gas to markets. The congressional intent of the Natural

Gas Act was to protect consumers from the market power of interstate pipelines. The structure of the industry is such that pipelines constitute a transportation bottleneck. Pipelines purchase gas from producers in the field and transport it to distributors or end users. Consequently, without producer price regulation, any price charged by the producer to the pipeline is fully passed through to consumers. Because of this automatic pass through, consumer pressure was brought to regulate producer prices. Federal regulation of natural gas producers first occurred in *Interstate Natural Gas Co. v. FPC* (S.Ct.1947). In *Interstate*, natural gas prices of producers affiliated with the pipelines were subjected to federal regulation because of the direct pass through. In 1954, the Supreme Court justified federal price setting for the non-affiliated interstate producer prices in *Phillips Petroleum Co. v. Wisconsin* (S.Ct.1954).

The direct effect of the *Phillips* ruling was to subject thousands of individual producers to trial-type ratemaking hearings before the regulatory agency set up to handle each such matter under the Natural Gas Act—the Federal Power Commission (FPC). However, the FPC was unable to administer the increase in its docket. Natural gas ratemaking evolved from individual adjudications, to area ratemaking, and finally to national ratemaking through rulemaking. Instead of individual hearings for each natural gas producer, the FPC set rates prospectively for large areas of the country; then it set national rates.

Area and national ratemaking were based on the concept of "vintaging," or two-tier pricing in which "old" gas prices (regulated under the Natural Gas Act) were based on historic or embedded costs, and "new" gas prices (post-NGA regulation) were allowed to float to market levels. The direct effect of two-tier pricing and cost-based ratemaking was to create two natural gas markets—interstate and intrastate. Federally regulated natural gas prices in interstate markets were kept down because the price of "old gas" was based on embedded or historic costs rather than being based on current market prices, which was the case with "new" gas. Prices in the intrastate market were set at the current market level and were allowed to rise, while federally regulated interstate prices were depressed.

The problems associated with this dual market were further aggravated by strict abandonment rules that prevented federally regulated producers of gas dedicated to the interstate market from switching to the more lucrative unregulated intrastate market. See 15 U.S.C.A. § 717f(b). Federal regulatory policies kept gas prices artificially low, which reduced domestic production and caused natural gas shortages. This regulatory structure hamstrung the industry and had to be dismantled.

The first governmental response to this distorted market was not complete deregulation, however, but rather regulatory reform and partial deregulation occurred through the Natural Gas Policy Act of 1978 (NGPA) 15 U.S.C.A. § 3301 et seq. The intent of the NGPA was to unify the dual markets and to begin to deregulate prices. Today, although most gas is now deregulated, pipelines continue to present regulatory problems that are discussed more fully below.

c. Oil

World War II marked the emergence of oil as the dominant energy resource, largely as a result of oil's dominance in fueling the country's transportation sector. Shortly after the war, imports exceeded exports, causing concern among domestic producers. The recurring problem with foreign imports is that the foreign imports shrink the market for domestic producers. A further problem with foreign imports is the political instability that makes oil supplies unreliable.

In order to shore up the domestic oil industry, government placed quotas on imports. With quotas, domestic producers were assured a share of the market. Consistent with past practices, government first relied on the market to limit imports, and then government asked industry to limit imports voluntarily. Not surprisingly, volunteerism did not prove to be an effective way to cut imports because imported oil was cheaper than domestically produced oil and was attractive to domestic refiners. During the 1950's, various political and rhetorical arguments were made to reduce imports for national security reasons, but the economic reality tilted in favor of cheap oil. At the end of the 1950s, oil import quotas were made mandatory, and they continued until the early 1970s when domestic production peaked, making them superfluous.

The 1970s caught oil in an unfamiliar setting—price regulation. Oil prices initially were set as part of President Nixon's wage and price controls. These regulations took on a life of their own after the Nixon economic stabilization program ended, and oil prices became regulated as a result of soaring gasoline prices caused by the OPEC oil embargo of 1973–74. Oil price regulations required an elaborate bureaucratic machinery for their administration. Oil price controls, like natural gas price regulations, were thought to have distorted the market rather than stimulated it, and they were ultimately dismantled by President Reagan in January, 1981.

d. Nuclear Energy

The single most notable energy event in the post-World War II period was the major commitment of capital to commercial nuclear power. This several hundred billion dollar industry began at the end of World War II as a way to channel the destructive force of nuclear power into more benign and beneficial uses. In 1946, the Atomic Energy Act, 42 U.S.C.A. § 2011, was passed for the purpose of moving nuclear power away from the military into civilian hands. The Act, however, still allowed the government a monopoly on uranium. That monopoly existed until the Act was significantly amended in

1954 to permit private ownership of uranium. This control was crucial for private sector investment to harness nuclear power for electricity production. Such investment became substantial in 1957 with the passage of the Price–Anderson Act, 42 U.S.C.A. § 2210, which limited the liability of nuclear facilities in the case of a nuclear accident.

After the passage of the Price–Anderson Act, thousands of megawatts of nuclear generating capacity were ordered by private firms. The expansion of commercial nuclear energy continued throughout the 1960s and into the early 1970s, spurred by a pro-nuclear consensus. The prevailing wisdom was that private producers had a new, modern, "safe and clean" technology, that consumers were pleased to receive a cheap product, and that the government found beneficial civilian uses for this technology of the future.

Toward the end of the 1960s and into the 1970s, however, the promises that had built the pro-nuclear consensus showed signs of fatigue. Instead of being safe, clean, cheap, and abundant, the nuclear enterprise was discovered to have large social costs, involving enormous environmental, health, safety, and financial risks. By the 1990s the industry was moribund. No new nuclear plants have been ordered since 1978, and all plants ordered since 1974 have been canceled. Although there were 111 plants in operation in 1990 and eight more with construction permits, nuclear power, particularly large-scale plants of 1000 megawatts and more, is stalled.

D. PRESIDENTS CARTER AND REAGAN TEST THE DOMINANT MODEL, 1973–1988

The history of energy law and policy until 1973 demonstrates the development of a dominant model of energy policy. The decade following 1973 tested that model as world energy markets experienced dramatic changes. In response to those changes, President Carter attempted to centralize energy policymaking and decisionmaking and tried to develop a comprehensive and coordinated national energy plan. That plan never coalesced. President Reagan tried to deregulate energy on a broad scale and dismantle the Department of Energy. He failed as well. In short, neither the Carter hyper-regulatory approach nor the Reagan deregulation approach was effective in radically altering energy regulation, which continued to hew closely to the dominant policy model that had developed over the previous century. The inability of these two presidential administrations to control energy policy demonstrates the tenacity of the model.

1. President Carter and Centralized Energy Policy

There were four significant energy events during the Carter Administration which generated a cascade of energy regulations. First, Carter sought to centralize energy administration in the cabinet level Department of Energy (DOE). The DOE was unable, however, to design a comprehensive national energy plan because energy decisionmaking and policymaking responsibilities were scattered over several branches of the federal government, and even within the DOE itself authority was fragmented as we discuss in the next chapter.

Second, Carter's "moral equivalent of war" speech on April 18, 1977, outlined the substantive principles of a national energy policy which led to the passage of the National Energy Act in October of the following year. The National Energy Act consists of five pieces of major legislation: the National Energy Conservation Policy Act, Pub.L. No. 95–619; 92 Stat. 3206 (codified as amended in scattered sections of Titles 12, 15, 25, 31 and 42 U.S.C.A.); the Powerplant and Industrial Fuel Use Act of 1978, Pub.L. No. 95–620, 92 Stat. 3289 (codified as amended in scattered sections of Titles 15 and 42 U.S.C.A.); the Natural Gas Policy Act of 1978, Pub.L. No. 95–621, 92 Stat. 3350 (codified at 15 U.S.C.A. §§ 33013432 & 42 U.S.C.A. § 7255); the Public Utilities Regulatory Policies Act of 1978, Pub.L. No. 9517, 92 Stat. 3117 (codified as amended in scattered sections of Titles 15, 16, 26, 42,—: and 43 U.S.C.A.); and the Energy Tax Act of 1978, Pub.L. No.95–618, 92 Stat. 3174 (codified as amended in scattered sections of Titles 26 and 42 U.S.C.A.).

The component parts of the National Energy Act addressed conventional fuels in several ways. Their purpose was to move the country away from a dependence on foreign oil, promote the use of coal, increase energy efficiency, modernize utility ratemaking, stimulate conservation, encourage the creation of a new market for alternative energy sources in electricity, and restructure a distorted market in natural gas.

The third major event was President Carter's energy address on April 5, 1979, which stressed the need to decontrol oil prices as a means of increasing domestic oil production. The address led to the passage of the Crude Oil Windfall Profit Tax Act of 1980, Pub.L. No. 96–223, 94 Stat. 229 (codified [a]s amended in scattered sections of Titles 7, 19, 26 and 42 U.S.C.A.), designed to capture the economic rents realized by domestic oil producers as a result of the rise in world oil prices.

Fourth, on July 15, 1979, the President delivered another major energy address, returning to his moral equivalent of war rhetoric. Again, Congress responded, this time with the passage of the Energy Security Act of 1980. The Energy Security Act, Pub. L. No. 96–294, 94 Stat. 611, (codified as amended in scattered sections of Titles 7, 10, 12, 15, 16, 30 and 42 U.S.C.A.), also consists of several pieces of legislation, including: the Defense Production Act Amendments of 1980, Pub.L. No. 96–294, 94 Stat. 617 (codified in 50 U.S.C.A. §§ 2061–2166); the United States Synthetic Fuels Corporation Act of 1980, Pub.L. No. 96–294, 94 Stat. 633 (codified as amended in scattered sections of 42 U.S.C.A.); the Biomass Energy and Alcohol Fuels Act of 1980, Pub.L. No. 96–294, 94 Stat. 683 (codified as amended in scattered sections of Titles 7, 15, 16 and 42 U.S.C.A.); the Renewable Energy Resources Act of 1980, Pub.L. No. 96–294, 94 Stat. 715 (codified as amended in scattered sections of Titles 16 and 42 U.S.C.A.); the Solar Energy and Energy Conservation Act of 19980, Pub.L. No. 96–294, 94 Stat. 719 (codified as amended in scattered sections of Titles 12 and 42 U.S.C.A.); and the Geothermal Energy Act of 1980, Pub.L. No. 96–294, 94 Stat. 763 (codified in scattered sections of 16 U.S.C.A.).

The Energy Security Act was a dramatically conceived package of legislation that turned energy policy away from conventional resources and toward the development and promotion of synthetic oil and gas, derived from coal, oil shale, and tar sands. The Act also attempted to stimulate a third energy transition, from fossil fuels to renewable resources such as solar, biomass, alcohol, wind, and geothermal steam. The Act also sought to make conservation a larger part of the country's energy planning.

The legislation that emerged during the Carter Administration did not coordinate national energy policy. Regulatory authority throughout the federal government was fragmented, and competition among and within the several energy industries resisted comprehensive planning. Nor did it stimulate the so-called third energy transition, from fossil fuels to renewable resources and conservation. Instead, Carter's energy program went contrary to the country's entrenched model of energy policy. The attempted coordination failed because of the model's resistance to centralization; the transition also failed because of the model's traditional reliance on the market to signal a move into other resources. Simply put, centralization and planning conflicted with competition and private markets.

2.   President Reagan and Deregulation

If President Carter's highly centralized, pro-government energy policy failed, it would seem to follow that President Reagan's private sector, supply-side, anti-governmental deregulation efforts surely would succeed and that the DOE would be dismantled. Indeed, President Reagan made his energy intentions clear in one of his first acts in office by decontrolling oil prices on January 28, 1981. The oil price decontrol was largely symbolic, however, because controls were scheduled to terminate on October 1st of that year.

The Reagan deregulation program did not spring from whole cloth. Natural gas deregulation, like oil deregulation, was scheduled to occur consistent with a phased deregulation contained in President Carter's Natural Gas Policy Act of 1978. Similarly, although President Reagan campaigned to dismantle the United States Synthetic Fuels Corporation, the synfuels program failed because the market was unable to support it. Synfuels producers were not able to process coal into natural gas or extract oil from tar sands or oil shale at costs competitive with traditionally extracted oil and natural gas.

In President Reagan's campaign against big government, the Department of Energy and the Solar Energy Research Institute (SERI), a federal laboratory devoted to renewable energy research, were to be abolished as part of the new president's program of supply-side economic deregulation. The continued existence of DOE and SERI (renamed in 1991 the National Renewable Energy Laboratory), and President Reagan's failure to deregulate energy in substantial ways, may be explained by the intransigence of bureaucracies. That explanation is, however, too superficial. A more refined explanation, like the explanation for President Carter's failure to centralize national energy planning, can be found in the dominant model. This model demonstrates that government regulation of energy is embedded in the country's political economy. By acting inconsistent with that model through overreliance on the market and underreliance on government support of conventional fuels and producers, President Reagan's initiatives at deregulation were destined to fail.

E. 1992–PRESENT

If it is accurate to say that Presidents Carter and Reagan both attempted to significantly change energy policy and that those policies failed, it is equally accurate to say that Presidents Bush, Clinton, and Bush II only tinkered with the basic energy policy during their administrations.

President Bush signed the 1992 Energy Policy Act (EPAct), Pub. L. No. 102–486, 100 Stat. 2776 (1992) to provide a comprehensive national energy policy that "gradually and steadily increases U.S. energy security in cost-effective and environmentally beneficial ways." H.R. Rep. No. 474 (I) (1992). The Act consisted of over 30 titles and several major provisions, including amending the Public Utility Holding Company Act; stimulating new entrants in the electricity market; opening access to the electricity grid to non-utility generators; stimulating state regulatory authorities to think about integrated resource planning; and providing subsidies and tax credits for electric vehicles. EPact involved deregulation of imported natural gas and liquefied natural gas and provided tax relief for independent oil and gas producers, while extending tax relief and tax credits for the production of oil from shale, tar sands, and other nonconventional sources.

The Act provided for R & D for advanced clean coal technologies; provided certain relief for coal companies under the avoided cost provisions of PURPA; provided for the export of clean coal technology; and provided some relief from the Surface Mining Control and Reclamation Act. Procedures of the Nuclear Regulatory Commission were streamlined and the United States Enrichment Corporation, a government-owned entity, was created to provide uranium enrichment services in the international market. Alternative fuel vehicles were required for government use; tax deductions for investments in clean fuel vehicles were permitted; and tax credits were provided for wind and biomass facilities. Additionally, as part of

Bush II's National Energy Policy Plan, the Secretary of Energy was directed to prepare a least cost energy strategy that was environmentally sensitive, specifically with the goal of reducing greenhouse gases. The Act also sought to stimulate energy efficient construction and demand side management for electricity.

About this time, however, significant deregulation initiatives in the natural gas and electricity industries had been promoted by FERC. These initiatives continue and have stimulated legislative and regulatory activity for retail electricity sales at the state level. These development are explored in subsequent chapters.

During the Clinton administration, the DOE issued its *National Energy Policy Plan* (July, 1995) followed by its Strategic Plan (1997) and its *Comprehensive National Energy Strategy* (1998). Each of these documents set out similar goals:

(1) Energy production and efficiency.

(2) National security.

(3) Environmental sensitivity.

Similarly, Vice President Cheney chaired the National Energy Policy Development Group which issued its *National Energy Plan* (May, 2001) from the White House. The subtitle of the report captures the main theme "Reliable, Affordable and Environmentally Sound Energy for America's Future." Again, we can note a change in rhetoric over the decades since the passage of the National Environmental Policy Act in 1970. We can also notice policy language sympathetic to sustainable development since the publication of a United Nations report entitled *Our Common Future* (1987). Nevertheless, energy policy in the United States remains well entrenched as we can witness in the fate of the *Energy Security Act of 2003*.

In November 2003, the Energy Policy Act of 2003 was tabled for the remainder of the year with promises to be reintroduced in 2004. The bill had the full support of the

President and was touted as a major goal of the Bush Administration's domestic agenda. Introduced originally in the House of Representatives H.R. 6 it was later merged with Senate Bill S. 14 and contained a controversial list of tax incentives and revised energy standards totaling anywhere from $31 billion to over $60 billion.

The bill's major provisions include more than $18 billion in tax incentives primarily to boost the development of oil, natural gas, coal, and nuclear power. The major goals of the bill that did enjoy bipartisan support were tax incentives to build a $21 billion pipeline to bring natural gas from Alaska to Chicago. Alternative energy resources were given some attention and were addressed through earned credit and tax incentive systems.

Another provision of the bill that had been long debated in Congress was the repeal of the Public Utility Holding Company Act of 1935. PUHCA strictly regulated business dealings of multistate holding companies that operate electric utilities. The bill also sought to amend the Public Utility Regulatory Policies Act of 1978, particularly repealing the mandatory purchase and sale requirements of wholesale electricity. We will discuss those requirements later in the book.

The most controversial provision of the bill dealt with gasoline additives known as methyl tertiary butyl ether (MTBE). The bill intended to double the use of corn-based ethanol as a gasoline additive and was a provision which attracted support from farm state Democrats otherwise opposed to other of the bill's provisions. Eventually the legislation would protect MTBE producers from product liability suits filed after September 5, 2003. Critics of the bill said that MTBE has been the cause of widespread groundwater pollution and other environmental degradation. Another controversial provision of the bill was to open up the Arctic National Wildlife Refuge to oil drilling and that provision was dropped from the final version of the legislation. One of the provisions that gained in importance since the bill's introduction concerned regulatory electrical reliability standards which would have had the effect of establishing reliability standards to be applied uniformly throughout the electric grid. The idea of rationalization of reliability standards makes great sense. There is controversy over who should operate this system and whether it should be left in the hands of the federal government or the states.

Although the Clinton and Bush administrations made energy policy pronouncements including a significant legislative proposal that failed to pass the first half of the 108th Congress as noted at the beginning of this chapter, these pronouncements have not led to significant policy changes. We can make two generalizations about these activities. First, the plans share general strategic goals. Second, even though the plans contain language sensitive to the idea of sustainable development, this language is more lip service than substance. Indeed, these plans, like putting old wine in new bottles, continue to adhere to the basic fossil fuel model.

F. THE DOMINANT MODEL OF ENERGY POLICY

Energy policies since the Nixon administrations have not lasted much beyond their immediate causes. Nixon and Ford addressed a disrupted economy caused by an oil embargo. The Carter and Reagan policies were similar in that both were inconsistent with the dominant energy policy model and with the prevailing market and neither Presidents Bush nor Clinton have seriously challenged the prevailing energy ideology. The dominant model requires support of conventional resources, and recognition that some segments of the energy industries possess market power requiring regulation. Stable energy production, distribution, and consumption occur as a consequence of the interplay of government and industry within the boundaries of our mixed-market political economy.

Domestic energy policy, from the late nineteenth century to the early 1990's, was based on the fundamental assumption that a link exists between the level of energy production and the gross national product (GNP). Consistent with this assumption is the hope that economies of scale in energy production can still be realized. As more energy is produced, prices will remain stable, or relatively low, and the GNP will grow. Implicit in this simple formula is the supposition that the general welfare increases in direct proportion to the GNP. Energy policy continues to rely on this fundamental market-based assumption.

As a consequence, domestic energy policy favors large-scale, high-technology, capital-intensive, integrated, and centralized energy producers which rely on fossil fuels. These archetype energy firms are favored over alternatives, such as small solar or wind firms, because energy policymakers believe that larger firms can continue to realize economies of scale. Policymakers gamble that greater energy efficiencies can be achieved by traditional fossil fuel-reliant firms, rather than by alternative firms. Such traditional firms seemingly have an advantage through technological innovation, discovery of new reserves, and discovery of new energy sources. This belief may or may not be accurate. Nevertheless, it persists, and the favoritism it engenders will continue as alternative firms carry the burden of persuading policymakers otherwise. Put another way, as long as energy production, consumption, and prices remain stable, the embedded assumptions of the dominant energy policy model will continue.

This dominant model of energy policy thus has the following general goals:

(1) to assure abundant energy supplies, even if these supplies have to be imported;

(2) to maintain reasonable prices;

(3) to limit the market power of archetype firms;

(4) to promote inter- and intrafuel competition;

(5) to support conventional fuels (oil, natural gas, coal, hydropower, and nuclear power); and

(6) to allow energy decisionmaking and policymaking to develop within an active federal-state regulatory system.

This policy, developed over the last 100 years, has served the country well by providing long periods of reliable energy at relatively low prices and with the respectable degrees of economic stability. In light of this historical intransigence, one can assume that the dominant policy will continue in the future, and that alternatives to conventional systems will be an insignificant component of domestic energy policy.

To the extent that an alternative energy policy exists, that is opposed to the dominant model, it would be one that is sensitive to domestic and international sustainable development, global environmentalism; and the economy of developing countries. Suffice it to say at this point, since the mid–1960s with the subsequent rise of the environmental movement, policymakers have been increasingly concerned about the effect of human activity on the environment. The effects come in various forms. Increased energy use contributes to environmental pollution of a worldwide nature including global warming. Increased energy use also contributes to the disparity of income among first world and third world countries and it gives rise to questions about environmental justice and ethics. In Chapter 11 we will discuss in more detail what an alternative policy would look like.

CHAPTER 3

THE ADMINISTRATION OF ENERGY REGULATION

Introduction

Energy Law is made and administered largely by that uniquely American legal institution, the administrative agency. These agencies were virtually invented in the United States and contributed by it to the legal systems of the world. It is generally recognized that the first modern federal administrative agency was the Interstate Commerce Commission (ICC), established to regulate the railroads in 1887. Generally, administrative agencies combine legislative with adjudicative and with executive functions; they issue regulations (legislative), which they then enforce (executive) and they adjudicate disputes (judicial). Administrative agencies are unlike courts in that the agencies attempt actively to formulate and implement prospective policies. Hence, in their adjudicative roles, their policy-making role may intrude upon their claim to be a neutral decision maker.

Within the last 30 years, a cabinet-level department concerned with problems of energy has been created with a mission of providing a reliable supply of energy in all its forms and of conserving energy. The Department of Energy (DOE) contains within it a so-called independent regulatory agency, the Federal Energy Regulatory Commission (FERC), which is charged with implementing and enforcing the Federal Power Act, the Natural Gas Act, the Natural Gas Policy Act and various other important pieces of federal energy legislation. Administrative procedures with respect to energy matters are governed both by the organic legislation creating the agencies and delegating powers to them, and by the Administrative Procedure Act (APA), which applies generally to administrative agencies within the federal government.

A.   AN INTRODUCTION TO ADMINISTRATIVE LAW

Although administrative agencies are said to constitute a fourth branch of government, it is important to remember that they are creatures of Congress. Congress has delegated to them the task of implementing the statutes that Congress has enacted. However, as a matter of constitutional law, Congress may not attempt to delegate the legislative power to agencies, and the prohibition against doing so is known as the nondelegation doctrine. As a practical matter, many thought that this doctrine was a relic without current significance and would never again be invoked by the courts since it was last called on in *A.L.A. Schechter Poultry Corp. v United States* (S.Ct.1935), to invalidate on constitutional grounds the Live Poultry Code of the National Industrial Recovery Act. There the Supreme Court held that the Congress had in effect attempted to delegate unconstitutionally legislative power to a private industry group (let alone to a government agency) to establish a code of fair competition in the poultry industry. See also, *Panama Refining v Ryan* (S.Ct.1935).

The clearest articulation of the nondelegation doctrine is usually ascribed to *J. W. Hampton v. United States,* (S.Ct. 1928), a tariff case in which authority had been delegated to the President to adjust duties on imported goods. In that case, the Court expounded upon the distinction between the power to make the law and the power to exercise discretion as to its execution. A temporary resurrection of the nondelegation doctrine occurred in 1999 when the District of Columbia Circuit invalidated a new ozone standard established by the Environmental Protection Administration (EPA), on the grounds that the EPA had not provided a "limiting standard" or "intelligible principle" to guide its discretion in applying the Clean Air

Act. See *American Trucking Ass'ns Inc. v EPA* (D.C. Cir. 1999). The Supreme Court reversed this conclusion almost perfunctorily by distinguishing *Panama Refining* and *Schechter Poultry* and by citing a number of instances where it had upheld a rather broad delegation of powers by the Congress to a regulatory agency. Although the nondelegation doctrine continues to exist, there is little likelihood of its gaining traction currently. See *Industrial Union Dept. v. American Petroleum Inst.* (S.Ct.1980) (J. Rehnquist concurring). See Richard D. Cudahy, *The Nondelegation Doctrine: Rumors of Its Resurrection Prove Unfounded* 16 St. John's J. Legal Commentary 1 (2002). A more vital concern today is the issue whether the agency has in fact exercised its discretion within the constraints of the congressional legislation.

The traditional method of regulating economic activity in the United States is through the operation of markets. This approach supposes effective competition to establish prices, and prices have not generally been the subject of administrative control. However, in instances when competition has been excluded or impaired, administrative action substitutes for market forces. In Chapter 1, and throughout this book, we list and discuss a variety of market failures and regulatory responses. Today, you should be aware that deregulation has thrust administrative agencies into new and unaccustomed areas of concern. Deregulation has had a marked impact, for example, in such energy industries as natural gas and electricity that will be discussed in detail in Chapters 6 and 8. In a few isolated cases, deregulation has resulted in an elimination of administrative activity.

In most cases, however, the apparent supplanting of administrative activity has been more a matter of aspiration than reality. The most well-known example of this was the abolition of the ICC, one of the foremost symbols of economic regulation. The functions of the ICC, however, and in fact its commissioners and much of its staff, were transferred intact to a new agency called the Surface Transportation Board under the Department of Transportation, making the abolition of the ICC more an exercise in politics than in government administration. In other areas of regulation, including that applicable to the energy industries, deregulation has not led to a real diminution of regulatory activity. It has merely changed the shape and form of the issues and may, in fact, increase regulatory oversight. Continuing efforts to promote deregulation of electric power, as an example, has led to extensive regulatory activity to ensure access to transmission by electric generators and to organize and monitor electric markets to minimize market power and to further other economic ends.

Another example of increased regulation in the face of efforts to deregulate is exemplified by the crisis in California when that state's electricity restructuring plan ran head-on into escalating prices for electric power and power shortages. California officials called repeatedly on the FERC to intervene to establish ceiling prices for wholesale electric power. At first these requests were rejected, but, as time went on, and the crisis deepened, the FERC became increasingly involved in attempts to moderate prices. Another area where the FERC will no doubt have to become increasingly involved in pursuing regulatory initiatives in electric power will involve the issue of reliability. Reliability is one aspect of electric power restructuring where no one has seriously suggested that competition is an answer to the problems. These examples suggest that the subject matter of regulation may change over time, but the continuing need for regulation is not in doubt.

B.   A CRITIQUE OF ADMINISTRATIVE LAW

Over the years, there has been a great deal of criticism of government regulation and of the administrative agencies that implement it on the ground that the agencies have been captured by the industries that they regulate. The basic argument regarding capture is that the relationship of the agencies with the regulated industries is close and continuous, while the access of outside groups such as consumers and environmentalists is limited. Partly to meet these criticisms, measures for public participation before administrative agencies have been introduced. See e.g., Richard B. Stewart, *The Reformation of American Administrative Law*, 88 HARV. L. REV. 1667 (1975).

A related criticism to capture is the issue of the "revolving door." Staff members of commissions, and in fact commissioners not infrequently seek and find employment with companies that have been subject to their attention as regulators. Sometimes the door revolves in the opposite direction, and those who have represented clients before agencies attempt to function effectively as members of agencies representing the public. See e.g. Robert E. Rubin, IN AN UNCERTAIN WORLD: TOUGH CHOICES FROM WALL STREET TO WASHINGTON (2003) (from CEO of the investment bank of Goldman Sachs to Secretary of the Treasury under President Clinton to chair of the Executive Committee with the financial institution Citigroup.) Many are able to manage such transitions successfully, but there is no denying the human proclivity to carry over the attitudes and prejudices associated with one role into the adoption of another. Ethics-in-government legislation seeks to prevent people serving with administrative agencies from quickly converting their contacts into cash for the benefit of supplicants before the same agencies. This sort of legislation tends to make the problem a little more manageable, but it does not eliminate it—no rules can. The expertise employed in the interests of the public for an administrative agency is the same expertise that just as easily serves a regulated industry. There is no doing away with the problem of the "revolving door;" all that can be done is to provide limits and to reduce the circumstances where appearances of conflicts of interest can occur.

A related problem involves the expectation of infallibility. One of the prime requisites of agencies is their possession, or supposed possession, of expertise in a particular field. However, regulatory problems may arise from an indeterminancy of the costs or of the benefits of taking certain action. Such a problem arises with drug regulation by the Food and Drug Administration (FDA). The drug in question may have benefits for some but may be harmful to others. There is very little that the FDA can do to actually resolve with certainty the question of whether or when the drug should be released to the public.

Perhaps, the most serious charge lodged against administrative agencies is the question of regulatory lag. Sometimes exacerbated by the need for multiple authorizations, the length of time consumed in acquiring regulatory authorizations—especially for energy projects—can become a serious problem. Regulatory lag was vividly demonstrated during the period when efforts were being made to secure licenses to build and operate nuclear power plants. The time required to obtain the permits and to build the plants averaged about twelve years. The difficulties inherent in such a time lag showed up when demand for electric power stabilized and growth declined in the late 1970s and early 1980s. Estimates of load growth twelve years in advance of operation could be wildly erroneous, and in some cases nuclear plant construction projects had to be canceled when the plants were no longer needed. Of course, there have been efforts to provide legislated time limits for agency decisions. But what is an appropriate sanction for violating such a rule? One can hardly say that, if the nuclear plant has not been disapproved before a legislative deadline, it will then be automatically approved or canceled. "One-stop shopping" has been proposed as the answer. This means letting one agency make all the determinations. But, of course, there are valid objections to trying to ask one agency to evaluate all the environmental and safety factors of a plant as well as the need for power.

In an effort to achieve fairness as well as the appearance of fairness, agency measures seeking to make the proceedings of these agencies more like proceedings in the courts have been introduced. But this trend has led to the criticism that the agencies have become over-judicialized, and that their effectiveness in policymaking has been compromised. Agencies also have been criticized for their apparent excessive bureaucratization. The argument is that agencies have so complicated some aspects of economic activity as to become an obstacle to innovation and growth. Agencies concerned with energy matters have been highly dynamic in recent years and have created vast bodies of rules and regulations. Additionally, the deregulation movement has led to an accretion of regulation seeking to further competition. The movement toward competition, particularly in electric power, has also helped create new problems regarding the reliability of the power supply and the need for new regulations. It has become something of a misnomer to speak of deregulation when one of the principal results of that policy has been to create many new regulations.

Finally, we come to the issue of political accountability. The objection that there is an absence of political accountability has been lodged primarily against the so-called independent agencies, those that are not headed by an official serving at the pleasure of the President. Thus, with energy regulation, the DOE is headed by a Secretary, who is directly accountable to the President. On the other hand, although the commissioners of the FERC are appointed by the President, they may not be removed by the President at will, and therefore the agency is not fully accountable politically. This circumstance has caused some observers to question the legitimacy of such independent agencies.

One response to the charge of lack of political accountability is to provide for more public participation in the deliberations and decision-making processes of the agencies. Public participation does not respond in theory to the absence of political accountability, but, as a practical matter, it may provide a democratic constraint on agency decisions. Judicial review is going to continue to carry much of the burden of keeping administrative agencies on the straight and narrow.

Clearly, regulation and democracy clash. However, given the needs of modern society especially in a mixed market economy, administrative agencies are inevitable. Legislators cannot set out detailed specifications in all legislation and even if they could, 538 Senators and Representatives could not implement and enforce those laws. Consequently, as noted, authority to do so is delegated mostly to Executive Branch agencies. We turn now to the rules of the regulatory state.

C. THE ADMINISTRATIVE PROCEDURE ACT

The basic federal statute governing procedures to be followed by all of the federal agencies is the Administrative Procedure Act (APA) 5 U.S.C. §§ 551 et. seq., which was enacted in 1946 to provide a procedural framework for the sprawling bureaucracy that proliferated under the New Deal. The APA, however, is not always controlling because the procedural provisions of an agency's organic statute (like the Department of Energy Organization Act creating the DOE) may be in conflict and may take precedence. But, even in the energy area, the APA controls most administrative procedure.

The APA was adopted in a spirit of compromise between the extreme claims of the critics and of the defenders of the administrative process, which had so proliferated under the regime of the New Deal in the 1930s. The weight of informed opinion before adoption of the Administrative Procedure Act was that administrative procedure was in need of standardization but that there should be a degree of agency flexibility in organization and decision making practices.

Before adoption of the APA, there had been various proposals for reform of the administrative process. One of these proposals contemplated creation of an administrative court to conduct all the adjudications required by the agencies. This arrangement would presumably make these proceedings "fairer," and this proposal was favored by many lawyers regularly appearing before agencies. However, because this suggestion would thoroughly separate the quasi-judicial agency functions from their policy-making, quasi-legislative functions, the proposed change would seem to impair the agencies' policymaking role. The APA was in large part an effort to maintain the link between policymaking and adjudication while attempting to safeguard procedural fairness.

Under the APA, agencies have two major modes of decision-making—adjudication and rulemaking. Adjudication is basically retrospective dispute resolution and attempts to deal with a conflict that affects an individual entity or group of entities. The APA provides for trial-type hearings for adjudication in contrast to legislative-type proceedings, which may be appropriate for rulemaking. Section 554 of the APA sets out the general rules for conducting an adjudication. A Section 554 hearing must be provided in every case of adjudication required by statute to be determined "on the record after opportunity for an agency hearing," with limited exceptions.

Case law is in some conflict as to what presumption is to be applied to ambiguous statutory language prescribing a "hearing." In *Seacoast Anti–Pollution League v Costle* (1st Cir. 1978), the court accorded a presumption to the need for an adjudicative proceeding, but in *Chemical Waste Management v. EPA* (D.C. Cir. 1989), such a presumption was rejected, because it was thought to be at odds with the usual policy of deferring to the agencies' interpretation of their own enabling legislation.

In contrast to adjudication, the APA also provides for rulemaking, which involves a legislative-type procedure. Rulemaking is prospective and affects large numbers of individuals. It is a means of establishing policy. The most common mode of rulemaking is classified under the APA as "informal" or "notice and comment" rulemaking. Informal rulemaking involves notice in the Federal Register about the subject of the proceeding and related information and invites responses by the participants through the submission of written comments. 5 U.S.C. § 553. The APA also has a provision for "formal" rulemaking, which is triggered when a statute requires that rules be made "on the record after an opportunity for an agency hearing." Formal rulemaking provides for oral submissions and cross-examination and other features more like those prescribed for adjudications, but formal rule making has proven unwieldy and excessively time-consuming in practice and is now seldom used. See, *National Nutritional Foods Ass'n. v FDA* (2d. Cir. 1974).

The APA also provides for judicial review and specifies the bases upon which agency actions may be set aside by courts. These include the familiar "arbitrary, capricious, and abuse of discretion or otherwise not in accordance with law" standard, the "unsupported by substantial evidence" standard, the "contrary to constitutional right" standard and certain other standards specified in Section 706 of the APA.

1. Adjudication under the APA

Formal adjudications, so called "on-the-record hearings" or "trial-type hearings" are presided over by an administrative law judge (ALJ) and are governed by Sections 554, 556 and 557 of the APA. There are also proceedings that are frequently called "informal adjudications," which may be governed by special statutory requirements or by an agency's own regulations but which presumably do not fall under the mandate of the APA. In addition, ratemaking for electric and gas utilities is forward looking and is classified as rulemaking but is conducted very much like a formal adjudication before an ALJ. It is not possible here to review all the requirements established for formal adjudications under the APA, except to say that in general they track many of the same issues addressed by the Federal Rules of Civil Procedure. Notice must be provided to persons entitled to a hearing, and all interested parties have an opportunity to submit evidence to the agency.

Agencies may issue subpoenas if authorized by law, under Section 555. Evidence is taken under oath, and the hearing officer, who is an ALJ, is authorized to issue subpoenas, allow depositions and otherwise control the proceedings. One of the most significant attributes of formal adjudication is the opportunity to cross-examine witnesses. Administrative adjudications also apply rules for the admissibility of evidence that are more liberal than those recognized in court proceedings. For example, hearsay evidence, inadmissible in court, may be generally admissible in administrative proceedings. A transcript of proceedings in formal adjudications is required to be made, and this constitutes the exclusive record. 5 U.S.C. § 556.

Discovery is generally available but is considerably more limited than it might be in a court proceeding. Thus, the APA contains no provisions for discovery against the agency. As a practical matter, most formal agency adjudications are preceded by staff investigations which, in general, can unearth a wide range of evidence.

Formal adjudication also involves what has been termed the institutional decision. This means that, although the ALJ who presides over the hearing makes an initial or recommended decision, the final decision is made by the agency in the person of the commissioners or members of the agency's governing body. The agency is not required to accept the determinations of the ALJ, either of matters of fact or of law, or even his or her credibility determinations; however, if the agency rejects the credibility determination of the ALJ, it must furnish persuasive reasons for doing so in order to pass muster on judicial review. The issue of the institutional decision was first raised in the well-known case of *Morgan v. United States* (S.Ct.1936). There the Supreme Court held that a statute giving a private party the right to a "full hearing" required a personal decision by the agency head. However, this decision was too strict to be taken literally, and the Court subsequently made it clear that the deciding administrator was not required to be physically present at the taking of testimony.

Another concern that arises in the context of a formal adjudication is the issue of the separation of functions; thus, certain staff members of the agency may be designated to act as advocates in trial-type hearings. It would be unfair if these staff members designated as prosecutors were allowed to consult with and advise the decision makers; therefore, § 554(d) provides that any employee who is "engaged in the performance of investigative or prosecuting functions" may not participate in the decision or advise the decision makers in that case or any factually related case. Any input from the prosecuting staff must come "as a witness or counsel in public proceedings." § 554(d) provides that the separation of functions requirements do not apply to initial licensing or rate cases—proceedings that are intended to decide technical or policy questions rather than to impose sanctions. Additionally, agency decisionmakers, when they are considering the record of a formal proceeding, may not obtain additional, nonrecord evidence from staff members. Going beyond the limits on internal consultation that are imposed by the APA, it has sometimes been contended that agencies should enforce a structural separation of functions. However, the idea that the mixture of prosecuting and deciding powers in a single agency is so unfair as to amount to a denial of due process of law was rejected by the Supreme Court in *Withrow v. Larkin* (S.Ct.1975).

Formal adjudication is completed with the issuance of a written decision, and the APA has detailed requirements governing the contents of the agency's final submission. 5 U.S.C. § 557(c) requires that the parties receive an opportunity to provide proposed findings and conclusions, as well as "exceptions" to the proposed decision before the agency announces a recommended, initial or final decision. The APA then provides that "All decisions, including initial recommended, and tentative decisions ... shall include ... findings and conclusions, and the reasons or basis therefor, on all the material issues of fact, law, or discretion presented on the record." 5 U.S.C. § 557(c). These requirements force the responsible decisionmaker to deal with each party's points attentively and systematically; assure the exposure of the agency's reasoning for the benefit of a reviewing court or others; and, help to assure that administrators will be publicly accountable for their decisions. Some agencies, including the FERC, have specialized opinion-writing staffs, who perform the task of articulating the decisions to be adopted by the top administrators, and this delegation may serve to dilute the benefits otherwise accruing from the imposition of the discipline of opinion writing upon the officials rendering the decision.

2. Rulemaking

Informal or "notice and comment" rulemaking has been employed extensively by administrative agencies, including those involved in energy matters, for the formulation of regulations, statements of policy and the like. Under the APA, a rule is "the whole or a part of an agency statement of general or particular applicability and future effect designed to implement, interpret, or prescribe law or policy" or to establish rules of practice. 5 U.S.C. § 551 (4). In rulemaking, the agency initially publishes a notice of proposed rulemaking that sets forth "either the terms or substance of the proposed rule or a description of the subjects and issues involved." 5 U.S.C. 553(b). Comments are solicited from regulated industries, competitors, and interested citizens and organizations. Many facets of the problems to be addressed are uncovered and developed, as well as the perspectives from which various players viewed the problems. With this information in mind, the agency can formulate rules that serve its policy goals while giving due consideration to the rights and interests of the diverse entities involved. In the energy area, ratemaking in the natural gas industry has proceeded by rulemaking rather than by individual hearings since the mid–1970s. See *Shell Oil Co. v. FPC* (5th Cir.1975).

During the 1970s and 1980s, the use of notice-and-comment rulemaking as a method for agencies to address issues grew markedly. Richard J. Pierce, Jr., *The Choice Between Rulemaking and Adjudication for Formulating and Implementing Energy Policy*, 30 HASTINGS L. J. 1 (1979); Cornelius M. Kerwin, RULEMAKING: HOW GOVERNMENT AGENCIES WRITE LAW AND MAKE POLICY (2003). The rulemaking process can be more efficient than case-by-case adjudication because rulemaking can resolve many issues in a single proceeding. By the same token, rulemaking can inspire more focused opposition from many sources, including an entire industry, to an agency course of action than would an adjudication. Nonetheless, rulemaking has become a preferred mode of action in the agencies and has been encouraged by Congress. In general, the courts have been liberal in permitting agencies to use notice-and-comment rulemaking. See *National Petroleum Refiners Ass'n v. FTC* (D.C. Cir. 1973).

For a time, however, the courts mandated something called "hybrid" rulemaking, which required procedures intermediate in formality between adjudication and rulemaking, usually consisting of an evidentiary hearing with cross-examination. These developments were essentially brought to an end by *Vermont Yankee Nuclear Power Corp. v. Natural Resources Defense Council, Inc.* (S.Ct.1978), which involved the weight to be assigned by the Nuclear Regulatory Commission (NRC) to the environmental effects of radioactive waste in licensing nuclear power plants. The District of Columbia Circuit held that the agency had not permitted adequate exploration of certain testimony about its plans for disposal of nuclear waste and that interveners were entitled to additional procedural opportunities such as discovery and cross-examination. The Supreme Court reversed unanimously, saying that except in "extremely rare" circumstances courts may not require agencies to use rulemaking procedures beyond those required by the APA or by other statutes or the Constitution. The Court was concerned that, if hybrid processes could be imposed, agencies, to anticipate judicial demands, would lean toward using highly adversarial procedures in every case.

Vermont Yankee and its blocking of courts' efforts to prescribe hybrid procedures for agencies has not been interpreted to impair the courts' ability to engage in exacting review of the substance of agency rulemakings. Courts have continued to employ "hard look" review and have prescribed "reasoned decisionmaking" to establish the rationality of agency rules as discussed below.

Another significant factor in rulemaking by agencies is the role of the Office of Information Regulatory Affairs (OIRA), an entity within the Office of Management and Budget (OMB), which is in turn an organization within the Executive Office of the President commonly referred to as The White House). OIRA engages in systematic examination of proposed "significant" rules to determine whether they are cost-justified and consistent with Administration policy. This form of executive oversight can play a significant role in the development of rules.

Rulemaking by negotiation or "reg-neg" was originally explored by the Administrative Conference and later codified in the Negotiated Rulemaking Act of 1990, 5 U.S.C. § 561 *et seq.* Under this concept, concerned interest groups and the concerned agency could send representatives to bargaining sessions led by a mediator. This process might produce a proposed rule, which would then be published by the agency and would go through the standard APA rulemaking process. The agency, of course, would be under no obligation to accept the compromise offering of the negotiators, but the concept might encourage the development of a cooperative attitude on the part of the various interest groups in approving an eventual rule.

The APA does not contain any requirement that, if new policy is to be announced, it be formulated, on the one hand, by an adjudication or, on the other, by a rulemaking. And the courts, in general, have not made it mandatory for agencies, in making policy, to use one of these procedures in preference to the other. Some agencies at certain times seem to have preferred adjudication as a policymaking device more or less along the same lines as the courts developed the common law incrementally. Affected entities have from time to time challenged this preference in the courts, primarily in National Labor Relations Board cases, but the courts have not enforced any requirement that rulemaking be employed in these cases.

In recent years there has been some dissatisfaction with notice-and-comment rulemaking on the grounds that, particularly with the demands of Congress and the White House for various analyses of the potential effects of significant proposed rules, the rulemaking exercise has become too burdensome. This trend has been called by some the "ossification" of the rulemaking process. See e.g. Paul R. Verkuil, *Comment: Rulemaking Ossification—A Modest Proposal*, 47 ADMIN. L. REV. 453 (1995). The fundamental problem now is to determine how society can establish adequate control of the rulemaking process without so burdening it as to destroy its usefulness. See e.g., Thomas O. McGarity, *Some Thoughts on "Deossifying" the Rulemaking Process*, 41 DUKE L. J. 1385 (1992).

D. JUDICIAL REVIEW

Judicial review of administrative decisions is usually available, and the scope of review is prescribed by the APA—or as the APA may be modified by organic statutes. However, there are certain categories of administrative actions that are not judicially reviewable. In some cases, judicial review may be precluded by statute. This, for example, was at one time fully the case with the provision of benefits for veterans by the Veterans Administration. Certain categories of immigration decisions have also been removed from the review jurisdiction of the federal courts. Another area in which judicial review is not available involves matters which have been committed to agency discretion. This is a wide, if not numerous, category of excepted cases, and the most general exception arises in situations where there is "no law to apply." Thus, when the agency's decision involves matters that are completely discretionary, and there can be no arguable violation of any law, the exception of commitment to agency discretion might reasonably apply.

Another issue which may affect the availability of judicial review, involves the matter of standing. This body of law has evolved through several doctrinal phases in modern times but now seems to impose a requirement that there be a "substantial likelihood" that the defendant is causing harm to the plaintiff and that a favorable decision will actually redress the harm. Just how direct or indirect may be the process of causation and the prospects of redressability requires a careful study of the case law.

There are also important questions of timing in judicial review. One of these involves the requirement of exhaustion of administrative remedies before review may be sought in court. If the administrative proceeding is still ongoing, there is every chance that the case will be dismissed in court. It is also necessary for an agency action to be "final" in order to seek judicial review. In fact, the APA states that only "final agency action" (in addition to agency action made reviewable by statute) is subject to judicial review. 5 U.S.C.§ 704. The "ripeness" doctrine also affects timing. This doctrine is essentially of a prudential nature and requires that the issue in question have progressed to a point where it might be resolved by a court.

Assuming that a matter is reviewable, however, it is important to understand what the scope of that review might be. The APA specifies various standards under which the courts may set aside administrative action. The various grounds on which an agency decision may be reversed are listed in § 706(2) of the APA. Two clauses deal only with questions of law, whether the Constitution has been violated (§ 706(2)(B)) and whether the agency has violated its statutory mandate (§ 706(2)(C)). There are two other clauses that deal only with issues of fact: § 706(2)(E) codifies the "substantial evidence" test, which is most often applied in proceedings in which there has been a trial-type hearing; and § 706(2)(F) provides for *de novo* review of the facts, which is rarely applied. § 706(2)(A) codifies the APA's "arbitrary and capricious" test, which, in various contexts, can involve legal, factual or discretionary issues. Finally, § 706(2)(D) provides authority to reverse an agency in case of a procedural error. These standards of review are quite deferential, particularly if questions of fact and matters committed to discretion are involved.

In matters of law, such as statutory interpretation, the courts purport to be the ultimate authority, and to some extent judicial independence is at stake. However, courts must also be duly observant of Congress' delegations to the agencies in terms that are frequently left open-ended in the expectation that the agencies will supply the necessary detail. It would not seem inappropriate for courts to arrogate to themselves, in most cases, the ultimate power to decide questions of law and to interpret statutes, an enterprise in which they would seem to be well qualified. This may particularly be the case in defining the jurisdictional bounds of an agency's authority, where the courts would seem to be less self-interested than the agency. On the other hand, there are numerous technical determinations involving, for example, the allowable level of pollutants in air quality prescriptions or the capability of emergency core cooling systems in nuclear reactors to prevent releases of radiation, which are certainly more within the range of knowledge of administrative agencies than of the generalists sitting on the reviewing courts. Similarly, proper regard must be given to the conclusions of the finder of fact who has heard the witnesses and taken the testimony.

This allocation of functions on judicial review also tends to promote economy and efficiency. A court's one-time interpretation of the law will constitute a standard that an agency may apply in all future cases. Such a decision is not wasteful of judicial resources. Courts, however, do not undertake the burden of determining the facts in each case, but apply a deferential standard of review to the efforts of the agencies who carry out this function. Were it otherwise, the courts would soon be swamped with litigation. Despite the somewhat deferential standard which the courts apply both to determinations of fact and to exercises of discretion, in recent years the courts have in their supervisory role become more demanding.

It is always difficult to make classifications between matters of law and matters of fact and especially so in dealing with the halfway house consisting of "mixed questions of law and fact." The courts have appeared to dispose of mixed questions in inconsistent ways. For example, in *NLRB v. Hearst Publications, Inc.* (S.Ct.1944) the Labor Board determined that "newsboys" who peddled Hearst newspapers on street corners were "employees" within the meaning of the National Labor Relations Act and hence entitled to bargain collectively. The Supreme Court ruled that its function as a reviewing court was "limited" because "the question [was] one of specific application of a broad statutory term." A few years later, however, the Court sustained the Board's determination that foremen could join unions, notwithstanding their ties to management. *Packard Motor Car Company v. NLBR* (S.Ct.1947). In that case, however, the court did not employ a deferential standard of review as it did in *Hearst*, even though the same statutory term "employee" was involved. The court instead decided the issue on its own authority.

An agency in applying law to facts is required to make two distinct determinations: the agency must decide what legal constraints control the problem at issue, and then decide what action to take within those bounds. Essentially, the agency's view of the law must survive a relatively independent judicial examination and, if the court then proceeds to the second step—the task of law application—the court's role is substantially more deferential. The agency's application of the law to the facts is governed by a standard of rationality or reasonableness.

Courts normally review an agency's legal conclusions with a greater degree of independence than would be shown toward the agency's findings of fact and policy judgments. Nevertheless, judicial review of agencies' construction of statutes involves a good deal of deference, as was emphasized by the Supreme Court in *Chevron U.S.A., Inc. v. NRDC* (S.Ct.1984). *Chevron* concerned a challenge to the EPA's "bubble" policy, an approach designed to reduce the costs of pollution controls to manufacturers. The issue was whether the agency could construe the Clean Air Act term, "stationary source," to refer to a whole industrial plant, rather than to an individual apparatus within the plant. The Supreme Court upheld the policy by prescribing a sequence of inquiry that a reviewing court should follow when reviewing an agency's construction of a statute. The first inquiry to be made was whether "Congress has directly addressed the precise question at issue." If so, the court should "give effect to the unambiguously expressed intent of Congress." On the other hand, if the statute in question is "silent or ambiguous with respect to the specific issue," the question becomes whether the agency's answer is "permissible" or a "reasonable interpretation." This prescription gives effect, by a presumption, to the regulatory power that has been delegated to the agency. Therefore, if the statute remains ambiguous, it must be presumed that Congress has delegated to the agency the task of filling in the gap in some reasonable way.

Despite the directives of *Chevron*, courts sometimes remain wedded to the view that they are the ultimate arbiters of questions of law and statutory interpretation. On any particular issue, courts are inclined to the view that Congress has "directly addressed" it. In addition, the existence of ambiguity is itself ambiguous, and on this basis a court may well reject an agency interpretation. As a practical matter, and in the language of *Chevron*, the question becomes how "unambiguous" must the legislation be, or how "unreasonable" must the agency's interpretation be, to justify reversal.

Thus, in one case, the court found that the word "modify" connoted only moderate change and held that the Federal Communications Commission's wholesale dismantling of a rate regulation program was too sweeping to qualify as a "modification." *MCI Telecommunications Corp. v. American Tel. and Tel. Co.* (S.Ct.1994). Nor has *Chevron* precluded courts from employing the traditional tools of statutory interpretation, such as the over-all structure of the statute and legislative history. In some cases, courts have followed the traditional maxim to reject an otherwise reasonable agency interpretation because it would raise a constitutional question. And, it is interesting that the aspect of *Chevron* which permits a court to find an agency's view "unreasonable" has never been employed by the Supreme Court to set aside an agency interpretation.

In *United States v. Mead* (S.Ct.2001), the Supreme Court imposed some limitations upon *Chevron* by indicating that there must be some evidence that Congress intended to delegate to the agency authority to make rules carrying the force of law and applicable to the question at issue. So-called "ruling letters" of the United States Customs Service setting tariff classifications did not qualify for *Chevron* treatment. However, these ruling letters should be accorded the respect indicated by *Skidmore v. Swift and Co.* (S.Ct.1944), according to their persuasiveness in view of the knowledge and experience of the agency. Although there are some other limitations upon *Chevron*, it continues to furnish an important guide to balancing the roles of agencies and of courts.

In reviewing the facts found in a formal adjudication, a court normally may apply the "substantial evidence" test.

Substantial evidence has been defined as "such relevant evidence as a reasonable mind might accept as adequate to support a conclusion." *Consolidated Edison Company v. NLRB* (S.Ct.1938). This is an inquiry to determine that the agency has done a careful and competent job of collecting and evaluating the available data. Sometimes in this connection, the courts speak of the obligation of the agency to take a "hard look" at the important factual issues. In applying the "substantial evidence" test, the reviewing court is obliged to consider the "whole record." The court is not supposed to look only for evidence that supports the agency's decision; it is required to consider all of the relevant evidence for and against the agency's findings and determine whether they are within the "zone of reasonableness." One of the problems that may arise in applying the "substantial evidence" test is an agency reversal of an ALJ's initial finding of fact—particularly a reversal of a credibility determination. An agency is authorized to do this, but it must supply persuasive reasoning for the benefit of the reviewing court, and the contrary decision of the ALJ may detract from the substantiality of the evidence supporting the agency's decision.

Another commonly applied standard of review is the inquiry whether the agency action is "arbitrary, capricious, an abuse of discretion, or otherwise not in accordance" with law. 5 U.S.C. § 706(2)(A). This test is sometimes applied to certain types of factual determinations, but ordinarily it applies to agencies' exercises of discretion. This kind of "arbitrariness" review has been described as determining "whether the decision was based on a consideration of the relevant factors and whether there has been a clear error of judgment," see *Citizens to Preserve Overton Park, Inc. v. Volpe* (S.Ct.1971). This test has involved scrutiny of the quality of an agency's reasoning, a "hard look" at the problems raised, and a requirement that the agency engage in "reasoned decision making."

Sometimes an administrative discretionary decision, although in accord with the controlling statutes, may be inconsistent with the agency's own rules; this may be a basis for the courts to invalidate it. Also, departure from the agency's precedents found in earlier adjudicative decisions can amount to an abuse of discretion, although a reviewing court is not compelled to reach this conclusion and may remand for a further explanation of the departure.

An agency can also abuse its discretion by violating certain principles of judge-made law, such as the principle of "equitable estoppel." In addition, a court may sometimes set aside an agency remedy on the ground that it is too severe, or courts may intervene when an agency applies a new holding retroactively if the courts believe that the interest in enforcement is outweighed by the inequity of imposing a sanction for conduct reasonably believed to be lawful. *See* e.g., *Retail, Wholesale and Department Store Union v. NLRB* (D.C. Cir. 1972).

It is important that an agency explain its findings and the reasons for them adequately, so that they may be examined by the reviewing courts. If the agency fails to do so, the courts may remand the matter for further explanation. Under the *Chenery* line of cases, a reviewing court may not affirm an agency decision on a basis other than that advanced by the agency. The reason for this is that only the agency has delegated authority from Congress to make discretionary determinations. And the courts may not make them for it. See. *SEC v. Chenery Corp.* (S.Ct.1947).

In *Morgan v. United States* (S.Ct.1938), the Supreme Court held that it was not "the function of the court to probe the mental processes of the Secretary in reaching his conclusions if he gave the hearing that the law required." Under this doctrine, a presumption of regularity attaches to the agency decision, and courts will not look for motives hidden under the surface of agency opinions. Problems may arise, however, when an agency acts without giving any explanation at all for its decision. In *Citizens to Preserve Overton Park, Inc. v. Volpe* (S.Ct.1971), the Supreme Court held that a reviewing court could make an inquiry into the agency's rationale either by obtaining affidavits from the decisionmakers or by having them testify in court. Alternatively, a court may take the preferred action of remanding the action to the agency for necessary explanation. But, if an agency does provide a contemporaneous explanation for its decision, the agency's opinion must ordinarily be taken as a *bona fide* expression of the agency's reasoning.

Many of the principles of scope of review that we have mentioned were originally conceived for courts to employ when an agency acts after formal, trial-type proceedings. Additional approaches must be employed when reviewing more informal decisions, including the review of rulemaking. Ordinarily the substantial evidence test does not apply to these informal proceedings, and usually factual review proceeds either with recourse to *de novo* consideration (now very rare) or to the arbitrary and capricious standard. In *Citizens to Preserve Overton Park v. Volpe* (S.Ct.1971), the court held that an informal action, such as a highway funding decision, must be reviewed for abuse of discretion on the basis of the "full administrative record that was before the Secretary at the time he made the decision."

The *Overton Park* principle that review should be applied on an "administrative record" has been extended to informal rulemaking cases. Under this approach, the possibility of subsequently exploring in the courts the factual basis for an agency's decision has been superseded. Agencies and regulated parties now understand that they must make their case at the administrative level because the reviewing court will disregard any evidence subsequently advanced.

In an informal rulemaking proceeding, the administrative record generally consists of a notice of proposed rulemaking, the final rule itself and its accompanying statement of basis and purpose, together with filed comments and any unprivileged working papers compiled by the agency. The rule will survive review under the arbitrary and capricious test if the record contains evidence that could lead a reasonable person to accept the factual basis of the regulation (taking into account the contrary evidence opposing the rule). The concept of the administrative record has been a key step in the development of "hard look" review of rulemaking.

Like other forms of agency action reviewed under the APA, rules must conform with the agency's statutory mandate, with the Constitution and with procedural requirements and must also not be arbitrary and capricious. In the rulemaking context, the principal issues concern policy judgments and "legislative facts," which often are not susceptible of proof as might be the case in a typical adjudicative proceeding. Also, the issues can be highly technical, as is the case in many determinations of energy questions. The informal rulemaking record is very much like materials collected in the proceedings before a legislative committee hearing on a proposed bill. There are letters, e-mails and written statements from proponents and opponents and occasional oral testimony not subjected to cross-examination. In reviewing such a record, courts must be cautious about not pursuing their own policy preferences and donning the garments of the legislator. The courts must seek to confine their efforts to correcting any overreaching by the administrative agencies while at the same time not nullifying democratic principles.

The Supreme Court approved the requirement of "reasoned decisionmaking" in *Motor Vehicle Mfrs. Ass'n. v. State Farm Mut. Auto Ins. Co.* (S.Ct.1983). This case concerned the rescission by the Department of Transportation in 1981 of a 1977 rule requiring the installation of "passive restraints" in automobiles—either airbags or automatic seatbelts. The agency explained its determination by finding that "detachable" automatic seatbelts would not necessarily advance safety because consumers would detach them. The Supreme Court located two deficiencies in this explanation. First, consumers who would not bother to fasten seatbelts might well allow self-fastening belts to remain in place, and the agency did not address this crucial argument. In addition, the agency did not explain why, even if the automatic detachable belts were ineffective, the agency had not instead substituted a requirement of airbags or "nondetachable" seatbelts, both of which the agency itself had earlier found to be effective. The Supreme Court in *State Farm* carefully pointed out that the alternatives ignored by the agency were clearly contained in the record and that the agency was reversing a settled course of action. The court said that the agency must discuss the available evidence and "provide a rational connection between the facts found and the choice made."

Of course, the principles of "hard look" and "reasoned decisionmaking" are difficult of application to the highly technical questions that must be considered by many agencies, especially those concerned with environmental and energy problems. Most courts have recognized their own weaknesses in ability to deal with these kinds of a questions. The Supreme Court itself has recognized the need for judicial restraint in the area of technical determinations. In *Industrial Union Department, AFL–CIO v. American Petroleum Institute* (S.Ct. 1980), the plurality read a statute to demand a showing of significant risk before toxic substances could be regulated. But it concluded that there was no requirement on the Secretary of Labor to support his finding "with anything approaching scientific certainty." The finding of risk required support only by "a body of reputable scientific thought." And in *Baltimore Gas & Electric Company v. NRDC* (S.Ct.1983), the Supreme Court commented that, "a reviewing court must generally be at its most deferential" when an agency is "making predictions, within its area of special expertise, at the frontiers of science."

Another question which occasionally arises concerns the judicial reviewability of agencies' failure to act, usually failure to enforce the law in certain situations. This problem arose in *Heckler v. Chaney* (S.Ct.1985), where eight death row prisoners wrote to the Food and Drug Administration (FDA)with the argument that states' use of lethal drug injections in human executions violated the Food, Drug and Cosmetics Act. They wanted the FDA to bring suit to stop the practice, but the FDA refused. The Supreme Court backed the agency, holding that an agency's declination to initiate an enforcement proceeding is "presumptively unreviewable."

Obviously, the standards of judicial review remain imprecise and leave a considerable area for the discretion of individual judges. Whether the exercise of judicial review is on balance beneficial or detrimental to jurisprudential values is an area of contention. Of course, defenders of judicial review have emphasized its contribution to the rule of law and its implementation of a quality control function remedying sloppiness and failure to observe every requirement at the administrative level. A very important point in defense of judicial review is that it substitutes a generalist's perspective for the narrowly focused outlook of specialized agencies. Skeptics about judicial review like to point out that agencies, with their technical sophistication and experience, can deal with problems more effectively than courts that lack their resources.

E.   FEDERAL ENERGY REGULATION

The Department of Energy Organization Act, 42 U.S.C. § 7101, established the DOE in 1977 for the purpose of coordinating and focusing national energy efforts in response to the energy crisis of the 1970s, when the Arab countries' oil embargo reduced supply and raised oil prices stratospherically. The oil embargo directly affected the availability and price of other forms of energy. Within the DOE, which was a cabinet-level agency, was placed the Federal Energy Regulatory Commission (FERC), an independent regulatory agency, which carried on all the functions of the former Federal Power Commission.

1. Department of Energy

Before the creation of the DOE, the federal regulation of energy resources was spread throughout almost every cabinet department, not to mention eight or nine independent regulatory agencies with jurisdiction over various energy programs. The field of energy regulation was fragmented throughout the government. Originally, the DOE assumed all the powers of the Federal Energy Administration, the Energy Research and Development administration and the Federal Power Commission; and these agencies were eliminated, at least in name. In addition to the FERC, with which it is linked on an equal basis, the DOE contains and is responsible for, among other organizations and program efforts, the National Nuclear Security Administration, various research programs and facilities (including one for electric transmission and distribution), the Energy Information Administration, which is a statistical agency collating and analyzing energy information, the Assistant Secretary for Policy and International Affairs, and the Power Marketing Administrations, such as Bonneville and the Southwestern Power Administrations. The National Nuclear Security Administration is responsible for maintaining and enhancing the safety, reliability and performance of the United States nuclear weapons stockpile and related issues. Within the DOE there is an Under–Secretary for Energy, Science and the Environment who has important responsibilities for such matters as energy efficiency, energy conservation and renewable energy. Despite the 1977 consolidation, however, there are still important energy agencies and programs which are not under the umbrella of the Department of Energy and are mentioned below.

The APA is applicable to all of DOE's actions. However, the DOE Organization Act has prescribed certain modifications of APA-approved procedures for application to the DOE. For example, if a proposed DOE rule is likely to have a substantial impact on the nation's economy, then an opportunity for oral presentation of views, data and arguments must be provided. In the same vein, if the Secretary determines that a substantial issue of fact or law exists, then an opportunity for an oral presentation must be offered, while, under § 553 of the APA, due process would be satisfied by the submission of written comments. The Secretary is authorized to waive these additional requirements if strict compliance with them is likely to cause harm or injury to the public health, safety or welfare. These additional rulemaking safeguards do not apply to the FERC, whose procedures are generally covered by the APA. The principal rulemaking efforts in the energy area have in fact been undertaken by the FERC rather than by the DOE as such.

2. The Federal Energy Regulatory Commission (FERC)

The FERC has assumed the powers and responsibilities previously possessed by the Federal Power Commission (FPC). The FERC has five commissioners appointed by the President and confirmed by the Senate, of whom only three may be from one political party.

The FERC staff, which consists of specialists in various aspects of energy development, is organized into a number of offices, including an Office of Energy Projects, which has oversight over hydroelectric facilities and natural gas pipelines and energy projects that are in the public interest. The Office of Markets, Tariffs and Rates deals with matters involving markets, tariffs and rates relating to electric, natural gas and oil pipeline facilities and services. The emphasis on the word "markets" suggests the importance of deregulation. Traditionally, of course, rates for natural gas, wholesale electric power and oil pipelines were set in adversary proceedings with cross-examination before an ALJ. The FERC has historically been engaged in exercising powers under the Federal Water Power

Act, the Federal Power Act, the Natural Gas Act, the Natural Gas Policy Act and other energy-related statutes.

In the ratemaking area, for example, wholesale rates for regulated electric utilities are subject to regulation by the FERC under Sections 205 and 206 of the Federal Power Act. No change in rates, charges, classifications or service may be made except after sixty days notice to the FERC and to the public. A new schedule of rates may be suspended for investigation by the FERC for a period no longer than five months. If the FERC has not made a determination with respect to the new rates within the five-month suspension period, these rates may be collected subject to refund if finally disallowed. The standard for approval of rates is that they be just and reasonable and not confer any undue preference or involve any unreasonable difference.

Similarly, the rates of regulated natural gas companies are subject to regulation by the FERC under Sections 4 and 5 of the Natural Gas Act. The notice requirement (thirty days in the case of gas) and the five-month suspension period are similar to the requirements for electric utilities and, like the electric requirements, after the suspension period, rates may be collected under bond subject to refund. The just and reasonable standard and the prohibition of undue preferences and unreasonable differences—similar to the provisions governing electric utilities—are in force for natural gas companies.

3. Other Energy-related Agencies

Although the Department of Energy Organization Act was an effort to consolidate the principal energy programs of the government, some of these for various reasons remained outside the new department. One of the most prominent of these is the Nuclear Regulatory Commission (NRC). The NRC is headed by a five-member commission, appointed by the President and confirmed by the Senate. The President designates one member to serve as Chairman and official spokesperson. The Commission as a whole formulates rules and regulations governing nuclear reactor and materials safety issues, issues orders to licensing boards and adjudicates legal matters brought before it. The Executive Director for Operations carries out the policies and decisions of the Commission and directs the activities of its program offices. The Commission issues construction permits and operating licenses for nuclear power plants with paramount emphasis on health and safety issues.

The NRC was one of the agencies to come out of the former Atomic Energy Commission, as to which there was some concern that by covering both regulatory and promotional activities it had a built-in conflict of interest; hence its functions were divided between the NRC and the Energy Research and Development Administration, which was to carry on research, development and promotion of the use of atomic energy. The principal reasons the NRC's regulatory duties were not folded into the Department of Energy were the emphasis on the safety of nuclear power plants and the concern that this function not be diluted by absorption into a more broadly based agency. The NRC has four regional offices to carry on its activities throughout the United States.

Another agency whose activities have a profound impact upon energy is the U.S. Environmental Protection Agency (EPA). The EPA develops and enforces regulations that implement environmental laws enacted by Congress. The EPA is responsible for researching and setting national standards for a variety of environmental programs, and delegates to states and tribes the responsibility for issuing permits and for monitoring and enforcing compliance. Where national standards are not met, the EPA can impose sanctions and take other steps to assist the states and tribes in reaching the desired levels of environmental quality. Since the development and use of energy has powerful environmental impacts, the regulatory activities of the EPA are a major factor in energy production, development, transportation and distribution. Many EPA rules and regulations have a direct impact on energy activities. The EPA's mission is to protect human health and to safeguard the natural environment—air, water and land—upon which life depends. It would not have been appropriate, because of the potential conflict of their missions, to place the EPA within the Department of Energy. The principal obligation of the Department of Energy is to assure an adequate and reliable supply of energy, while that of the EPA is to assure that the exploitation of energy resources does not unduly adversely impact the environment.

Another large agency with major energy responsibilities is the Department of the Interior (DOI), which was created by Congress in 1849. One of its missions, among many others, is to provide wise stewardship of energy and mineral resources. The DOI manages 507 million acres of surface land, or about one-fifth of the land in the United States. Energy projects on federally-managed lands and offshore areas supply about 28% of the nation's energy production. This includes: 34.5% of natural gas, 32% of oil, 35% of coal, 17% of hydro power and 48% of geothermal resources. The Bureau of Reclamation (BOR), which is an agency of the DOI, operates 58 hydroelectric power plants. The Bureau of Land Management (BLM), another DOI agency, administers on-shore minerals underlying federal lands, a total of about 700,000,000 subsurface acres of minerals. Production from on-shore federal lands accounts for 33% of national coal production, 11% of natural gas production and 5% of domestic oil production. The Office of Surface Mining (OSM), another agency of the Department of the Interior, was created to help implement the Surface Mining Control and Reclamation Act of 1977. The mission of the OSM is to insure that surface coal mines are operated in a manner that protects citizens and the environment during mining, assures that the land is restored to beneficial use following mining and mitigates the effects of past mining by aggressively pursuing reclamation of abandoned mine lands.

Thus, the venerable DOI plays a major role in energy policy in the United States, and the reasons for its non-inclusion in the relatively recently created DOE include DOI's size and age.

There are numerous other programs impacting energy, carried on by other agencies of the United States government too numerous to mention.

F.   ENERGY REGULATION BY THE STATES

1.   The Historical Roots of State Regulation

The roots of regulation in the public interest may be traced back as far as the "just price" doctrine of medieval times ascribed to the early Church Fathers and their doctrine of *justus pretium*, which was contrasted with the doctrine of *verum pretium*, or "natural price," which the Roman Law had derived from Stoic philosophy. This natural price doctrine justified any price reached by agreement in effecting exchanges between willing buyers and willing sellers and is therefore not unlike modern economic doctrines. The "just price" school, on the other hand, held that, for trading to be legitimate, the trader having paid a just price to the producer, might add in selling only so much to the price as was customarily sufficient for his economic support. See e.g. Jerry Z. Muller, THE MIND AND THE MARKET: CAPITALISM IN MODERN EUROPEAN THOUGHT, ch. 1 (2002).

During the Middle Ages these ideas guided commerce among the guilds, which were to provide service to all comers at reasonable prices. When the common law courts came to displace the authorities of the guilds, manors and towns, certain occupations or callings were singled out and made the subject of special rights and duties. These occupations became known as "common callings" and were explained primarily by the way business was conducted; that is, a person who practiced such a calling, as distinguished from the conduct of a private calling, sought public patronage. Lord Chief Justice

Hale (1609–1676) in his treatise, *De Portibus Maris*, was apparently the first to use the term, "affected by a public interest," as applicable to the common callings. The list of common or public occupations regulated by the English Parliament included those of bakers, brewers, cab drivers, ferrymen, innkeepers, millers, smiths, surgeons, tailors and wharfingers.

These ideas continued to develop in colonial America where efforts were made to regulate prices for such products as beer, bread, corn and tobacco, although the most detailed control was exercised over common carriers by land and water. After the War of 1812, many of these restrictions lapsed, and the general view was that competition was the best form of control for the general welfare. Following the Civil War the doctrine of public interest control was revived, since competition did not seem to prove as effective as economic theory might indicate. The railroads were the first major exemplar of monopoly or quasi-monopoly, and Granger legislation sprang up in the 1870s to establish state commissions for regulation of the railroads. In 1877, the U.S. Supreme Court decided the case of *Munn v. Illinois* (S.Ct.1877), which held that the State of Illinois could regulate the rates of grain elevators in Chicago under Lord Hale's theory that these were businesses "affected with a public interest." After 1890, however, public interest regulation of economic activity fell into disfavor and laissez-faire doctrine reigned supreme in the courts. Nonetheless, certain enterprises called public utilities were subjected to public regulation. In general, but not always, public utility status was conferred on monopoly enterprises. Generally, public utilities were given exclusive franchises to deliver their services in defined areas and were obligated to serve all who applied for service on equal terms and at just and reasonable prices.

Regulation of public utilities by state commissions evolved after regulation by the courts, directly by legislatures and under local franchises proved unworkable for one reason or another. Regulation by states through public services commissions is of great importance in the energy area, particularly in the area of electric power, since the states (or their municipalities) originally granted exclusive franchises to the utilities within their borders and regulated electric service from the generator through transmission and distribution to the local customer. There was no legal basis for federal regulation of electric power until the passage of the Federal Power Act in 1935. The first public service commission law was enacted in May, 1907, in New York State, and created jurisdiction over rapid transit, railroad, gas and electric companies. This was followed only a month later by the action of the Wisconsin legislature to expand the powers and duties of an existing railroad commission to cover such utilities as gas, light, power and telephone companies.

The idea of state regulation of electric power had been proposed and advocated by none other than Samuel Insull, one of the great developers of electric utilities in the United States, in a speech to the National Electric Light Association in 1898. The Wisconsin Commission, in large measure, followed the work of John R. Commons, a noted economist. By 1920 more than two-thirds of the states had regulatory commissions. After the Great Depression, the powers of many of these commissions were strengthened, and today all 50 states plus the District of Columbia have commissions known as public utilities or public service commissions, corporation commissions or commerce commissions. Most of these commissions have authority to issue licenses, franchises or permits for the initiation of service, for construction or abandonment of facilities and related matters. With respect to rates, commissions generally have power to require prior authorization of rate changes, to suspend proposed rate changes, to prescribe interim rates and to initiate rate investigations. Most commissions have authority to control the quantity and quality of service, to prescribe uniform systems of accounts and to require annual reports. More than three-quarters of the commissions are authorized to regulate the issuance of securities.

Boundary lines between federal and state regulation of public utilities, which include energy companies, are usually now well established. The Federal Power Act is at pains to preserve state jurisdiction, and the respective regulatory commissions have, for the most part, abstained from infringement. In the case of natural gas, federal regulation is more inclusive, since it covers gas transmission and only local distribution is reserved to the states. On the other hand, electric power has been primarily under state control, but due to deregulation is now coming increasingly under federal oversight.

G.   CONSTITUTIONAL PRINCIPLES AFFECTING REGULATORY JURISDICTION

Certain provisions of the United States Constitution are important, either in allocating regulatory powers between the states and the federal government or in placing limitations upon regulatory powers, either at the state or the federal level or at both. One of these provisions is the Commerce Clause, another is the Supremacy Clause and another is the Takings Clause of the Fifth Amendment and as applied by the Fourteenth Amendment to the states.

1.   Commerce Clause

The Commerce Clause of the United States Constitution gives Congress the power to regulate commerce with foreign nations, among the several states and with the Indian tribes. It is both an affirmative grant of Congressional authority and a limitation on state regulatory powers. In its negative aspect, it prohibits state regulatory measures designed to benefit instate economic interests by burdening out-of-state competitors. The Commerce Clause is of particular importance in energy law because energy resources are produced and sold locally and they are transported and sold in interstate commerce. See *New England Power Co. v. New Hampshire* (S.Ct. 1982). In other words, these businesses are susceptible to two or more regulatory authorities and with the potential for market disruption which has, in fact, occurred as will be explained in other chapters. Telephone service has been for many years divided between local service under state surveillance and long distance under federal control. An interesting question is presented by the question, "Who has jurisdiction over intrastate railroad service?" At first glance, intrastate service would seem to lie in state jurisdiction, but this service may be only a segment of an interstate movement. Intrastate rates may thus have a substantial impact on interstate rates. And a federal agency may have to have the last word on both categories of rates. An interesting problem was also presented by efforts of the Illinois legislature to further the cause of Illinois coal at the expense of coal from out-of-state sources. This constitutional question was resolved against Illinois by the United States Court of Appeals for the Seventh Circuit in *Alliance for Clean Coal v. Miller* (7th Cir. 1995).

Congress' power to regulate is not absolute. Congress has no authority under the Commerce Clause to regulate anything that is not related to commerce and no authority to do anything about commerce, except to regulate it—that is, Congress' exercise of the commerce power must have a real and substantial relation to some part of commerce. A statute that regulates an activity that has nothing to do with commerce or an economic enterprise or is not an essential part of a larger regulation of economic activity in which the regulatory scheme could be undercut unless the intrastate activity were regulated is subject to invalidation as an enactment in excess of Congress' authority under the Commerce Clause. At least this is true if the statute in question contains no jurisdictional element which would insure, through a case-by-case inquiry, that the prohibited activity in question affects interstate commerce so that the statute's reach would be limited to a discrete set of activities that have an explicit connection with or effect on interstate commerce. And, the measure might still be salvaged if it is accompanied by congressional findings as to the substantial burdens the prohibited activity has on interstate commerce that would enable judicial evaluation of the legislative judgment that the activity in question substantially affects interstate commerce. See *United States v. Lopez* (S.Ct. 1995); *New York v. United States* (S.Ct.1992); *FERC v. Mississippi* (S.Ct.1982).

2. The Supremacy Clause

The Federal Constitution provides that the laws of the United States made in pursuance thereof shall be the supreme law of the land, anything in the Constitution or the laws of any state to the contrary notwithstanding. Therefore, an act of Congress, constitutionally passed within the limits of its authority, becomes a part of the supreme law of the land. Hence, a state law is void if it is contrary to the valid will of Congress, since Congress clearly has the power to pre-empt state laws. *Pacific Gas & Electric Co. v. State Energy Resources Conservation and Development Comm.* (S.Ct.1983).

The critical question in any preemption analysis is whether Congress intended that federal regulation supersede state law. In a preemption case, a state law should be displaced only to the extent that it actually conflicts with a federal law or when the scope of a federal statute indicates that Congress intended the federal law to occupy the entire field exclusively. Obviously, preemption doctrine is of great importance in defining the boundaries between federal and state regulation of the same kind of activities, including, for example, energy activities. In *Louisiana Public Service Commission v. FCC* (S.Ct.1986), the Supreme Court held that depreciation rates for intrastate telephone equipment set by the Louisiana Public Service Commission were not pre-empted by the Federal Communications

Commission, which had adopted depreciation practices pursuant to validly adopted federal policies.

In matters involving electric power, Congress has been careful to avoid infringing on the prerogatives of the state commissions and their jurisdiction over local electric distribution service. However, the Federal Power Act gives the FERC jurisdiction over transmission in interstate commerce. This jurisdiction is presumably exclusive and was upheld in *New York Public Service Comm'n v. FERC* (S.Ct.2002). There is reason to believe that, as deregulation continues and regional power markets increase in importance, federal jurisdiction will tend to supersede and prevail over state jurisdiction.

In connection with concerns about reliability and the adequacy of the transmission system, a federal agency may ultimately be designated to regulate a national power grid and to prescribe the construction of transmission links as well as conceivably to authorize the powers of eminent domain to acquire transmission corridors. Although it may be an unintended consequence of the deregulation movement, there is a considerable likelihood of power and jurisdiction in this area continuing to move from the state to the federal level.

3. The Takings Clause

The Fifth Amendment to the Constitution of the United States and as applicable to the state through the Fourteenth Amendment provides that private property shall not be taken for public use without just compensation. The federal government is required to compensate the owner for what actually has been taken. The question of takings is relevant to energy law primarily with respect to the issue of regulatory takings: that is, regulatory actions that permanently deprive private property of all use, *c.f. Tahoe–Sierra Preservation Council, Inc. v. Tahoe Regional Planning Agency* (S.Ct.2002), or which attach conditions to land-use permits requiring the dedication to public use of property where the condition does not serve a public purpose related to the permit requirement. For purposes of constitutional takings, under limited circumstances, a state may resist payment of compensation even though regulation denies an owner all the economically beneficial or productive use of the land; those circumstances include instances in which the state can show that the owner's bundle of rights never included the right to use land in a way that regulation prohibits. *Iowa Coal Mining Co., Inc. v. Monroe County* (Iowa 1996).

Takings arguments in the energy area have mostly involved regulatory procedures which assertedly deny a public utility the right to earn a fair return on its property. Thus, in *Duquesne Light Company v. Barasch* (S.Ct.1989), Pennsylvania law required that rates for electricity be fixed without consideration of a utility's expenditure for electric generating facilities which were planned but never completely built, even though the expenditures were prudent and reasonable when made. The Supreme Court said:

> The Supreme Court of Pennsylvania held that such a law did not take the utility's property in violation of the Fifth Amendment to the United States Constitution. We agree with that conclusion and hold that a state scheme of utility regulation does not "take" property simply because it disallows recovery of capital investments that are not "used and useful in service to the public."

Takings claims, however, have been made repeatedly over the history of utility regulation, and remain an important weapon in the arsenal of regulated companies.

You will encounter these several legal principles throughout the remainder of the book. Suffice it to say that the topic of energy involves matters of policy as well as law. Nevertheless, no regulatory policy can be effectuated without strict adherence to the substantive and procedural laws that govern the regulatory state.

CHAPTER 4

ENERGY DECISIONMAKING

In the previous three chapters, we introduced the fundamental ingredients of the regulatory state—economics, politics, and law. In this chapter, these three elements combine in the energy decisionmaking process.

We cannot predict with any degree of certainty which regulations are likely to be proposed by the legislative process, but there is something we can say about government regulation with some confidence. For any given regulatory proposal, let's say a proposal to drill for oil in the Arctic National Wildlife Refuge as an example, we can say that the proposal will be implemented *if and only if*, the proposal is politically, economically, and legally sound. A regulatory proposal must make rational economic sense in terms of efficiency and fairness, have political support from legislators or administrators, and satisfy statutory and constitutional requirements. Joseph P. Tomain & Sidney A. Shapiro, *Analyzing Government Regulation*, 49 ADMIN. L. REV. 377 (1997). In other words, as students of government regulation, while we cannot *predict* which regulatory proposals are likely to emerge from legislative or political processes, we can *evaluate* those that do as to whether or not they are likely to survive those processes.

Regulatory proposals often start in the legislature. It is the case that most often legislation is drafted in general language and administrative agencies, which are mostly executive branch agencies, are directed to fill in details and implement the goals and objectives of the legislation. One can easily imagine that for a legislator, general language has several attractions. First, legislators cannot be expert in every field.

115

Second, agencies are charged with the responsibility of expert administration. Third, general language allows a legislator to claim credit for the passage of legislation and avoid blame for its implementation.

Herein lies the rub. Once an agency is given direction from the legislature, it is required to act by law on that direction. Agencies, of course, must satisfy statutory and constitutional law. Nevertheless, agencies can be caught in political cross-winds. Imagine, for example, the situation of a divided government with a president from one party and a Congress controlled by the other. Since most agencies are in the Executive Branch, one might suppose that an agency's allegiance should be to the president. Yet, agencies are directed to act and are sometimes monitored by the Legislative Branch. How can or should agencies behave in such situations, not to mention survive?

One way to fulfill their legal mandate and reduce (they can never eliminate) political pressure is through decision-making methods that are as objective and non-political as possible. One might think that, with all of the power that computers can provide, technical and scientific decision-making rules which are non-partisan and objective can be developed and relied upon. Life, however, is not so neat and politics, another behavioral science, cannot help but intrude into government regulation. Still, agencies do what they can to develop reliable, transparent, objective rules, particularly where economic and financial issues are at stake.

In this chapter, we expose you to two decision-making techniques used by administrative agencies in the field of energy law. Both methods—ratemaking and cost-benefit analysis—are intended to be quantitative for the explicit purpose of finding economically efficient solutions to regulatory problems. Be forewarned, though, that neither method is free from non-quantitative, normative political influences.

We start with an introduction to public utility regulation for two reasons. First, public utility law is the precursor to energy law and while the history of the field is instructive in itself, public utility principles still obtain. Second, public utilities provide an excellent example of our theory of government regulation as an interaction between government and markets. More specifically, a public utility is the quintessential example of market failure due to natural monopoly followed by government intervention. We should also note that while we concentrate on natural gas and electricity utilities, public utilities also cover such industries as water, cable television, and telephone. Indeed, today it is fashionable to label all of the above "network industries," which is just putting old wine in new bottles. Joseph P. Tomain, *networkindustries.gov.reg*, 48 U. KAN. L. REV. 829 (2000).

A. PUBLIC UTILITY REGULATION

The basic justification for what is today's energy regulation can be dated at least to the 19th century. The basis for public utility regulation lies in the very name of the object being regulated, that is, the *public* utility. Can a private firm affect the public interest such that government regulation of that firm can withstand a legal takings challenge? To pose the question in this way goes a long way to answering it. The antecedents of contemporary regulation are of historical interest and they indicate the breadth and the bases for regulation. In 1670, for example, England's Lord Chief Justice Matthew Hale authored a treatise entitled *De Portibus Maris* which justified government regulation of seaports precisely because seaports were affected with the public interest. John Stuart Mill in his *The Principles of Political Economy* (1848) adopted the same idea. On this side of the pond, government regulation traces its roots to early Commerce Clause litigation, including *Gibbons v. Ogden* (S.Ct.1824) asserting federal supremacy over steamboat regulation.

While it is understandable that the Commerce Clause of the United States Constitution would affect federal regulation on a wide variety of matters, utility regulation is based on a more narrow concept—the regulation of monopoly. For monopoly regulation we can turn to the early case of *Proprietors of Charles River Bridge v. Proprietors of Warren Bridge* (S.Ct. 1837). At issue in the *Charles River Bridge* case was whether or not the state would protect (in effect, grant a monopoly to) a toll bridge operator. The Charles River Bridge company operated a toll bridge across the Charles River and the company was granted a state charter. The charter, however, did not grant the company an explicit monopoly and the court refused to imply such a provision. However, the idea that the state would have protected the franchisee's investment and financial expectations if they bargained for monopoly protection is sound.

The immediate precursor to public utility regulation is railroad regulation and the basic justification for regulating both industries is the same. The first modern and most significant case of public utility regulation is the case of *Munn v. Illinois* (S.Ct.1877). At the heart of *Munn* is the question whether or not the State of Illinois could set prices on grain elevators. The Supreme Court held that the legislature could set prices in order to protect the public interest. *Munn v. Illinois* involved two elements: (1) the object to be regulated, in this case grain storage, was deemed to be in the public interest; and, (2) elevators operators occupied a position of natural monopoly. In short, the elevator operators were found to be setting prices above market prices to store farmers' grain.

The fundamental issue, however, is how can government constitutionally justify intrusions into private markets? That question may seem quaint now given the expanse of government regulation. Nevertheless, its underlying importance remains and our constitutional law demonstrates how much we have struggled with the fundamental relationship between government and markets.

To make this point imagine you operate a private business and the government decides to tell you what and where you can sell and what price you can set. Such government commands are anathema to any conception of a free market. Nevertheless, in today's regulatory state, the ability of government to limit territories and set prices is exactly the basis for ratemaking.

Over the 20th century, we have experienced a sea change in the view of government regulation. Prior to the New Deal, the Supreme Court engaged in strict judicial scrutiny of rate and economic regulation, as exemplified in the case of *Lochner v. New York* (S.Ct.1905), in which the Supreme Court invalidated workers' hours legislation holding that a state's interference with the freedom of contract violated the 14th Amendment. Later, exactly that type of regulation was upheld by the New Deal Court in *Nebbia v. New York* (S.Ct.1934), in which the Court held that a state could regulate prices as a part of its police power as long as the laws have a *reasonable relationship* to a proper legislative purpose.

The legal requirement that there be a reasonable relationship between the purpose of regulation and the object being regulated continues to this day. Regarding price setting, in *Nebbia*, the Court held:

> "[A] state is free to adopt whatever economic policy may reasonably be deemed to promote the public welfare, and to enforce that policy by legislation adapted to its purpose. The courts are without authority either to declare such policy or, when it is declared by the legislature, to override it. If the laws passed are seen to have a reasonable relation to a proper legislative purpose, and are neither arbitrary nor discriminatory, the requirements of due process are satisfied, ... And it is equally clear that if the legislative policy be to curb unrestrained and harmful

competition by measures which are not arbitrary or discriminatory it does not lie with the courts to determine that the rule is unwise. With the wisdom of the policy adopted, and with the adequacy or practicability of the law enacted to forward it, the courts are both incompetent and unauthorized to deal."

The *Nebbia* principle also applies to public utility rate-making because public utilities are deemed to be "affected with a public interest." Public policy is that these products and services should be made available at reasonable, competitive prices. Unfortunately, the industrial structure of a utility enables it to set monopoly prices and that is the mischief that regulation seeks to cure.

B. THE THEORY OF NATURAL MONOPOLY

Utilities are referred to as "natural monopolies" because of their structure. A natural monopoly occurs when a firm is able to grow larger and reduce prices simultaneously until it is the only firm in a market. Judge Richard Posner describes the situation of natural monopoly in the cable television industry:

The cost of the cable grid appears to be the biggest cost of a cable television system and to be largely invariant to the number of subscribers the system has. We said earlier that once the grid is in place ... the cost of adding another subscriber probably is small. If so, the average cost of cable television would be minimized by having a single company in any given geographical area; for if there is more than one company and therefore more than one grid, the cost of each grid will be spread over a smaller number of subscribers, and the average cost per subscriber, and hence price, will be higher.

If the foregoing accurately describes conditions in Indianapolis ... it describes what economists call a "natural monopoly," wherein the benefits, and indeed the very possibility, of competition are limited. You can start with a competitive free-for-all—different cable television systems frantically building out their grids and signing up subscribers in an effort to bring down their average costs faster than their rivals—but eventually there will be only a single company, because until a company serves the whole market it will have an incentive to keep expanding in order to lower its average costs. In the interim there may be wasteful duplication of facilities. This duplication may lead not only to higher prices to cable television subscribers, at least in the short run, but also to higher costs to other users of the public ways, who must compete with cable television companies for access to them. An alternative procedure is to pick the most efficient competitor at the outset, give him a monopoly, and extract from him in exchange a commitment to provide reasonable services at reasonable rates. *Omega Satellite Prods. Co. v. Indianapolis* (7th Cir. 1982).

This situation of natural monopoly is also the case for energy industries. For example, once a natural gas company lays a pipeline or an electric utility erects a transmission line, there is no good economic reason to lay another pipeline or transmission line. The additional lines are duplicative and wasteful. In order to eliminate such waste and to avoid the sins of misused market power caused by monopolistic pricing, government and utilities enter the regulatory compact. Thus, government's answer to the problem of natural monopoly may seem counterintuitive, but its response is a government-protected monopoly! The government permits the utility to maintain its monopoly status, but it regulates the utility in an effort to set the price and quantity of service at what would be competitive levels. As the following description elaborates, the regulatory compact benefits both the utility and the ratepayers:

> The utility business represents a compact of sorts; a monopoly on service in a particular geographical area (coupled with state-conferred rights of eminent domain or

condemnation) is granted to the utility in exchange for a regime of intensive regulation, including price regulation, quite alien to the free market.... Each party to the compact gets something in the bargain. As a general rule, utility investors are provided a level of stability in earnings and value less likely to be attained in the unregulated or moderately regulated sector; in turn, ratepayers are afforded universal, non-discriminatory service and protection from monopolistic profits through political control over an economic enterprise. *Jersey Cent. Power & Light Co. v. F.E.R.C.* (D.C. Cir. 1987) (Judge Kenneth Starr).

The regulatory compact imposes significant obligations on both the government and the public utility at levels that are fair and reasonable and non-discriminatory. In exchange for a government-protected monopoly, the public utility lets government set its prices. The utility is given the power of eminent domain, is given a franchise or a service area, and is the only firm authorized to sell its product in that area. In fact, the utility acquires an obligation to serve that exclusive territory. The government, through ratemaking, sets the price of the service. Generally, rates will be set so that a prudently managed utility will cover its operating expenses and earn a reasonable return on its capital investment, thus enabling the utility to earn a profit. The regulatory control of natural monopoly, then, occurs by: (1) limiting entry; (2) setting prices; (3) controlling profits; and, (4) imposing a service obligation. The heart of the regulatory compact is the ratemaking process which, as you will learn next, has both political and economic dimensions.

C. RATEMAKING GOALS

Ratemaking has an economic dimension because it attempts to set prices at efficient (nonmonopolistic, competitive) levels. Ratemaking is political because the product is determined to be a social necessity and rates must be fair across different classes of consumers. Additionally, ratemaking can be designated to serve other social purposes. Although it can be said that all regulation is a combination of politics and economics, a view of that combination is frequently lost in an area as technical as ratemaking.

Ratemaking has five functions:

(1) Capital Attraction;

(2) Reasonably Priced Energy;

(3) Efficiency Incentive;

(4) Demand Control or Consumer Rationing; and

(5) Income Transfer.

See generally J. Bonbright, A. Danielson & D. Kamerschen, *Principles of Public Utility Rates* (2nd ed. 1988); C. Phillips, Jr., *The Regulation of Public Utilities: Theory and Practice* (3rd ed. 1993).

These regulatory goals can conflict. It can be the case, for example, that Goal 2, *Reasonably Priced Energy* conflicts with Goal 3, *Efficiency Incentive*. When prices are kept below market, then the efficiency goals suffers. Also, when prices exceed the market, then the goal of reasonable prices suffers. Both events have occurred during the history of utility regulation. These five goals attempt to serve the several interests of the utility, its shareholders, consumers, and the public generally.

1.   Capital–Attraction Function

Even though utilities are regulated industries, they are, for the most part, privately owned, and for a private business to function, it must borrow money or find investors. In short, private firms must attract capital. Accordingly, because of constitutional takings law, government must assure private firms that a fair revenue is available. Otherwise the firm would not be able to borrow money or attract investors. Thus, regulators must balance two competing demands. First, the private firm must be given the opportunity to make a profit. Second, the regulator must make sure that the utility does not gouge customers by charging monopolistic price. Prices cannot be kept so low that it simply is not worth it economically for a firm to stay in the public utility business; nor so high that the customers are disadvantaged. Therefore, regulators attempt to set rates which keep the utilities competitive. Firms are allowed to charge "reasonable rates," which are rates that allow them to encourage people to invest in utility stocks and bonds at the same rate of return as they would in comparable non-regulated industries.

In addition to covering operating costs and expenses, rate-making has been structured to allow a firm to expand plant and production. The capital-attraction function is another way of saying that rates should be set which allow utilities to seek investment capital for growth. Traditionally, investment in public utilities has been safe, promising a steady return. During the expansion and growth of the industry, until roughly 1970, utilities were seen as a steady growth industry. Utilities were a prudent investment for portfolio managers and individual investors. Any diversified investment portfolio would certainly have its share of utility stocks whose dividends were almost certain. During that period the return to shareholders was a little lower than that of competitive industry because utility stocks and bonds had been perceived to be a much less risky investment.

Since the 1970s, however, utilities find themselves in a more financially risky environment. Resource prices were affected by international cartels, business costs increased, inflation soared, and the political climate stressed resource and energy conservation. Each of these variables contributed to high energy prices and greater public and consumer awareness. Public utilities began to compete aggressively for investment capital, and rate setting agencies had to pay closer attention to the ability of a utility to find capital in the market. The direct consequence of such increased financial pressure on utilities was a demand by the utilities for higher rates of return. Regulators cautiously granted requests for rate increases until there was a public backlash over escalating utility prices, sometimes referred to as rate shock. The utility industry became even more complicated in the 1990's as federal and state regulators began deregulating network industries. Each of these events affects competition for investment dollars. Further, as the industry became more competitive, prices became more volatile. This period of industry change will be explained more fully in the chapters on natural gas and electricity.

2. Reasonably Priced Energy

As noted in Chapter Two, one element of the nation's general energy policy is low-cost energy. High utility rates are inconsistent with a policy favoring low-cost or reasonably priced energy. Therefore, as prices rose, utility commissions took a much harder look at the requests by utilities for rate increases. The consumer pressure to reduce rates, and the reluctance on the part of regulators to raise rates, have resulted in an era of greater competition in the electricity and natural gas industries. In the electricity industry, greater competition comes in the form of new producers. In the natural gas industry, greater competition was spawned by an increased supply of natural gas. Deregulation further complicates pricing because under microeconomic theory competition should put downward pressure on prices. Deregulation, as we shall see in later chapters, has not been smooth and is continuing in fits and starts. In other words, the electric and natural gas industries are in competitive limbo, remain partially regulated, and the effects of deregulation on the regulatory goal of reasonable energy prices is uncertain.

3. The Efficiency Incentive Function

What is an efficient price? Perhaps surprisingly, there is no single definition of efficiency and economists continue to debate the best measure. Nevertheless, under microeconomic theory, efficient pricing is a function of competition. In a regulated industry, however, there is no competition so the rate must be set to mimic the market. For regulated utilities, an efficient price is one which is designed to yield revenues to cover costs plus a "fair rate of return" for the investors. Regulators approximate this price by allowing a utility to recover its prudent operating costs and earn a reasonable rate of return on its capital investment. Below we describe the rate formula in more detail. The resulting rate must be one which keeps the utility competitive compared with firms with similar financial risks, thus, hopefully, approximating efficiency. In short, the regulated price will never get it exactly right and will be too high or too low given insufficient data combined with competing policies.

4. The Demand Control or Consumer Rationing Function

Another aspect of microeconomic theory is that price affects consumption. The lower the price the more of a product people will buy. A single firm can encourage people to purchase more of a product by lowering its prices. Likewise, a price increase decreases demand. Therefore, simply by setting prices ("rates" in the case of utilities) the regulator can affect consumption.

Through a concept known as *rate* design or *rate structure*, regulators can promote different energy policies. Until the mid–1970s, for example, utility rates were set according to a declining block method to encourage consumption. The declining block rate structure is graphically depicted below:

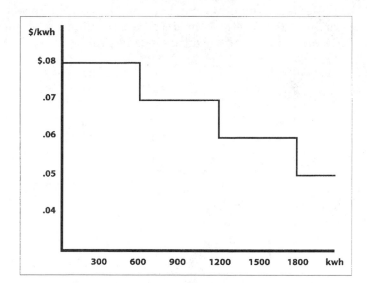

The above graph shows the cost of electricity in kilowatt hours. A kilowatt hour is the use of 1,000 watts of electricity in an hour. A residence will consume approximately 2000 kwh per month. The graph above shows that a utility will charge $.08 per kilowatt hour for the first 600 kwh consumed; then $.07 for the next 600 kwh; then $.06 for the next 600 and, then $.04 for all electricity consumed thereafter. Because the price declines, this rate design encourages consumption. With declining block rates, utilities are satisfied to sell as much as they can even at declining rates because they will have covered their fixed costs with the early purchases. And, consumers are satisfied because supply is plentiful and cost is declining. This rate structure works well when electricity is plentiful and works well when the market is expanding.

When electricity is not plentiful, at peak times such as the hottest days in the summer when air conditioners are working at capacity, utilities strain to produce and rates can be used to discourage consumption by raising the price of electricity with an increase in consumption. Such a rate structure is rare and this graph of a theoretical inverted rate is intended to show how consumption might be constrained at peak.

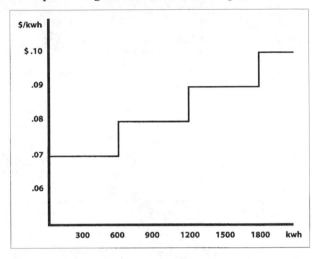

You can see from this above graph that as a consumer uses more electricity, the higher the cost of kilowatt hour. Therefore, if conservation is seen as a desirable goal, regulators can promote conservation by letting prices rise. Another design is a flat rate which charges the same price for all consumption for a period of time.

5.   Income Transfer Function

At the most general level, ratemaking distributes wealth from consumers to utility owners. Thus, one function of ratemaking is to affect the amount of money that is transferred from ratepayers to the shareholders that own the utility. In other words, ratemaking is not only a form of price control, it is also a form of profit control.

Ratemaking also involves redistributions of wealth among *and* within classes of customers. Utility customers generally can be grouped in three categories—residential, industrial, and commercial. Each group can be further subdivided. Residential customers, for example, can be classified by income level, or as owners of primary residences or vacation homes, as examples.

Each of these general categories has different costs associated with it. A large industrial plant, for example, consumes large amounts of electricity but does not require costly distribution for customer service. Individual residential customers, though, consume quite a bit less electricity, yet they require an electric line into each residence which incurs relatively high service costs and they have higher customer costs. Regulators can allocate rates differently among these various consumer classes through the rate structure.

One way to lower the cost of electricity to residential consumers is to set slightly higher rates for industrial customers, thus resulting in the subsidization of residential customers by industrial customers. Another form of wealth distribution comes under the heading of lifeline rates. Lifeline rates are lower utility rates for poor and elderly consumers who are thus being subsidized by other consumers.

The ability of a utility to discriminate in the pricing of the product is not without an economic explanation or justification. Different consumers have different demand elasticities. As the price of electricity rises, industrial consumers will find it easier than residential consumers to use other forms of energy. Compared to industrial consumers, residential customers have a greater demand inelasticity. Consequently, their "willingness to pay" is higher than that of industrial customers, and differential rates can reflect that "willingness."

We can see, then, that these several ratemaking goals are achieved primarily through two devices. The first device, *rate design* or *rate structure*, was discussed above through the examples of declining block, inverted block, and lifeline rates. This device also assigns rates across customer classes to achieve particular policy goals. The second device to which we now turn is the *rate formula* which assesses the amount of revenue a utility can earn. Recall that to be constitutional the rate cannot be so low as to be confiscatory and, by statute, it must be just, reasonable, and non-discriminatory.

D. THE RATE FORMULA

The traditional rate formula is intended to produce a utility's revenue requirement. The formula is simple to state:

$R = O + (V - D)r$

The elements of the traditional rate formula are defined as:

R   is the utility's total revenue requirement or rate level. This is the total amount of money a regulator allows a utility to earn.

O   is the utility's operating expenses.

V   is the gross value of the utility's tangible and intangible property.

D   is the utility's accrued depreciation. Combined $(V - D)$ constitute the utility's *rate base*, also known as its capital investment.

r   is the rate of return a utility is allowed to earn on its capital investment or on its rate base.

Defining the variables is simple, determining their content and application is more difficult.

1. Operating Expenses

A firm's operating expenses, such as wages, salaries, supplies, maintenance, taxes, and research and development, must be recouped if the utility is to stay operational. Operating costs are most often the largest component of the revenue requirement, and the easiest to determine. Occasionally, operating expense items have caught the attention of supervisory agencies and courts for such items as: automatic fuel cost adjustments; rate case and regulation expenses; salaries, wages, and benefits; advertising and public relations fees; and, charitable contributions and these items have been examined more closely.

Regulators must make two determinations. First, they must determine which items should be allowed as expenses. Second, regulators must determine the value of those expense items. The determination of value has generally been left to the management of the utility under the theory that these are essentially business decisions which will not be second guessed by a regulatory agency or a court. Managerial good faith is presumed. Although both agencies and courts have the legal authority to supervise the utility's management, they will not substitute their judgment unless there is an abuse of managerial discretion. *State of Missouri ex rel. Southwestern Bell Tel. Co. v. Public Service Comm'n of Missouri* (S.Ct.1923). Hence, litigation involving operating expense issues has been light.

2. Rate Base

The next step in determining the rate level is to ascertain the net amount of capital investment that a utility has made. This net, or depreciated, value includes tangible and intangible property and is known as the rate base. Tangible property includes plant and equipment used to provide the utility's service. Intangible property would include such items as some working capital items, leases, and franchises. This variable is crucial for the profitability of the utility because it is this variable against which the rate of return is measured. The rate base has been the subject of much litigation. The determination of what constitutes the rate base also forms the basis for the constitutional standard for judging whether or not rates are confiscatory.

Central to determining rate base is to determine the value of the capital investment. It should not be difficult to recognize that valuation methods vary. Let's take the simple example of a new power plant. How should that investment be valued? For commercial and residential buildings, valuation is relatively easy because comparable sales provide good data. There is no market for a new utility plant; so comparable sales are unavailable. Is the value of the plant the original cost of construction? Or the current reproduction cost? Or how the plant is valued on the company's books? Or the tax assessment? Or the cost of borrowing? What about investment in the plant during construction but before completion? What about the nuclear part of an investment made in a plant that is converted from nuclear power to coal? Or, the investment made in a project that is canceled before completion? These are all rate base questions.

In a period of static costs or no inflation, an original cost valuation may be sufficient. With a period of inflation, a rate base which values plant and equipment at original cost substantially undervalues the plant. In these circumstances, utilities argue in favor of reproduction cost valuations. In either case, depreciation on plant and equipment is subtracted from the rate base and carried as an operating expense. The theory behind including depreciation as an expense is that capital may be accumulated for further expansion and growth.

We have already mentioned that rates cannot be confiscatory. Early on in the history of ratemaking the legislature set the standard for what constituted a confiscatory rate. *Munn v. Illinois* (S.Ct.1876). Later, that legislative standard setting gave way to the judiciary. In *Smyth v. Ames* (S.Ct.1898) and later in *Bluefield Waterworks & Imp. Co. v. Public Service Commission* (S.Ct.1923), the Supreme Court listed factors that regulators should consider in evaluating a company's property, and in determining a rate of return to which a company is entitled. In *Smyth*, the Court wrote:

We hold, however, that the basis of all calculations as to the reasonableness of rates ... must be the fair value of the property being used by it for the convenience of the public. And in order to ascertain that value, the original cost of construction, the amount expended in permanent improvements, the amount and market value of its bonds and stock, the present as compared with the original cost of construction, the probable earning capacity of the property under particular rates prescribed by statute, and the sum required to meet operating expenses, are all matters for consideration, and are to be given such weight as may be just and right in each case. We do not say that there may not be other matters to be regarded in estimating the value of the property. What the company is entitled to ask is a fair return upon the value of that which it employs for the public convenience. On the other hand, what the public is entitled to demand is that no more be exacted from it for the use of a public highway than the services rendered by it are reasonably worth.

Justice Brandeis was a critic of *Smyth v. Ames* because some of the elements of the formula were contradictory and others circular. He announced another formula in his concurrence in *Missouri ex rel. Southwestern Bell Tel. Co. v. Missouri Pub. Serv. Comm'n* (S.Ct.1923)

" ... The investor agrees, by embarking capital in a utility, that its charges to the public shall be reasonable. His company is the substitute for the State in the performance of the public service; thus becoming a public servant. The compensation for which the Constitution guarantees an opportunity to earn is the reasonable cost of conducting the business. Cost includes not only operating expenses, but also capital charges. Capital charges cover the allowance, by way of interest, for the use of the capital, whatever the nature of the security issues therefore; the allowance for risk incurred; and enough more to attract capital. The reasonable rate to be prescribed by a commission may allow an efficiently managed utility much more. But a rate is constitutionally compensatory, if it allows to the utility the opportunity to earn the cost of the service as thus defined. . . .

The adoption of the amount prudently invested as the rate base and the amount of the capital charge as the measure of the rate of return would give definiteness to these two factors involved in rate controversies which are now shifting and treacherous, and which render the proceedings peculiarly burdensome and largely futile. . . . It would, when once made in respect to any utility, be fixed, for all time, subject only to increases to represent additions to plant, after allowance for the depreciation included in the manual operating charges.

The Brandeis formulation did not remove the courts from valuation determinations. Rather, it shifted the courts' focus to a choice between prudent investment and reproduction cost.

In a seminal, and lasting, opinion, Justice William O. Douglas, in *Federal Power Commission v. Hope Natural Gas Co.* (S.Ct.1944), took the Court out of the valuation business and established the "end result" test, which is a constitutional standard to determine when rates are confiscatory. *Hope* began an era of court deference to decisions of federal and state public utility commissions. In *Hope*, the Court established the principle that the judiciary should defer to the rate determinations of utility commissions as long as the "end result" was "fair" or "reasonable." If the factors were applied by regulators in a manner acceptable to the courts, then the regulator's decisions would not be disturbed. If not, then the regulators could expect that their decisions would be overturned by the courts. After *Hope*, the generally accepted test for the rate base is prudently invested original cost less depreciation.

In the late 1960s and 1970s, the nuclear power industry stalled. Utilities planned the construction of dozens of plants in part because uranium was a much cheaper fuel. Unfortunately, the cost of construction was much higher for a nuclear utility as opposed to a coal utility, for example, and the construction period was much longer. As energy prices rose and as concerns about nuclear safety escalated, utilities were in the impossible position of having invested billions of dollars in plant construction and then being forced to either cancel the project or convert to a fuel source other than nuclear power.

In short, the nuclear investment resulted in the production of no electricity even though the investments were prudent when made. The ratemaking issue was clear—how should such investments be treated? Should they be included as expenses? Or should they be included in the rate base? Or not at all? At bottom, the question was "Who should pay?" The choice was between shareholders or consumers.

Regulators and courts had two competing tests that they could apply. The "prudent investment" test included such investments in the rate formula under the theory that investors acted in good faith and should, therefore, not be penalized. The "used and useful" test excluded from the rate formula any investment that did not result in the production of electricity under the theory that consumers should not pay for a product that they did not receive. Thus, regulators had to decide between recognizing a utility's "prudent investment," in which case shareholders would receive protection, or whether the investment was "used and useful," in which case consumers would receive protection. Not surprisingly, federal and state regulators developed a range of answers to these questions and achieved a rough justice by a variety of apportionments between shareholders and customers. Joseph P. Tomain, *Nuclear Power Transformation* (1987). See also *Dusquesne Light Co. v. Barasch* (S.Ct.1989); *Jersey Central Power & Light Co. v. FERC* (D.C. Cir. 1987).

3. Rate of Return

Finally, a fair rate of return must be determined. Recall that one of the ratemaking goals was capital attraction. To attract investors, they must have a reasonable opportunity to make money (a return) on that investment. The rate of return, thus, is the percentage return on investment in the rate base.

There are two basic classes of investors—debt (bonds) and equity (preferred and common stock). The investment return to each class, based on anticipated risk, must be taken into account. In effect, the rate of return reflects interest on debt, and dividends from stock adjusted for growth. The final percentage is the weighted average of debt and equity and is intended to reflect the return necessary to attract investment from each class of investor. Therefore, the rate of return to attract these various investors must reflect the varying risks.

The rate of return can also be used as an incentive mechanism to reward utilities for desirable behavior. Regulators, for example, may choose to reward conservation or greater economic efficiency by awarding a higher rate of return to the utilities that achieve gains in these areas. Naturally, the rate cannot be so high as to cause injury to customers nor so low as to cause unjustified loss to investors. There is no precise economic or financial formula to find the appropriate rate. Instead, financial experts will testify to a variety of market factors and regulators will set the rate of return within a zone of reasonableness. *Federal Power Com'n v. Natural Gas Pipeline Co.* (S.Ct.1942).

E. CONTEMPORARY RATEMAKING ISSUES

The traditional rate formula encourages capital investment because it provides a rate of return on the rate base. In other words, the more a utility invests, the more money it earns. Encouraging capital investment makes sense when the industry and the general economy are expanding as was certainly the case for most network industries for most of the 20th century. Such encouragement also makes sense for a firm or industry that is experiencing declining costs because productive capacity is being added to the economy. When costs are rising, however, a regulatory scheme which encourages capital spending has the undesirable effect of contributing to overinvestment of capital and to excess capacity. The tendency of the traditional ratemaking formula to encourage overinvestment is known as the Averch–Johnson (A–J) effect. When demand for electricity began to level off in the late 1970s, for example, the country found itself with excess electric capacity and with potential economic waste. During this period, utilities overinvested due to wrong estimates about demand, mistaken assumptions about demand elasticity for electricity, and inflation among others, in addition to a rate formula that rewarded capital investment. In such circumstances, regulators examine more closely the utility's inclusion of capital investment in the rate base.

For the last two decades or more, traditional cost-based ratemaking has been subject to close scrutiny because of the rising prices of traditional utility generated electricity. If an industry, such as the electric industry, has sufficient capacity, should the ratemaking formula continue to encourage capital expansion? Policymakers recognized that in the face of excess capacity energy prices under the traditional formula will be supracompetitive and they began to explore alternative ratemaking methods.

1. Marginal Cost Pricing

Marginal cost pricing is a rate structure that attempts to move away from the traditional method. This structure was adopted notably by the Wisconsin Public Service Commission in *Re Madison Gas & Electric Co.* (Wis. 1974). See also Richard D. Cudahy & J. Robert Malko, Electric Peak–Load

Pricing: *Madison Gas* and Beyond, 1976 WISC. L. REV. 48 (1976). This rate method is based on the economic concept of marginal cost pricing previously explained in Chapter One. The traditional rate method sets rates based on historic average cost. Under that method, a regulator gathers financial data from the utility for a historic test year usually the year just prior to the rate hearing. Rates are set roughly by apportioning costs based on kilowatt hours (kwh) of electricity or thousands of cubic feet (mcf) of natural gas sold. This method has the effect of charging customers the average cost of their utility product. Recall that average costs do not necessarily reflect the actual current cost of production. Marginal cost rates are instead based on the total cost of producing the next increment (kwh or mcf) of a utility's service. If a utility is operating at 100% of its capacity, then the next customer that requires service literally forces the utility to add capacity. The cost of the necessary additional capacity is the true cost of production because resources are being allocated to produce that next incremental unit.

Proponents of marginal coat ratemaking argue that marginal coat pricing better reflects the true cost of a utility's product than does historic or average cost ratemaking. See 1 Alfred E. Kahn, THE ECONOMICS OF REGULATION: PRINCIPLES AND INSTITUTIONS ch. 3 (1 vol. Ed. 1991). In fact, if utility rates were actually based on their true marginal cost, users would pay the exact value of the product at the exact time of use. A simple example of marginal cost pricing is a concept called time-of-day rates. With time-of-day rates, electricity consumers pay a rate based on the electricity's cost at the time it is being consumed. At peak hours electricity costs more to produce than at non-peak hours and rates should reflect these costs. Another example is seasonal pricing. During heat waves the use of air conditioners increases demand. Similarly, commercial users place a high demand on electricity production during office hours. Consequently, time-of-day or time of season rates should reflect those costs.

2. Incentive Rates

As we will explain in more detail in the electricity chapter, as a result of the historic and regulatory development of the industry, traditionally structured utilities overinvested in plants and, consequently, added to the price of electricity. Because the price of electricity produced by traditional utilities was high, new entrants to the market saw an opportunity to produce less costly electricity and, therefore, capture a share of the market. Not surprisingly, customers wanted to purchase the lower cost electricity. This phenomenon of cheaper electricity has led to a series of deregulation and restructuring initiatives. One effort to encourage competition among traditional public utilities is through a change in ratemaking method.

Under the traditional formula, the clear incentive was to invest capital. If the price of the product is above market, then utilities clearly need a different incentive. An incentive rate method is a generic term meaning that rates should be set so that producers have a profit incentive. This can occur through a rate formula known as price caps or price levels. The fundamental idea is to decouple historic costs and expenses from the rate formula. In other words, a rate is either set at a particular level or a price cap is set above which rates cannot go. Then the producer's incentive becomes to lower costs below the level or cap and then retain the profits.

Incentive regulation is not free from difficulties of its own such as establishing the correct level or cap. Again, the problem for the regulator is to avoid setting the level or cap too high to the disadvantage of consumers or too low as to be confiscatory to producers. One response to this problem is to find a surrogate price mechanism such as the Consumer Price Index, Producer Price Index, or Gross National Product Index. Other problems include whether or not to allocate gains between producers and consumers; whether such a rate method leads to a competitive price; service reliability if the rates are insufficient; and adequate compensation to the producers for investment made under the previous regulatory regime.

In short, incentive rates have the positive effect of getting away from historic costs and they provide a profit incentive to producers. The open question is whether the method can be designed and implemented so as to better mimic the competitive market. There is also an important legal issue surrounding incentive rates. Federal and state legislation for the electricity and natural gas industries requires that rates be "just and reasonable." This standard protects both producers and consumers. While the legislation does not dictate that a particular rate method be adopted, any method must satisfy that standard. If the rate level is too high, then the legislative standard is violated. *Farmers Union Cent. Exchange, Inc. v. F.E.R.C.* (D.C. Cir. 1984).

Another alternative rate method which abandons historic costs is being used currently in the telecommunications industry and has received the endorsement of the United States Supreme Court. *Verizon Communications v. FCC* (S.Ct.2001); *AT & T Corp. v. Iowa Utilities Bd.* (S.Ct.1999). The technical name is "total element long-run incremental cost" or TELRIC, and it is based on the forward (economic) costs rather than the historic (embedded) costs, of a part of a telecommunications firm. The idea behind TELRIC is to compensate the firm that must, by law, allow another firm to use its property for the purpose of opening access to telecommunications markets. The trick with TELRIC rates is not to set the rate too high to the detriment of new entrants or too low to the detriment of incumbents. Notice, though, in both cases competition suffers even though the idea is to open access to local telecommunications. In the natural gas and electricity industries, the transmission portion of each retains monopoly power. In telecommunications, the local exchange carrier does. Consequently, access must be opened to foster competition.

Open access regulations will be explored in the natural gas and electricity chapters.

3. Market–Based Rates

One way to avoid the problem of choosing the efficient price level or cap is to set rates by mutual agreement between sellers and buyers. Public utilities would negotiate to purchase bulk power under FERC-approved circumstances. These negotiated rates are known as market-based rates. The key to implementation of a successful market-based rate method is that the parties must have equal bargaining power. Put in other words, neither party must exercise market power to the disadvantage of the other. Otherwise, market manipulation can occur, which is the painful lesson of the California electricity crisis in 2000. See, William T. Miller, "Rates and Tariffs" in 4 *Energy Law and Transactions* § 80.01 [3] (David J. Muchow & William A. Mogel (eds.) 2002).

Fair bargaining can take place if there are a number of buyers and sellers and if information is reliable. One technique that FERC has used to reduce the exercise of market power is to require as a condition of approval of a market-based rate that the parties have open access to transmission. "The Commission [FERC] allows power sales at market-based rates if a seller and its affiliates do not have (or can mitigate) market power in generation and transmission and cannot erect other barriers to entry, such as full inputs and control of generation siting. Generally, the affiliated public utility must have an approved open-access transmission tariff on file with FERC." James H. McGrew, *FERC: Federal Energy Regulatory Commission* 163 (2003).

4. Stranded Costs

Ratemaking in many ways constituted the core of public utility regulation for most of the 20th century. At the end of that century, the traditional rate formula came under scrutiny and new methods are being used as a transition to more competitive markets. That transition is not complete and as the old regulatory regime confronts the new order, old investments must be addressed and are being addressed through rates among other devices. The most intractable old investment problem is known as stranded costs.

Clearly, energy industries, most notably electricity and natural gas, are undergoing significant restructuring as we move from one regulatory regime to another. But what should be done about a utility that relied upon the traditional regime and invested accordingly? Regulatory restructuring poses significant threats to regulated firms who have invested their shareholders' capital in a company that was operating in a regulated environment and was complying with government requirements and regulations. The problem of stranded costs should be getting clear. If government significantly changes the regulatory scheme, then to the extent that a regulated firm's assets are devalued by their inability to meet competition does the new regulatory scheme constitute a taking?

Imagine the situation of a utility which relied on the traditional rate formula. In a changing economic environment, that utility is between a rock and a hard place. On the one hand, the utility has a service obligation to its customers and a fiduciary obligations to its shareholders. Those obligations are to be satisfied through a rate formula that rewards capital investment. Of course, these investment decisions must be sound and that has not always been the case. On the other hand, further capital investment may place rates higher than the market as the presence of new entrants demonstrates. Imagine further that the utility's management prudently and in good faith decides to build a new electricity generation plant for $500 million to satisfy projected demand, knowing that the $500 million investment will be recovered over the

40–year useful life of the plant under the then current rate-making formula.

How should that $500 million investment be viewed if regulators decide to abandon the traditional ratemaking formula and go to more competitive rates specifically for the purpose of allowing new entrants into the market, thus threatening the competitive position of the regulated firm? Does the regulated firm have cause to complain that their $500 million investment has been taken? See generally, J. Gregory Sidak & Daniel F. Spulber, *Deregulatory Takings and the Regulatory Compact: The Competitive Transformation of Network Industries in the United States* (1997).

The answer to this question is quite interesting. The answer is yes and no. The answer is yes because regulators, policy-makers, and commentators generally agree that such a change in the regulatory regime should provide compensation for assets so affected—the so-called stranded costs. The answer is "no" insofar as no court has ruled that a taking has occurred although courts have upheld legislation providing for the recovery of stranded costs. Therefore, while there is a clear consensus that stranded costs are properly recoverable, complex issues remain. First, how should stranded costs be defined? Second, once defined, how should they be recovered? Defining stranded costs becomes a battle of the experts with the firm and its shareholders seeking to include as much investment as possible and with regulators and customers seeking lower valuations.

Ultimately, payment comes from the utility's customers, the utility's shareholders, new entrants, or taxpayers. The utility's customers would pay through a surcharge on their utility bills. The utility's shareholders would pay to the extent that all costs are not recovered. New entrants pay through a fee to use a utility's assets. And, if all else fails, taxpayers may be put in a position to bail out a utility.

F. COST–BENEFIT ANALYSIS

1. Introduction

Cost-benefit analysis (CBA) is a staple of the regulatory process. A general textbook definition is that CBA:

"[S]ets out to answer [ ] whether a number of investment projects, A, B, C, etc., should be undertaken and, if investible funds are limited, which one two or more ... should be selected." E. Mishan, *Cost Benefit Analysis: An Informal Introduction* xxvii (4th ed. 1988).

Thus, CBA is a methodology for public decisionmakers to choose an efficient solution from an array of options such that benefits should exceed costs B > C. So stated, CBA seems not only reasonable, but unassailable. Beware, however, of simple formulas because CBA has had a long history of vigorous criticism on normative, value grounds and on positive, technical grounds.

CBA helps policymakers choose among alternative, competing public projects. Tracing its history to welfare economists such as Vilfredo Pareto, Nicholas Kaldor, and Sir John Hicks, CBA was first incorporated into United States law in the Flood Control Act of 1936, 33 U.S.C. § 701a. Later, the National Environmental Policy Act (NEPA), especially the environmental impact statement section, 42 U.S.C. § 4332, extended the federal government's use of this method. See e.g. *Sierra Club v. Morton* (5th Cir. 1975). Although cost-benefit analysis language does not appear explicitly in this section of NEPA, courts have held that the use of the method in some form is permitted. Several statutes and numerous federal regulations require the implementation of cost-benefit analysis and a few statutes effectively prohibit its use. *Industrial Union Dept. AFL–CIO v. Am. Petroleum Inst.* (S.Ct.1980); *American Textile Manufacturers Inst., Inc. v. Donovan* (S.Ct. 1981). Although not every regulatory decision is based on cost-benefit analysis, the device is a useful way to gather and sort relevant decisionmaking data, and it is useful to identify and explore the many ramifications of complex decisions involving public energy projects.

CBA has been used by executive branch decisionmakers for decades. President Reagan's *Executive Order 12,291* required that all executive agencies use CBA and that each "major rule" undergo "regulatory impact analysis." "Major rule" is defined as one likely to result in:

(1) An annual effect on the economy of $100 million or more;

(2) A major increase in costs or prices for consumers, individual industries, federal, state or local government agencies, or geographic locations; or

(3) Significant adverse effects on competition, employment, investment, productivity, innovation, or on the ability of United States-based enterprises to compete with foreign-based enterprises in domestic or export markets. 46 Fed. Reg. 13193 (February 17, 1981).

President Clinton implemented similar requirements with Executive Order 12, 866 with the following regulatory philosophy:

"Federal agencies should promulgate only such regulations as are required by law, are necessary to interpret the law, or are made necessary by compelling public need, such as material failures of private markets to protect or improve the health and safety of the public, the environment, or the well-being of the American people. In deciding whether and how to regulate, agencies should assess all costs and benefits of available regulatory alternatives, including the alternative of not regulating. Costs and benefits shall be understood to include both quantifiable measures (to the fullest extent that these can be usefully estimated) and qualitative measures of costs and benefits that are difficult to quantify, but nevertheless essential to consider. Further, in choosing among alternative regulatory approaches, agencies should select those approaches that maximize net benefits (including potential economic, environmental, public health and safety, and other advantages; distributive impacts; and equity); unless a statute requires another regulatory approach." 58 Fed. Reg. 51735 (September 30, 1993).

While there are some language differences between the two orders, agencies use the same general procedures. The Executive Order applies to executive branch agencies like the Department of Energy and the Department of the Interior. It does not apply to independent agencies like the Federal Energy Regulatory Commission.

CBA can be applied to several energy projects. The CBA literature regarding air pollution, for example, is vast and has particular application to coal-fired electricity generating units. At the time of this writing, the Bush Administration's EPA has dropped investigations into 50 powerplants for past violations of the Clean Air Act so that less stringent environmental rules will be applied. In this case, the CBA issue involves the costs and benefits of energy versus the environment. Note the difficulty in posing the proper question. Is the proper question: Do the benefits of electricity production outweigh the costs to clean the air? Or should the question be: Do the benefits of clean air outweigh the benefits of additional electricity production? In other words, framing the CBA issue is an important step in the process.

CBA is also useful in determining trade-offs between competing projects. Should oil drilling be permitted in the Alaska National Wildlife Refuge or should the wilderness be preserved? Should a hydroelectric plant license be renewed, or should salmon fisheries be protected? Should we build new nuclear power plants or continue to construct coal-fired plants? These questions arise throughout the CBA process and each involves cost-benefit tradeoffs as well as a major dose of politics.

2. Applying CBA

The CBA process can be divided into four stages: benefits and costs must be identified and classified; second, risks must be translated into costs; third, benefits and costs must be quantified; and, fourth, the cost-benefit information must be presented in a usable form. Each of these steps presents difficult issues and choices and has given rise to criticism.

a. Identification

Identification involves deciding which variables should be considered in the cost-benefit equation and whether the variables are costs or benefits. When deciding whether to require a coal burning electric utility to install smokestack scrubbers to reduce air pollution, for example, how should the costs and benefits of the scrubber requirement be weighed? Direct benefits might include the contribution to the domestic economy of the value of the use of a domestic natural resource (i.e. local coal rather than imported oil) and the value of the generated electricity. The scrubber requirement may impose costs. If the decision is made to enforce the scrubber requirement, some coal-fired plants may never be built because the cost of scrubber installation is too high, or if built, the resulting high cost of the electricity will limit the amount of electricity produced. What about the scrubber equipment itself? Is it a cost or a benefit?

If electricity produced from coal rather than from oil, natural gas, or nuclear power is thought to be a valuable commodity, then industry research money and time will be spent looking for cleaner ways to generate electricity from coal. How is the money that is used in anti-pollution research and development in the industry to be carried in the cost-benefit equation? Is it really a cost because otherwise the money would not have been spent for such research? Or, is it truly a benefit because a new industry of clean coal research and development is created? If that research ultimately is success- ful, then there will be cleaner air and more coal burning plants, which will be more competitive as industry concentra- tion is lessened. Thus, the price of the product will decline and consumers will be satisfied. Likewise, alternative assumptions can be made. The coal pollution control technology industry may fail; clean burning coal plants may not be feasible; industry concentration will increase; air pollution will in- crease; people will pay higher prices for the product; fewer jobs will be created, and so on and so on.

The extrapolation of costs and benefits can be carried out indefinitely. In the discussion of the scrubber, for example, the effect on jobs, economic productivity, cleaner air and water were implied at best. An exhaustive cost-benefit analysis would include such items and more. The criticism is twofold. First, identifying what counts as a cost or a benefit is an issue which itself is not free from questions. Second, there is no logical place to terminate cost-benefit analysis. In both cases, value decisions must be made. Nevertheless, the reality is that we make decisions all of the time in light of numerous uncertainties and this reality alone does not invalidate CBA.

b. Risk Analysis

Next, the risk component of costs must be identified and translated into costs. In weighing the costs and benefits of building a nuclear power plant, for example, the small risk of a core meltdown multiplied by the large negative conse- quences of that type of accident is part of the cost-benefit equation and must be taken into account in the analysis. What is the risk of a nuclear accident occurring? If it should occur, how many lives will be lost? How many short-term and long- term injuries are likely? What is the cost of those lives and injuries? How should that cost be discounted to the present? See, Stephen Breyer, *Breaking the Vicious Cycle: Toward Effective Risk Regulation* (1993).

Think about analyzing the risk of a core meltdown in a nuclear power plant. The number of variables and calculations are substantial. Is the risk of a meltdown once in 200 years? In 500 years? In 10,000 years? Where is a meltdown most likely? How many lives are at risk? How many years of life are at risk due to short-term, mid-term, and long-term cancers? Perhaps most difficult: What is the value of a life? Do we consider age, life expectancy, work years, wealth, contributions to society? Clearly these are not only technically difficult questions, they are normatively controversial as well.

Still, there are certain truisms about risk analysis. Risk is inherent in everything we do. Yet, all risks are not perceived in the same way. Risks voluntarily assumed by individuals are perceived differently from risks publicly imposed. Individuals make private choices about risks everyday. Some people risk their lives in hazardous occupations; other people risk injury playing sports. Individual homeowners, for example, have little voice as to where a nuclear waste site is placed. Many people prefer to drive rather than to fly even though flying is safer than driving. Similarly, natural disasters that cause multiple fatalities may be less costly to society than an equal number of separate fatalities although people usually perceive mass disasters as more costly. Still, the point to note is that regardless of the scientific accuracy of the nature and extent of different risks, risks are perceived differently. Unfortunately, living in any complex society necessitates the public imposition of risks, and public imposition engenders political conflicts. It is the publicly-imposed risk that is taken into account in cost-benefit analysis.

c. Quantification

Quantifying benefits, costs, and risks is the third stage of the analysis. Congress, for example, has passed statutes intended to protect the health and safety of coal miners, and these statutes necessarily increase the dollar cost of producing a ton of coal. A classic cost-benefit problem lies in trying to quantify the economic value of those coal miners' lives. How is the life of a miner to be carried in a cost-benefit equation? The difficulty of answering this question is illustrated by the great range in life value assessments by the federal government. One study reports that the government assessed the cost per life saved in various federal programs in a range from $35,550 to $624,976,000 per life.

One strategy in evaluating the worth of a human life is to equate the loss of 6000 work days as the monetary equivalent of one life. This may work within an industry but may not be effective when comparing industries. Is a work day lost in the coal industry economically equivalent to the lost work day of a neurosurgeon or an investment banker? Further, there are economic differences between groups based on age, sex, and race. Should these differences be accounted for in the human life calculation? If the value of all occupations and classes of persons are treated equally, the economic analysis will be distorted. The simple fact is that most neurosurgeons and major league baseball players earn more income than sanitation workers and college professors. Likewise, income is not equally distributed along either racial or sexual lines. Is it enough to say that decisionmakers treat everyone equally by monetizing every life according to earning capacity? Does this mean that the non-economic value or the quality of life is to be ignored? These are extremely sensitive and difficult questions for decisionmakers, and as a result, more often than not, they are not addressed in a direct and meaningful way. See Robert W. Hahn, *Risks, Costs, and Lives Saved* (1996); Deborah G. Mayo & Rochelle D. Hollander (eds.), *Acceptable Evidence: Science and Values in Risk Management* (1991); Cass R. Sunstein, *Risk and Reason: Safety, Law and the Environment* (2002); W. Kip Viscusi, *Fatal Tradeoffs: Public & Private Responsibilities for Risk* (1992).

d. *Presentation*

The final stage in cost-benefit is the presentation of cost-benefit information. This stage entails problems of interpretation and in the selection of data which will differ depending on who is doing the interpreting and why the presentation is being made. It is not unreasonable to assume that the presentation of information regarding the placement of a nuclear waste disposal site will differ according to whether the Department of Energy or the Union of Concerned Scientists or a local homeowners association is making the presentation. The presentation also is shaped by the audience. The presentation of information pertaining to the placement of a nuclear waste disposal site will differ if the audience is a judge, the Nuclear Regulatory Commission, or the local zoning board.

e. *Critiques of Cost–Benefit Analysis*

Cost-benefit analysis has not been without its critics. There are normative and positive criticisms of this method. Some critics argue that the method itself involves undesirable value choices insofar as the method requires the quantification and commodification of values that do not easily translate into money. After all, the method does require assigning dollar figures to a person's life or health. Similarly, such critics argue that you cannot quantify the aesthetic appreciation of nature or the value of the preservation of species. Other critics argue that CBA is a form of utilitarianism which favors the production and expansion of wealth rather than the preservation of resources in a small is beautiful world. Is bigger better? Or, is small beautiful? At bottom, the critics are right and wrong. They are correct to suggest that CBA has a normative dimension that excludes other ways of looking at the world. They are wrong, however, to attribute too large a role in decisionmaking to this procedure. After all, CBA most often is a means of analysis; it is not the sole decisionmaking tool.

The technical, positive criticisms center not so much on what cost-benefit analysis can do—gather data, sort information, and highlight sensitive normative and positive issues—as much as they focus on the extent to which it applies and the weight given to it by decisionmakers. Advocates of the method see it as a way to deal with large masses of complex and often conflicting quantitative data. Critics argue that the method is notoriously imprecise and that it should not be used to obscure delicate moral, social, and political issues that arise in the allocation of scarce natural resources.

Whatever the criticisms, public decisionmakers must choose from among competing alternatives and they must articulate the reasons for their choice. Cost-benefit analysis is useful in identifying costs, risks, and benefits to assist decisionmakers in articulating the reasons for their decisions. The rationale behind public decisionmaking must be explicit if the decision is to attain legitimacy. If the goals or the objectives of the public decisionmaker are not articulated, then the decision may not be publicly acceptable. It is the case that as a matter of constitutional law, the reasons for administrative decisions must be given in order to satisfy the constitutional due process requirement. Thus, the rationale behind public decisions must be given so that the decision is visible and accountable. Two useful recent surveys which discuss the methods and limits of CBA are: Matthew D. Adler & Eric A. Posner (eds.), *Cost–Benefit Analysis: Legal, Economic, and Philosophical Perspectives* (2001); Cass R. Sunstein, *The Cost–Benefit State: The Future of Regulatory Protection* (2002).

CHAPTER 5

OIL

Oil has occupied center stage in domestic and international energy policy and planning for over a century. See Daniel Yergin, *The Prize: The Epic Quest for Oil, Money, and Power* (1991); Robert Sherrill, *The Oil Follies of 1970–1980: How the Petroleum Industry Stole the Show (And Much More Besides)* (1983). As the Arab Oil Embargo in 1973 and the 1990 Iraqi invasion of Kuwait attest, the disruption of the oil supply affects domestic and world economies. Indeed, the U.S. invasion of Iraq in 2003 was also discussed, in part, in terms of the country's interest in Middle East oil. In short, the story of oil is a story of multinational corporations and global politics. In this chapter, we concentrate on domestic oil regulation while remaining mindful of international influences. Domestically, the year 1970 was a pivotal one for United States oil policy. In that year, domestic oil production peaked and it has been in decline ever since. Moreover, domestic oil production presents difficult environmental issues and the resource is increasingly expensive to extract. Since the mid–1970s, however, starting with President Nixon's Project Independence, the key aspiration of the country's oil policy has been to become free of dependence on foreign oil. Unfortunately, that independence has not been forthcoming because foreign oil, particularly in the Middle East, can be produced more cheaply than in the United States, thus making foreign oil attractive to domestic refiners and consumers.

It is a curiosity of United States energy policy that, even though oil is the central actor as a resource, oil is currently subject to few direct government regulations. The primary reason offered for the light regulatory hand is that the oil

153

industry purports to be fully competitive and does not exercise monopoly power; therefore extensive federal government oversight is unnecessary. The exercise of monopoly power was a major concern at the turn of the 19th century. That concern dissipated with the break-up of the Standard Oil Trust in 1911. See *Standard Oil Co. v. United States* (1911). Since then there have been only intermittent government antitrust assessments which continue to find the industry to be competitive and hence largely free of command-and-control government regulation.

A. INDUSTRY OVERVIEW

As consumers, we rely on one important petroleum product, gasoline, daily for our automobile transportation needs. Also as consumers we use petroleum products and petrochemicals regularly. Half of our energy economy is a function of oil, and it is not an overstatement to say that we are dependent on oil for the quality of our daily lives.

Such a claim would be relatively non-controversial but for two major consequences. First, our ability to maintain a steady supply of oil is a matter of national security and global politics. Second, oil is a fossil fuel and exploration for it and recovery of it involve several environmental problems.

The general theory is that crude oil is a result of organic residues, plants and animals that have been trapped underground for thousands of years. Underground pressures force the organic materials to migrate into porous and permeable rock such as sandstone and limestone, where it is transformed into its current form. Petroleum is generally trapped in specific geological formations known as petroleum deposits. Often, natural gas is trapped with oil and we call such gas, "associated gas." All crude oil is not a uniform substance. In fact, oil is chemically complex and is comprised primarily of hydrogen and carbon with trace amounts of oxygen, nitrogen, and sulfur.

In terms of consumption, world oil consumption is currently approximately 75 million barrels a day, half of which is consumed by western Europe and North America. The United States consumes about 19.5 million barrels of oil per day. At the same time, we produce domestically about 9.1 million barrels a day and import daily about 11.4 million barrels and export 1 million barrels of oil.

In terms of sector consumption, two-thirds of all petroleum products are consumed by the transportation industry. The next largest user of nearly 5 million barrels a day is the industrial sector. Residential users use oil for heating and a small portion is consumed for electric power production as depicted in the chart below.

Figure 1 Petroleum Flow, 2002

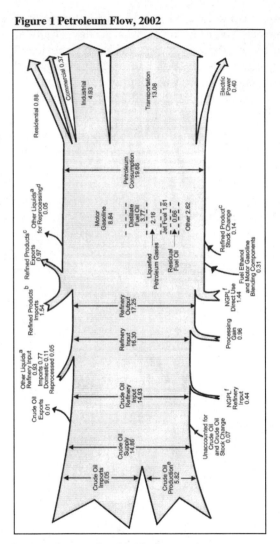

The oil fuel cycle can be divided into four parts: exploration and production, refining, transportation, and marketing. Large oil companies such as British Petroleum and Exxon are involved with every stage and are integrated and known as "major" oil companies. Such integrated firms operate at each stage from exploration to selling gasoline at the pump. Non-integrated or independent companies, of which there are about 40,000, are those that are engaged in one of these phases. Semi-integrated or partially integrated companies have two or more but not all phases.

The fuel cycles for oil and natural gas are structurally similar because oil and natural gas are often found together. Although the science of oil geology is technically sophisticated, the only way to find oil is through drilling wells. Surprisingly, more "dry holes" are found than wells and the process can be time-consuming as well as expensive. It has been estimated that only about 3% of exploratory wells become commercially successful. Once oil is located, it can be brought to the surface either through natural or mechanical pressure. Wells have natural pressure that moves oil through permeable rock to the well bore. After the natural pressure dissipates, however, mechanical energy, through the introduction of water or gas, creates pressure to bring oil to the surface. After the primary pressures have been exhausted, additional measures must be applied.

After a given oil reservoir produces a certain amount of oil, enhanced (more expensive) recovery techniques are required. When oil from older wells is depleted, new and deeper wells in harder to drill places such as the outer continental shelf are needed. Oil is then transported by tanker, truck, or pipeline to one of about 300 oil refineries in the United States. Refineries separate the petroleum into more than 3,000 products, ranging from jet fuel to petrochemicals used to make plastics. Gasoline is the largest component of petroleum production and accounts for about 50% of refined product consumption.

B. REGULATORY OVERVIEW

1. State Regulation

With the exception of antitrust enforcement in the early 20th century and regulation of the interstate transportation of oil pipelines, the federal government has not regulated the oil industry heavily for most of the century. Rather, the federal government, primarily through favorable tax treatments, such as resource depletion allowances and foreign tax credits, has supported the industry.

As noted, the exact location and placement of oil reserves cannot be completely known by surface owners. Wells must be drilled to tap into oil "pools," which do not perfectly coincide with surface boundaries. Consequently, special property law regimes must be developed. From an economic standpoint, anyone interested in exploring for and exploiting oil resources cannot afford to own all surface lands in fee simple. Instead, oil leases are purchased from surface owners and surface owners are paid royalties. Thus, these leases create mineral interests as well as royalty interests that are negotiated between the parties. Clearly, the mineral interest holder must have some rights to the surface estate and the extent and duration of those rights, again, is subject both to the lease and to statutory laws in some jurisdictions.

The first oil well was drilled in Titusville, Pennsylvania in 1859. At the time, the prevailing property right was the *ad coelum* doctrine. Briefly, this meant that the surface owner owned all of the land to the heavens and through the depths of the earth. The *ad coelum* doctrine works well with hard minerals, but not with migratory ones. Such a rule does not further the development of the petroleum industry because of the uncertainty inherent in the parameters of the property right.

Instead of applying the *ad coelum* doctrine to migrating resources such as oil and natural gas, the rule of capture was adopted, which allowed for the development of oil and gas resources. In short, the rule of capture meant that a well operator could drain oil and gas resources from beneath another owner's lands without liability. *Barnard v. Monongahela Natural Gas Co.* (S.Ct. 1907). Once extracted, title was vested with the person who captured those resources. As long as the well operators did not trespass on the surface of another's land, he was able to capture those resources. The rule of capture has a perverse economic effect, i.e. it is inefficient because it forces people to drill wells to capture oil, thereby overconsuming the resource. The rule of capture has been applied differently in different states. In Texas, for example, the doctrine of correlative rights was adopted, which holds that surface owners had a right to a fair and equitable share of oil and gas resources as well as a right to protection from negligent damage caused to other owners. Even with the doctrine of correlative rights, the rule of capture continued to create inefficiencies particularly during the period of the early 20th century in which large oil and gas fields were discovered.

At that time the overproduction of oil outstripped the demands of the market to buy it, the capacity of the pipelines to transport it, and the ability of the refineries to convert it into saleable products. Unsold oil often was stored in open surface pits, which were subject to fire and seepage, and some oil wells were abandoned before their productive lives were at an end.

In the first third of the 20th century, this wasteful situation was addressed through state oil and gas conservation laws. See Northcutt Ely, *The Oil and Gas Conservation Statutes (Annotated)*, (1933); *Oil Conservation through Interstate Agreement* (1933). Through such devices as pooling, unitization, well spacing, and prorationing, states attempted to affect how much oil was produced and put on the market at any given time. Producing states such as Texas, Louisiana, and Oklahoma, which were interested in keeping the petroleum industry viable, passed legislation to insure that oil did not glut the market and reduce oil prices to the point of incurring waste. See Interstate Oil Compact Commission, *Summary of State Statutes and Regulations for Oil and Gas Production* (1986).

Since the mid–1960s and particularly after the early 1970s, as domestic production peaked and imports increased, all states have permitted oil production at the maximum allowable level. Nevertheless, different forms of state regulation have continued. For example, most states impose a limit on the number of wells that can be drilled in a particular area and do so through well spacing regulations which are intended to optimize the cost of drilling by maintaining pressure in wells. States also use pooling regulations which require different land and interest owners to share the costs and benefits of drilling. States continue to require drilling permits and to impose completion requirements. In addition, states continue to have maximum efficient rate regulation (MER) in an attempt to maximize the efficient production of oil. Similarly, unitization is considered by many to be the best approach to avoid economic waste. Today unitization is seen as critical to secondary and tertiary recovery programs which require reservoir-wide programs to maintain pressure.

2. Early Federal Regulation

Not unlike many industries, energy industries including the oil industry began competitively; then became concentrated leading to federal oversight. In the oil industry, at the end of the 19th century, there was a significant movement toward industry concentration through corporate mergers and acquisitions to capture economies of scale both among oil companies and among oil companies, banks, and railroads. Oil industry concentration also gave rise to monopoly power in the hands of a few concerns. For example, John D. Rockefeller recognized that the vital link between oil production and the consumer was the oil refinery, and he founded the Standard Oil Company with the purpose of controlling the oil refinery stage of the fuel cycle. By the 1870s Standard Oil owned many refineries in the Northeast. Rockefeller then began buying railroads and pipelines to control the transportation stage of the fuel cycle. In 1879, the Standard Oil Trust was formed, which was comprised of many oil companies created or acquired by Rockefeller. The trust concentrated its initial activity on combining refineries. Later, it obtained pipelines linking both the oil fields to refineries and refineries to the marketplace. The trust owned relatively few oil producing properties as these correctly were considered by Rockefeller to be the financially risky end of the oil business.

In 1911, the United States Supreme Court in *Standard Oil Company v. United States* (1911), found that the acquisition by the Standard Oil holding company of the stock of over one-third of subsidiary oil companies violated the Sherman Antitrust Act laws as an illegal restraint of trade in interstate commerce in the oil business and ordered the dissolution of the trust. This decision resulted in the breakup of the Standard Oil Trust into independent companies. By 1920, the companies resulting from the breakup of the Standard Oil Trust had begun to compete with each other. By the early 1930s, eight of these severed companies themselves had become vertically integrated oil companies that were among the largest in the United States. See Arthur M. Johnson, "The Lessons of the Standard Oil Divestiture" in *Vertical Integration in the Oil Industry*, 191–214 (Mitchell ed. 1976).

Early federal efforts at regulation had been directed toward bringing oil production into line with market demands as well as toward monitoring concentration in the industry. In 1906, for example, the Hepburn Act, 34 Stat. 584, Pub. L. No. 59–337 (since repealed) limited the ability of railroads to transport oil in interstate commerce for oil companies in which they might have direct or indirect ownership interests, thereby reducing opportunities for self-dealing.

In the early 1930s, several rich oil fields were discovered in East Texas and Oklahoma and, as noted, existing state conservation laws were unsuccessful in stemming production. Oil prices plummeted and the federal government sought to supplement state regulation by restricting the amounts of oil placed in interstate commerce. In 1935, the Interstate Compact to Conserve Oil and Gas Act was enacted, 49 Stat. 939, and it has been renewed regularly. The compact was drafted by a committee representing governors of seven principal oil-producing states and sets non-enforceable, voluntary oil production quotas and encourages cooperative efforts to conserve oil and gas. Initially, six states executed the compact and today some 29 oil producing states participate and operate under the Interstate Oil Compact Commission. Despite such voluntary arrangements by oil producing states to restrict production, the states have regularly exceeded agreed quotas. Since the states could not restrict the movement of oil in interstate commerce, oil produced in excess of production quotas could not be effectively prevented from reaching a domestic market. Oil in excess of state conservation laws and placed in interstate commerce was known as "hot oil" and was first banned by President Franklin Roosevelt's Executive Order, then as part of his National Industrial Recovery Act, which was later invalidated in the two celebrated anti-delegation decisions, *Panama Refining Co. v. Ryan* (1935); *Schecter Poultry Corp. v. United States* (1935). The federal government responded to this problem with the Connally Hot Oil Act enacted into law in 1935, 15 U.S.C. §§ 715 et seq. The Act prohibits the transport in interstate commerce of oil produced in excess of state quotas. Thus, the federal government effectively assisted the states in enforcing their prorationing laws. Soon thereafter, the demand for oil increased as the country mobilized for war.

The oil market changed after World War II. First, oil replaced coal as the nation's dominant fuel, a transition that had begun during World War I. Second, oil production expanded throughout the world. And third, in 1948, U.S. oil imports exceeded exports for the first time. Consequently, global production by the major integrated oil firms has kept the world economy in a delicate balance.

The network of state, federal, and private company efforts at conservation and production controls worked fairly well in the following twenty years because the United States was essentially "oil independent" and free of competition in the domestic oil market from foreign producers. Much of the foreign oil, particularly that from the Middle East, was produced by subsidiaries of the eight major American oil companies operating independently or as part of oil consortia with French or British companies. Nevertheless, when foreign oil is cheaper than domestic oil, it is attractive to domestic refiners. Domestic producers, however, would prefer to limit imports as a protectionist measure. Consequently, oil imports caught the attention of business and political leaders alike.

The effective control of Middle East (e.g. Saudi Arabia, Kuwait, Bahrain, Iran, and Iraq) sources of oil by the major American oil companies began in the late 1920s and lasted until the early 1970s. The control was achieved primarily because the Middle Eastern countries needed the technology of the oil companies to find, extract, refine, and market their oil. Without the oil companies, the Middle East effectively was barred from entering the oil marketplace. The oil companies and their host governments created joint operating companies (comprised of a major American oil company and its host government) and entered long term supply contracts with terms, such as the level of oil royalties, that were favorable to the oil companies. This control eventually was broken through a series of expropriations and nationalizations of oil operations by the host governments and by the grant of concessions to independents.

Later, the Organization of Petroleum Exporting Countries (OPEC) was formed and began to exert coordinated influence on world oil supply and demand. OPEC presently consists of thirteen member nations: Algeria, Ecuador, Gabon, Indonesia, Iran, Iraq, Kuwait, Libya, Nigeria, Qatar, Saudi Arabia, the

United Arab Emirates, and Venezuela. OPEC countries have three-fourths of the known economically recoverable world oil reserves, of which over half is located in the Persian Gulf region. By comparison, the United States has about 5% of the world's known reserves.

In the mid–1950s oil companies, for a variety of reasons, including the increased cost of domestic oil production and the reduction in relative transportation costs of foreign oil, began to earn larger profit margins on foreign crude oil than on domestically produced oil. As a result, imports of foreign oil into the United States greatly increased. The majors enjoyed a decided competitive edge over independent domestic producers and refiners because they were able to import oil from their lower-cost foreign sources and refine and market the oil products themselves. The federal government became concerned that the less profitable domestic oil production would be curtailed to a point that would harm the domestic oil industry and would threaten the level of oil reserves for national defense. Initial federal efforts to control imports of foreign oil into the United States were voluntary and largely unsuccessful. See *The Report of the Presidential Task Force on Reform of Federal Energy Administration Regulations*, Appendix F (1977). The failure of the voluntary import control program, the increased access to foreign oil concessions by a greater number of companies, large new oil discoveries (especially in the Middle East), and an increase in the sale of Russian crude oil in Europe all combined to increase competition and production in international oil markets to the detriment of the domestic oil market. Domestic oil prices fell as a result of the competition from foreign sources and, with the lower prices, domestic oil production fell.

In 1959, the federal government instituted the Mandatory Oil Import Program (MOIP) by presidential proclamation under the original authority of the Trade Agreements Extension Act of 1958, Pub. L. No. 85–686, 72 Stat. 673. The MOIP limited the amount of foreign crude oil that could be brought into the United States primarily on grounds that imports above permitted amounts would threaten national security. The implementation of the program effectively insulated United States oil production from competition from lower-priced foreign oil. Domestic prices rose, profit margins increased, and demand for domestic oil grew. By the early 1960s, the MOIP had become very complex and was criticized for depleting the nation's domestic oil reserves and for increasing the prices of domestic oil products. By 1970, domestic oil production peaked and this reduced the pressure on the MOIP to limit imports. In 1973, the MOIP changed from a system of absolute quotas or limits on oil imports to one of licensing fees administered by the Department of Energy. For a review of the constitutional authority for the imposition of oil import restrictions, see, *United States v. George S. Bush & Co.* (1940); *Norwegian Nitrogen Products Co. v. United States* (1933); *J.W. Hampton, Jr., & Co. v. United States* (1928).

In the first half of the 20th Century, the relationship between major oil companies and foreign governments was one of shifting power and authority. At the beginning of the century, expertise resided in the majors, whereas ownership resided with foreign governments. As governments began to educate themselves and acquire technical expertise, oil contracts were renegotiated. As a consequence, power moved away from the majors and toward foreign governments. The most significant development in this regard was the formation of OPEC and its exercise of its power with the Arab Oil Embargo of 1973. In that year, several Arab nations in protest of the United States' support of Israel in the 1973 Arab–Israeli war, instituted an oil embargo against the United States. The embargo came at a time when the United States was experiencing a decline in its domestic oil production and increasing demand. The embargo was accompanied by a decrease in OPEC production, which created short-term shortages and price increases. Prices more than tripled from a 1973 average of $12 per barrel to over $40 per barrel. The embargo lasted approximately six months after which U.S. oil imports increased from nearly 26% in 1973 to 36% in 1977. The sharp increase in energy prices was widely considered to be a major cause of an economic recession that the country experienced in the mid–1970s. The embargo was also the occasion for significant amounts of energy legislation during that period.

Beginning in 1978, political problems in Iran resulted in a drop of nearly four million barrels per day of oil being put into production and resulting in tightening world supplies. The war between Iran and Iraq in 1980 contributed to decreased oil output and prices rising from $14 per barrel in the beginning of 1979 to over $35 per barrel in January 1981. These prices were eventually stabilized at between $28–29 per barrel. The high cost of oil stimulated exploration and production in areas such as the north slope of Alaska, Mexico, and the North Sea. In the United States, higher prices reduced consumption and encouraged fuel switching as well as conservation.

In early 1981, the United States government, in response to the oil crisis of 1978–1980, began to remove price and allocation controls. A direct result of oil price decontrol was to allow producers to raise prices to market clearing levels and domestic prices became more closely aligned with world oil prices. Not surprisingly, as prices rose, demand decreased. In 1986, the world experienced a price collapse. In July 1986, for example, OPEC crude oil had dropped from over $23 per barrel in December 1985 to under $10 per barrel, thus reversing the upward trend in U.S. oil production. Again, as prices declined, demand increased, and the United States continued purchasing foreign oil.

The fall in the price of oil in the mid–1980s was due, in part, to OPEC's failed efforts to control production. In the early and mid–1980s, over one quarter of the world's excess supply of oil came from the non-Persian Gulf members of OPEC, and United States' imports rose to 41% of its total consumption. Cartels are not very stable organizations and it is not unusual to have OPEC members exceed agreed-upon quotas. For a time, Saudi Arabia was willing to independently cut its production to offset this cheating. However, in 1985, Saudi Arabia saw its own oil exports fall by 80% to 2 million barrels a day from 10 million barrels and it attempted to recoup its market share of international oil sales. Other OPEC members did the same with the result that an oil glut was created. In 1986, Saudi Arabia's oil exports rose to 6 million barrels a day and the price of a barrel of oil fell to under $10. Shortly thereafter, OPEC returned to reductions in output with a view to stabilizing the price of oil at between $15 and $18 a barrel. See Energy Information Administration, Monthly Energy Review (April 1987). Since that time oil prices have ranged from an annual average of $12.50 in 1986 to $27.50 per barrel in 2003. See Energy Information Administration, Petroleum Marketing Monthly, Table 1 (March 2004).

C. THE ERA OF PRICE, ALLOCATION AND ENTITLEMENT CONTROLS, 1970–1980

1. Price Controls

The history of the price, allocation and entitlement controls on oil—which began on August 11, 1971 with President Nixon's institution of national wage and price controls, under the Economic Stabilization Act of 1970, Pub. L. No. 92–210, 85 Stat. 743, and ended with President Reagan's Executive Order, No. 12287, 46 Fed. Reg. 9909 (Jan. 30, 1981)—is a complex story of the federal government's attempt to respond to the domestic economic and political consequences of the limitations that it placed on the import of foreign oil into the United States. Today, these regulations are primarily of historical interest because they are no longer in place. Nevertheless, it has been the case in the United States that in difficult economic times, such as during major wars, government turns to price controls to control inflation or prevent price gouging or the like.

The oil regulation of the 1970s was accomplished primarily through three statutes: the Emergency Petroleum Allocation Act of 1973 (EPAA), Pub. L. No. 93–159, 87 Stat. 627; the Energy Policy and Conservation Act of 1975 (EPCA), Pub. L. No. 94–163, 89 Stat. 871; and the Energy Conservation and Production Act of 1976 (ECPA), Pub. L. No. 94–385, 90 Stat. 1125. To carry out these various statutory programs, the President established the Federal Energy Office (FEO). The FEO was succeeded in mid–1974 by the Federal Energy Administration (FEA) created by the Federal Energy Administration Act of 1974, Pub. L. No. 93–275, 88 Stat. 96. In 1978, the Department of Energy (DOE) was created and succeeded the FEA.

The problem that faced energy policymakers (in the sort of circumstances that existed in the 1970s) posed by federal intervention in international oil markets might be summarized in broad economic terms by characterizing it as an attempt to induce artificially a shift in United States demand for oil from foreign to domestic sources. A shift that increases demand for domestic oil can be accomplished by moving domestic oil prices below the price of foreign oil. At that point, the competition from foreign oil is diminished. In turn, both domestic production and prices tend to increase above levels that would exist without federal intervention. These price rises encourage new investment by domestic oil producers to explore for and produce new oil wells and to increase production at existing wells. At the same time, existing domestic oil wells of settled production will continue to produce at least at the same level as they would if the federal intervention in the oil marketplace had not occurred. If nothing more were done, as prices rise to market-clearing levels, domestic oil producers and suppliers would receive a higher return without any increase in the costs of production. That higher return has been labeled variously as economic rent, a transfer of wealth from the users to the producers, and windfall profits. Policymakers then are induced by political considerations to make adjustments in federal intervention to prevent such shifts or windfalls by adjusting prices downward or by taxing profits. Policymakers are further moved to impose allocation measures to assure that refiners (such as the major oil companies) and end users that have greater access to lower-priced settled production do not have an unfair advantage over independent refiners.

All of these events came to pass during the 1970s. The federal regulation of petroleum and refined oil products in the 1970s was instituted as part of a national statutory response to rising inflation rates in the form of a freeze on almost all wages and prices under the Economic Stabilization Act of 1970, Pub. L. No. 91–379, 84 Stat. 799. In general, the regulation by the executive branch of wages and prices ended by mid–1974 for nearly all commodities except oil because of the supply cutbacks which occurred as part of the Arab Oil Embargo.

The federal government's response to increasing domestic oil prices was to institute a system of multi-tiered price ceilings at the producing, refining, wholesaling, and retailing stages of the oil fuel cycle through the EPAA. The pricing system recognized three types of domestic oil that were subject to different pricing requirements at the production stage (the price at which the producer sells oil to the refiner). Oil produced by a specific oil field at or below its 1972 production level was priced at the May 15, 1973 price for oil from that field (plus a small addition or minus a small deduction per barrel) on the theory that this price reflected the fixed production costs for that oil. This oil was referred to as "old" oil. Oil produced from that same field in excess of "old" oil was not subject to price ceilings. This oil was called "new" oil. The price of "new" oil was allowed to rise for the express purpose of stimulating new production. In addition, for each barrel of new oil produced from that field one barrel of old oil was freed or released from old oil price ceilings. This oil was called "released" oil. Finally, imported oil was not subject to price control.

The economics of the old oil/new oil regulations are quite basic and could work well *if the oil industry were evenly structured.* We will return to this qualification about the industry in a moment. The basic economics mean that old oil prices were controlled so that economic rents (i.e. windfall profits) would not be generated. The new oil prices would be freed from controls in order to stimulate investment and increase production.

Because the oil industry is not evenly structured, which is to say that in addition to integrated oil companies there existed independent producers, importers, and refiners, the two tier system of old prices and new prices affected the industry unevenly. A consequence of this unevenness was the push for exemptions to the system. As a result, a set of rules was introduced which greatly complicated the system.

The Supplier–Purchaser Program, for example, established set prices among domestic petroleum producers, refiners, re-sellers, and retailers, as of 1972. The purpose of this rule was to prevent some refiners from engaging in transactions giving them access to additional qualities of the price controlled old oil which was much cheaper to refine than new oil.

Analogously, the Buy–Sell Program required refiners that had disproportionate amounts of less expensive oil to sell such oil at controlled prices to other refiners. Finally, the Crude Oil Entitlements Program attempted to equalize oil costs across domestic refiners, requiring those with access to cheaper old oil to buy rights to purchase this lower cost oil.

In a sense, the industry reaction to price controls was predictable as domestic exploration and production declined as the price of United States oil was kept below world prices. Simultaneously, with the reduction in prices, there was an increase in demand and shortages arose, which resulted in gas lines and allocation controls.

The national wage and price freeze, which began on August 11, 1971, was the first phase of price controls applicable generally in the economy. The freeze was replaced three months later, on November 13, 1971, with a program that limited price increases to three percent of existing prices. The mandatory price increase limitation phase was replaced with a third non-mandatory phase on January 11, 1973, which consisted of price increase guidelines that depended on voluntary compliance by the business community.

The price level at which refiners could sell their refined oil products to wholesalers and retailers generally consisted of the May 5, 1973 base price for those refined oil products adjusted by certain allowed increases attributable to costs. Certain costs (mostly non-product related costs), which could not be passed through to retailers in a particular month because of price ceilings, could be "banked" and reserved later in accordance with federal regulations. In addition, the pass-through rules required refiners to prorate the increased costs of certain special products like gasoline, diesel fuel, and heating oil.

Wholesalers and retailers that bought refined oil and oil products, in turn, could pass-through their purchase price to consumers subject to retail price ceilings. Initially, this often placed retailers in a profit margin bind. On the one hand, they had to pay increased product costs passed through by refiners but were limited in their ability to recover an adequate profit margin because the price at which they could sell to the consumer was subject to a ceiling sometimes unrelated to the pass-through costs incurred. Retailers eventually prevailed on Congress to amend the price ceiling system to allow a dollar-for-dollar pass-through of oil and oil product costs from production to end-use.

The next significant federal intervention into the oil economy was the Energy Policy and Conservation Act of 1975, Pub. L. No. 94–163, 89 Stat. 871. The EPCA was enacted to increase oil production through price incentives eventually leading to price decontrols, to establish a strategic petroleum reserve, and to increase automobile fuel efficiency. You will recall that old oil and new oil were priced differently, and the idea behind EPCA was to equalize those prices. The strategic petroleum reserve was designed to store up to one million barrels of oil in the event of additional supply disruptions. To date, the strategic petroleum reserve has acquired 500 million barrels of crude oil. The Act also established the Corporate Average Fuel Economy (CAFE) standards that mandated improvements in average automobile fuel economy. The idea was to require various fleets of vehicles to achieve certain fuel standards in terms of miles per gallon.

The pricing structure of EPCA had the effect of increasing production and exploration and also provided an incentive for oil companies to increase purchases of imported oil. In response to the CAFE standards, car manufacturers built and sold more subcompact and compact cars, with a consequent decline in the sale of large cars since the standards were set.

The CAFE standards seemed to have had a positive effect in increasing fuel efficiency from 1975 to 1978. The cars had to meet CAFE standards increased in efficiency from 15.8 miles per gallon to 28.6 miles per gallon. Since 1988, however, fuel economy for cars has declined as a result of the less demanding standards applicable to light duty trucks and sports utility vehicles.

2. Allocation Controls and Entitlements Controls

The Economic Stabilization Act of 1970, 12 U.S.C. § 1904, authorized the President to allocate oil and oil products. Allocation authority was thought necessary to help preserve the relative competitive positions of companies as they existed before the pricing distinctions between old and new oil. One fear was that vertically-integrated major oil companies would keep old oil for themselves, refine it and sell it at a lower price than could be achieved with new oil, which they would sell to competing independent refiners. Executive allocation authority was exercised initially to institute a voluntary program to induce suppliers to allocate oil and oil products that were in short supply on a pro rata basis to their customers. The increasing shortages of oil and refined oil products and the limited success of the voluntary allocation program prompted the federal government to mandatorily allocate available supplies among customer classes. The EPAA required the President to issue allocation regulations and final regulations went into effect on January 15, 1974, 39 Fed. Reg. 1924.

The FEO, under the regulations, froze allocations among oil and oil product suppliers and buyers as they existed in 1972 subject to a *pro rata* reduction in periods of shortages. Later the DOE froze allocations among suppliers and purchasers as they existed in 1976. Thus, suppliers along the fuel cycle had to make available to buyers, beginning in 1974, the same amount of oil or oil products bought in 1972. If suppliers and buyers of oil and oil products mutually agreed to end their relationship, they had to obtain FEO approval. In addition, new buyers, if they could not find a supplier could apply to FEO to assign them both to a supplier and to an allocation. The allocation scheme was made more complex by the addition of a system of priorities for categories of consumers that could disrupt the 1972 base period allocations. For example, certain consumers—like farmers, the Department of Defense and those providing essential services—were entitled to buy all their current requirements without reference to the 1972 base period allocations. Other consumers like individual driving cars were not guaranteed any supply of oil or gasoline. Suppliers had to meet priority customer needs even if it meant that non-priority consumers received less than their 1972 base period allocation. In short, the federal allocation program became a government rationing system.

Eventually, regulations were added to ensure that all refiners, large and small, major and independent, had the same ratio of crude oil supplies to refining capacity. Refiners with a greater ration had to sell their crude oil to refiners with a lesser ration. Finally, the allocation scheme was subject to a state set-aside program under which the FEO and later the DOE could require part of available supplies to be allocated to state energy offices in states where there was an energy supply shortage. The DOE also eventually had the power to move oil and oil product supplies from one section of the nation to another where relative supply shortages were particularly disproportionate to those in the rest of the nation.

At the end of 1974, an entitlements program was initiated in order to equalize the cost of crude oil among refiners. The price differential between "old" and "new" oil had increased dramatically, largely because of the oil price increases created by the Arab Oil Embargo. At one point, the differential in price between old and new oil had reached $8.00 a barrel. As a result, refiners that had access to large amounts of lower priced "old" oil came to have a significant competitive edge over refiners who only had access to higher-priced "new" oil.

Under the entitlements programs, refiners received "entitlements" from the FEA that corresponded to the national average use of old oil. If a refiner wanted to use a greater amount of old oil than the national average it had to buy the "entitlements" to old oil from refiners with surplus or unused entitlements. The FEA became the clearinghouse or broker for purchases and sales of these entitlements purchases and sales. The entitlements program also was subject to a bias in favor of the small refiner in the sense that these operators were assigned extra entitlements to old oil in order to keep them competitive with the large oil companies. See, *Pasco, Inc. v. FEA* (TECA 1975). There was no equivalent to the price entitlement program for the allocation of refined oil products.

The old oil entitlements program authorized the FEA to provide relief through exceptions to companies that were placed at a competitive disadvantage by its operation. In *New England Petroleum Corp. v. FEA,* (S.D.N.Y. 1978), the old oil entitlements program is described in a context in which the

FEA's exercise of its exceptions relief power was placed at issue. There, New England Petroleum Company (NEPCO), a foreign oil refiner and a domestic supplier of petroleum, challenged a series of FEA orders granting in part and denying in part NEPCO's requests for exceptions relief. Exxon Corporation intervened challenging FEA's (and its successor DOE) authority to grant any exceptions relief to NEPCO. On motions for summary judgment the district court upheld the FEA's orders except to the extent FEA denied NEPCO exceptions relief during the months of December 1975 and January 1976. The district court remanded to the DOE to determine the dollar amounts of NEPCO's entitlements during that two month period.

During the period under discussion, market distortions had been created between integrated and nonintegrated companies, and among large and small refiners and various producers. Price disparities also developed between domestic and imported oil. Some refiners argued that the two-tier system caused refiners to purchase more imported oil instead of reducing imports. In addition, price disparities appeared in different geographical markets within the United States. To deal with these peculiarities, the DOE was empowered to grant exceptions relief to the pricing regulations. *Rock Island Refining Corp. v. DOE* (S.D. Ind. 1979); *New England Petroleum Corp. v. FEA* (S.D.N.Y. 1978). Exceptions to the entitlements program protected the competitive position of oil firms that were adversely affected in the market because of government regulations. See Peter H. Schuck, *When the Exception Becomes the Rule: Regulatory Equity and the Formulation of an Energy Policy Through an Exceptions Process*, 1984 DUKE L.J. 163.

3. Enforcement

Price controls also contained an enforcement component. If sales of controlled products were made in violation of the pricing regulations, then the DOE had enforcement authority and violators could be ordered to refund overcharges. See generally, *Quincy Oil, Inc. v. FEA* (D. Mass 1979); *Plaquemines Oil Sales Corp. v. FEA* (D. La. 1978); *Naph–Sol Refining Co. v. Cities Service Oil Co.* (D. Mich. 1980). These overcharges could be large. In *United States v. Exxon Corp.* (D.D.C. 1979), the government sought to have Exxon refund over $183,000,000.00. Oil companies were ordered to refund large overcharges in *Phillips Petroleum v. DOE* (D. Del. 1978); *Standard Oil Co. v. DOE* (TEAC 1978); and *United States v. Metropolitan Petroleum Co., Inc.* (S.D. Fla. 1990).

On November 12, 1979, in response to the taking of hostages by Iran, President Carter issued a proclamation banning the importation into the United States of oil produced in Iran. The Iranian government then placed an embargo on the export of its oil to the United States. In an effort to alleviate the hardships caused by this supply disruption, the DOE implemented a mandatory allocation program. Under this program, a domestic refiner injured by the embargo could receive cheaper oil from other domestic refiners. *Marathon Oil Co. v. DOE* (D.D.C. 1979); *New England Petroleum Corp. v. FEA* (S.D.N.Y. 1978). The DOE also prescribed the amount of an oil product that suppliers could sell to their customers. *Shell Oil Co. v. Nelson Oil Co., Inc.* (TEAC 1980).

The power of the DOE to allocate supplies also became important to consumers affected by shortages throughout the market. The regulations under the mandatory allocation program distributed supplies to help keep firms competitive in the industry. When oil supplies were reduced as a result of the Iranian embargo, the fear was that some end-of-the-fuel-cycle customers would also be indiscriminately disadvantaged. Rules for rationing gas at the pump were a kind of allocation that affected consumers most directly. *Reeves v. Simon* (TEAC 1974). In an effort to allocate gasoline in a "fair and equitable" manner, Congress also passed the Emergency Energy Conservation Act of 1979, 42 U.S.C. § 8501, which required the President to develop a "standby" rationing plan for gasoline and diesel fuel.

Another enforcement mechanism used by Congress was to capture windfall profits. The existence of the OPEC cartel has had a peculiar economic consequence, known as economic rents, for domestic oil producers. Economic rents occur when the value of a good rises independent of a rise in costs. During the Arab Oil Embargo, for example, the world price of oil was driven from its market price about $20 per barrel to over $40 per barrel. Domestic oil producers who had produced oil for $20 per barrel now had oil worth $40 per barrel through no effort of their own. Politicians saw such gain as an unearned windfall and sought to capture that gain for the U.S. Treasury.

Congress, in conjunction with President Carter's 1979 initiation of a gradual phased decontrol of oil and oil products, enacted the Crude Oil Windfall Profit Tax Act of 1980, Pub. L. No. 96–223, 94 Stat. 229, in order to tax a fair share of the additional revenues received by oil producers and royalty owners as a result of oil price decontrols. The revenue raised by the tax was to be used for tax incentives to encourage energy conservation and production of alternate energy sources together with assistance to lower-income households to help them cope with higher energy prices. The constitutionality of the WPT and its exemptions was challenged and the statute was upheld in *United States v. Ptasynski* (1983).

4. Price Decontrol

As noted, price controls on oil were applied in times of emergency, such as both World Wars and as a result of the 1970s energy crisis. Price controls generally are difficult to monitor and, particularly for competitive industries, are inefficient. By the end of the 1970s decontrol mechanisms were in place. The first form of decontrol came through exemptions from price and allocation controls in various statutes and regulation. During the Ford and early Carter administrations, proposals were made to decontrol gasoline, which was the last petroleum product deregulated. By April 1979, the Economic Recovery Administration promulgated the first stage of regulations leading to the decontrol of oil prices. Finally, the Economic Recovery Administration adopted regulations which provided for the phased decontrol of crude oil beginning in January 1980, that was to be completed by September 30, 1981.

Oil price controls were always seen as a temporary measure and oil price legislation during the Carter Administration was intended to terminate oil price controls in October of 1981. President Reagan, however, as the first act of his presidency, decontrolled in January, 1981. Thus, for the first time since the early 1970s, domestic crude oil prices were allowed to rise to market levels. These decontrols also allowed for the relaxation of export restrictions of oil products. A negative consequence of deregulation was that many small refineries, who had been the beneficiaries of entitlements program, were forced to shut down and the United States saw a decline of more than 100 refineries from 1981 to 1995. The reduction in the number of refineries had the effect of increasing imports of certain types of oil for more technologically sophisticated refiners.

The price decontrol allowed producers to raise prices to market clearing levels with the consequent increase in oil exploration and production in the first half of the 1980s. The concern about decontrol, of course, was that without price controls, oil prices would rise. It turned out, however, that prices fell in the aftermath of decontrol. When oil prices collapsed in 1986, the production and exploration slowed considerably.

D.　FEDERAL LANDS

1.　Onshore Oil

Federal public lands comprise over 600 million acres, with the federal government owning half of the land west of the Mississippi River. The Department of the Interior, through the Bureau of Land Management (BLM), generally has jurisdiction over oil and gas assets of public lands. Historically, oil was known as a "locatable" mineral and classified as such under the Oil Placer Act of 1897. Oil was also subject to placer claims under the General Mining Law of 1872, 30 U.S.C. §§ 21–54. In the early 1900s, however, oil became strategically important and was removed as a locatable mineral for national security purposes by President William Howard Taft. See *United States v. Midwest Oil Co.* (1915). In 1920, Congress passed the Mineral Lands Leasing Act, Pub. L. No. 66–146, 41 Stat. 437 (codified as amended in scattered sections of 30 U.S.C.) which classified oil as a leasable mineral and under that act, the federal government reserves a royalty on the production of oil and gas located on its lands. In 1987, Congress passed the Federal Onshore Oil and Gas Leasing Reform Act, Pub. L. No. 100–203, 101 Stat. 1330, reforming the leasing requirements. In particular, all federal onshore lands, with few exceptions, must be offered for lease under competitive conditions. Today, both the Mineral Leasing Act and the Federal Onshore Oil and Gas Leasing Reform Act govern. Under those acts, as well as under other federal statutes, lands that are owned by the federal government that may not be leased must be identified.

The Mineral Leasing Act is administered by the Secretary of the Interior through the BLM, which issues both competitive and non-competitive leases to cover oil, gas, and other minerals under the jurisdiction of the Department of the Interior and in some instances under the jurisdiction of the Forest Service which is an agency of the Department of Agriculture.

Lands available for leasing are subject to bidding by interested parties and the lease is to go to the highest bidder. Annual rentals range from $1.50 per acre for the first five years of a lease to $2.00 per acre thereafter. See 43 C.F.R. § 3103.2–2(a). Although established by Congress, these rental fees may be raised by regulation. On discovery of oil or gas, the lessee must pay a minimum royalty of not less than what the rental would properly be. Generally, the lessee pays a 12.5% royalty to the federal government on discovered resources. Except for Alaska, half of the income is paid directly to the state in which the resources are found. Alaska receives 90% of the income.

Leasing is discretionary with the Secretary of the Interior. Lease terms are five years for competitive leases. If the lessee has not produced oil or gas in that time period, the lease expires. These leases, however, may be extended only for the period of production. If, however, production has not started, but drilling operations have, the lease may be extended for two years.

2. Offshore Lands

When we discuss offshore lands, we are referring to oil exploration on the outer continental shelf (OCS). The continental shelf is part of the sea bed which lies adjacent to the coast, also called the continental margin. This is an enormous territory estimated to be over 100 billion acres under the jurisdiction of the United States. For oil purposes, however, most of the oil development occurs in an area largely off the state of California and within the Gulf of Mexico which comprises about 25 million acres. In terms of volume, the OCS contributes about 25% of the United States' total gas and oil production as shown in Figure 2. Nevertheless, it is also the case that further into the ocean in deeper waters lie oil and gas reserves that are beginning to be exploited.

Figure 2 Crude Oil and Oil Well Productivity

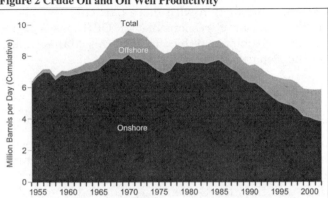

On September 28, 1945 President Truman signed a proclamation on the "Policy of the United States with Respect to the Natural Resources of the Subsoil and Sea Bed of the Continental Shelf," 4 *Whiteman's Digest of International Law* § 756 (D.O.S. 1987). The Truman Proclamation on the continental shelf was given domestic life in 1953, primarily through two pieces of legislation—the Submerged Lands Act (SLA), 43 U.S.C. §§ 1301–1315 and the Outer Continental Shelf Lands Acts, as amended in 1978, (OCSLA), 43 U.S.C. §§ 1331–1356.

The SLA confined the jurisdiction of the states to offshore sea-bed to a belt of submerged lands extending up to three miles beyond the low-water mark along the coast, 43 U.S.C. § 1301(b) (1985). The OCSLA defined the outer continental shelf (OCS) subject to federal jurisdiction as "all submerged lands lying seaward and outside of the area of lands" subject to state jurisdiction, 43 U.S.C. § 1331(a). Thus the OCS under federal government control comprised the continental shelf seaward and beyond three miles from the coast to a distance recognized by international law (for the most part 200 miles beyond the coast). The United States Supreme Court has determined that the continental shelf comes under federal regulation. *United States v. Louisiana* (1950); *United States v.*

Texas (1950); *United States v. California* (1947). Congress has specified that jurisdiction with more particularity. The Secretary of the Interior is responsible for OCS leases which are handled more particularly by the Minerals Management Services in the Department.

Under the 1978 Amendment to the OCSLA, states gained a more significant role in leasing and the amendment provided more coordination with the Coastal Zone Management Act of 1972, 16 U.S.C. §§ 1451 et seq. See, *Secretary of the Interior v. California* (1984). Also pursuant to the 1978 amendments, the Secretary of the Interior is required to conduct environmental studies for assessment as well as management of the areas leased. In addition, the Secretary is required to establish and maintain the OCS Oil and Gas Information Program for the public dissemination of oil and gas data resulting from exploration, development, and production on the outer continental shelf.

The heart of the OCSLA and its amendments is the leasing system. The process is complex and lengthy, balancing several interests, including natural resources as well as environmental matters. The leasing process calls for information and nominations of potential producers, identification of the area to be explored, as well as draft final environmental impact statements pursuant to the National Environmental Policy Act of 1969, 42 U.S.C. §§ 4321 et seq. After the publication of the final environmental impact statement, the Notice of Proposed Sale is followed by a final notice with a bidding system. Under the 1978 amendments, the Secretary is authorized to use a variety of bidding systems, 43 U.S.C. § 1337(a)(1). These systems involve both cash payments and percentage royalties. The leases allow for exploration and development. Bids are solicited on the basis of a cash bonus with a fixed royalty, a royalty bid with a fixed cash bonus, or various combinations of the two. The bidding system is designed and intended to balance the economic, social, and environmental concerns in developing these offshore lands, as well as to assure a fair market price to the government. *Watt v. Energy Action Educ. Foundation* (1981). In *Watt*, a group of environmental plaintiffs sought to halt all leasing activities until the Interior Department developed regulations requiring the Secretary to use a variety of systems. The Supreme Court said that it found nothing in the Congressional authorization to mandate such a requirement. Rather, the Court ruled that alternative bidding was permissive.

Given the value of these resources, the royalties that are paid to the United States Treasury can be significant and total billions of dollars. The royalties are governed by the Federal Oil and Gas Management Act of 1982, 30 U.S.C. §§ 1701 et seq. This act provides for the maintenance of records and files, audits and investigations, collection of monies, as well as distribution and disbursement. Failure to follow the rules prescribed by the Act can result in fines and penalties.

While it is the case that the federal government has wide ranging authority regarding leases, should it fail to honor its obligations to a producer, such failure is subject to judicial scrutiny. *Mobil Oil Exploration and Producing Southeast, Inc. v. United States* (2000). In *Mobil Exploration*, two oil companies sought restitution of $156 million that they paid to the government in lease contracts giving them the rights to explore for and develop oil off the North Carolina coast. The companies argued that the government repudiated its contracts when it denied them the opportunity to acquire additional permits that were necessary. The Supreme Court held that the government did break its promise and had to return those fees to the oil companies.

E. OIL AND THE ENVIRONMENT

The 1960s and early 1970s saw a proliferation of environmental laws and regulations. Oil exploration played no small part in our nation's awareness of the environment.

"One event, above all, was the catalyst for the wave of environmental legislation enacted from 1969 onwards: the Santa Barbara oil spill of January 28, 1969. In 1966 the first federal leases on the Pacific offshore were issued in the Santa Barbara Channel. As Union Oil drilled the fifth well on its platform A in the channel, the well blew out. Eleven days passed before the well was plugged and some 24,000 to 71,000 barrels of oil spilled into the channel and onto nearby beaches." Fred Bosselman, Jim Rossi, & Jacqueline Lang Weaver, *Energy, Economics, and the Environment* 349 (2000).

These authors then go on to argue that after the Santa Barbara oil spill, Congress enacted a slew of legislation including the National Environmental Policy Act of 1969, the Marine Protection, Research, and Sanctuaries Act of 1972, the Coastal Zone Management Act of 1972, the Marine Mammal Protection Act of 1972, the Endangered Species Act of 1973, the Clean Water and Clean Air Acts of 1977 and, in 1978, made significant revisions to the Outer Continental Shelf Lands Act of 1953

A notable environmental problem arises when pristine areas are explored. The Arctic National Wildlife Refuge (ANWR) was designated a federal wilderness area by President Eisenhower. Today with 19 million acres, ANWR is the size of South Carolina and sits hundreds of miles north of the Arctic Circle next to Prudhoe Bay hugging the Arctic Ocean. ANWR is an area of rolling tundra, migratory birds, polar bears, porcupine caribou, snow geese, and other wildlife; an area of lagoons, barrier islands, large bays, seashore, estuaries, river corridors, and thaw lake wetlands. The World Wildlife Federation describes ANWR as one of the only places on earth that protects the complete spectrum of sub-arctic and arctic habitats. Today, jeep tracks from decades ago are still visible on the ANWR tundra.

Contrast that picture of wilderness with 2,000 acres of oil pipelines and facilities projected to explore and exploit the 1.5 million acres of ANWR recognized as containing potential oil and natural gas resources. These 2,000 acres constitute the estimated area or "footprint" of oil production. A 2,000 acre footprint out of 1.5 million acres does not sound like much. However, to develop ANWR would require 20 different sites to exploit 30 or more oil fields with roads and oil transportation networks connecting those areas.

The choice should be clear: oil development or wilderness protection? The Department of the Interior in its environmental impact statement concluded that oil development in the coastal plain would have serious impacts on the wildlife and the ecosystem. The current Bush Administration wishes to go forward.

Vice President Cheney's Energy Plan proposes to develop the ANWR site and specifies that:

The total quantity of recoverable oil within the entire assessment area is estimated to be between 5.7 and 16 billion barrels (95% and 5% probability range) with a mean value of 10.4 billion barrels.... Peak production from ANWR could be between 1 and 1.3 million barrels a day and account for more than 20% of all U.S. oil production.

These numbers should be put in perspective. Currently, the United States produces slightly over 20.5 million barrels of oil a day (mbd) and exports one million mbd. The country thus consumes 19.5 million mbd, of which nearly 70% is consumed by the transportation sector. Other reserve estimates for ANWR range from a low of 3.2 billion barrels to the USGS estimate of 16 billion barrels. Going inside the reserve numbers, the low estimate of 3.2 billion barrels would provide 160 days of domestic oil consumption. Sixteen billion barrels would provide 800 days of domestic oil consumption. According to the Energy Information Agency, at its peak, at least 10 years from now, ANWR will produce only 800,000 barrels a day. The EIA also estimates that this production will reduce the net share of foreign oil used by the United States in 2020 from 62% to 60%.

The choice may have been best summarized, according to *New York Times* columnist Nicholas Kristof, by an oil industry geologist who said: "We can build cleanly, we can drill without hurting the caribou. But we can't drill and keep this a wilderness." Nicholas D. Kristof, *A Grizzly's–Eye View of the Land Above the Oil*, N.Y. TIMES op. Sept. 2, 2003. To drill, or not, of course is the question. The accepted way of deciding to drill or preserve is to balance extra energy against environmental damage; balance contributions to the local economy against degradation of the wilderness; or, balance the preservation of a land few will ever see against limited exploration by those willing to pay.

OCS exploration poses similar problems. The DOE has authority to develop the OCS so that the nation might increase its supply of oil and gas. In a real sense, the OSC and federal onshore lands are the last domestic frontiers, certainly in the foreseeable future. However, development of the OCS raises concerns that the ecological dangers inherent in tapping offshore resources will require a great deal of caution. The major challenge is whether the Department of Interior's environmental impact statement (EIS) for offshore leasing satisfies the requirements of the Natural Environmental Policy Act. *Suffolk County v. Secretary of Interior* (2d Cir. 1977); *Natural Resources Defense Council, Inc. v. Hodel* (D.C. Cir. 1988). If the EIS is inadequate, then the leasing can be enjoined. *Commonwealth of Massachusetts v. Andrus* (1st Cir. 1979).

In *Commonwealth of Massachusetts v. Andrus*, the U.S. Court of Appeals for the First Circuit considered a preliminary injunction, issued by the district court, which enjoined the Secretary of the Interior from proceeding with the proposed sale of oil leaseholds in the OCS off the coast of New England. The injunction had been granted on the basis that safeguards against oil spills were lacking. In response to the dangers inherent in oil spills, Congress amended the Outer Continental Shelf Lands Act to create an oil spill fund.

The second problem, oil spills, presents significant environmental risks which can occur as a result of a blow out, pipeline leak, or tanker spill, as the Exxon Valdez accident in Alaska's Prince William Sound demonstrated. The oil tanker disaster of the Exxon Valdez in March 1989 is perhaps the most significant tanker disaster. This tanker loaded with 53 million gallons of oil bound for Long Beach, California was captained by someone who had been drinking. The ship was grounded at Bligh Reef, having ruptured eight of its 11 cargo tanks and dumping 10.8 million gallons of crude oil into Prince William Sound. Although no human lives were lost as a result of the grounding, four deaths were attributable to clean-up efforts. The economic loss in terms of damage to fisheries, subsistence livelihoods, tourism, and wildlife was perhaps incalculable. The oil spill extended nearly 500 miles for the next two months following the grounding.

The legacy of the Exxon Valdez continues. In January, 2004 federal judge Russell Holland sitting in Anchorage imposed a punitive damage award of $4.5 billion on the Exxon Mobil Corporation. With interest, the award is about $6.75 billion in a suit brought by about 32,000 fishermen and residents of the area. This ruling was the third attempt to impose a punitive damages award, the previous two having been overturned by the U.S. Court of Appeals for the Ninth Circuit.

Oil spills are indeed vexatious on many fronts. In *Sun Oil Co. v. United States* (Ct. Cl. 1978) and *Pauley Petroleum Inc. v. United States* (Ct. Cl. 1979), numerous lessees of federal offshore lands brought lawsuits against the United States contending that their leasehold rights had been impaired by new restrictions on exploration following the Santa Barbara blow-out. The oil companies' claims for damages were denied. The costs of purchasing the now largely useless leaseholds, which ran into the hundreds of millions of dollars, had to be absorbed by the oil companies and passed through to consumers and shareholders.

Oil spills may endanger shorelines, aquatic life, wildlife, and the stability of the entire ecosystems. In *Commonwealth of*

Puerto Rico v. SS Zoe Colocotroni (1st Cir. 1980), the U.S. Court of Appeals upheld, in part, a district courts' award of damages for the clean up costs of an oil spill against a tanker. Costs can also be recovered by the government pursuant to the Clean Water Act. *United States v. Dixie Carriers, Inc.* (5th Cir. 1980). In *North Slope Borough v. Andrus* (D.D.C. 1980), environmentalists obtained an injunction against the Department of the Interior from issuing leases for the exploration of Alaska's North Slope until the EIS had been supplemented. In *North Slope*, suit was brought under NEPA, the Outer Continental Shelf Lands Act, the Endangered Species Act, the Marine Mammal Protection Act, the Migratory Bird Treaty Act, and the Agreement on Conservation of Polar Bears.

Congress, in response to the Exxon Valdez disaster, has further addressed the problem of oil spills in the Oil Pollution Liability and Compensation Act of 1990, 33 U.S.C. §§ 2701 et seq. This extensive legislation establishes a system of compensation and liability, including the creation of an Oil Spill Liability Trust Fund and a system of fines and penalties.

This legislation requires reporting, assigns liability, requires clean-up, and addresses prevention. The Oil Pollution Act initially places liability on the owner or the operator of the vessel or facility, giving them the burden of developing a statutory defense establishing the liability of a third party. The act contains limits on liability assignable to any on-shore facility of $350 million. The Act also imposes financial responsibility on vessel and facility owners to be achieved through insurance, a surety bond, a letter, or a letter of credit. The Act does preempt additional state regulation. By way of prevention, the Oil Pollution Act contains provisions for improving vessel design and operation, training, and emergency preparedness.

Clearly, oil will continue to be a major energy source for years to come. Oil will also continue to be a focus of domestic and global politics. As a fossil fuel, oil will continue to raise environmental concerns, also of world-wide concern.

CHAPTER 6

NATURAL GAS

Federal regulation of natural gas and electricity share several similarities. The organic legislation for each are very similar. Rates for both were, for most of the century, set under the traditional rate formula. Both industries were similarly structured insofar as they had multiple producers and limited means of transportation to end users or to distribution companies. In the electric industry, high voltage power lines are the main source of transmission and in the natural gas industry, pipelines constitute the transmission segment. Thus, transmission in both industries constitutes a privately owned bottleneck that currently constrains industry deregulation and was the basic reason for the initial regulation. And both are attempting to move into more competitive environments.

Further both industries grew tremendously after World War II until the mid–1960s. The electric industry grew with the expanding economy. The gas industry grew as a result of: (1) bountiful natural gas reserves and favorable prices; (2) improvements in long distance pipeline technology and storage; (3) increased demand for natural gas; (4) perception of natural gas as a competitively priced and desirable fuel; and, (5) favorable financing for interstate pipelines. James McManus, *Natural Gas* in 2 ENERGY LAW AND TRANSACTIONS D–9 (David J. Muchow & William A. Mogel (eds.) (2003)).

The post-World War II years were good for natural gas. Residential users increased their use of a clean burning fuel that did not have to be stored at home. Also, industrial users saw gas as another fuel that they could use for manufacturing processes. Developments continued for gas plants and pipelines. Additionally, technological improvements in gas and electricity continued until the 1960s, at which time the prevailing regulatory regime seemed to run its course.

The story of natural gas regulation is a favorite of free market advocates because, they argue, federal regulation has caused severe market dislocations and, therefore, constitutes an excellent example of regulatory failure. Those who favor regulation point to exercises of market power by gas pipelines and the continuing problem of natural monopoly in pipeline transportation. As you read the materials that follow you can judge whether natural gas regulation corrected a market failure or constituted a primary example of regulatory failure.

A. INDUSTRY OVERVIEW

The first gas utility in the United States opened in Maryland in 1817 as the Gas Light Company of Baltimore. The painter Rembrandt Peale and his associates had used coal gas (also referred to as manufactured gas) the year earlier to illuminate an exhibit at his museum and gallery. By 1859, there were nearly 300 manufactured gas plants in the country serving nearly 5 million customers. Small, privately owned manufactured local gas companies proliferated until between 1920 and 1945 natural gas pipeline technology enabled broader transportation and as electricity and coal replaced it in the residential and industrial sectors.

The natural gas fuel cycle is similar to that of oil. In the late 19th century and for most of the 20th century, oil and natural gas were found together and such gas is called "associated gas." Today it is more frequently the case that gas is non-associated or not found with oil. Natural gas, like oil and coal, is a fossil fuel which means that it is comprised of the remains of plants, animals, and microorganisms living millions of years ago. Natural gases can be made up of currently living plants and waste, but most of our natural gas is of the fossil fuel variety and is found trapped in geological formations under the ground. In the early part of the 20th century, oil was the more important natural resource and natural gas was seen to be a nuisance by-product of oil exploration and production. It was considered so much of a nuisance that it was burned off or flared at the wellhead rather than extracted and stored. Today, however, natural gas is an extremely important part of our nation's energy economy accounting for about 25% of all energy consumed in the United States and industry revenues top $50 billion per year. Two of the reasons for the continued importance of natural gas is that it is in relatively abundant supply and it is a relatively clean burning fuel.

Natural gas is measured either by heat content (one million British Thermal Units–MMBtu) or volume (one thousand cubic feet-Mcf). These measurements are roughly comparable. One Mcf has a heat content of about one MMBtu. Most of the gas produced comes from highly porous sedimentary rock at depths less than 15,000 feet. Gas below 15,000 feet or gas located in sedimentary rock with low porosity is said to come from unconventional sources. Thus, the economies of the gas industry are such that natural gas production from conventional and easily accessible sources can be done fairly cheaply. However, to recover gas from unconventional sources requires expensive recovery techniques that raise the price of natural gas. Any energy policy that depends on the further exploration and development of domestic supplies of natural gas must take into account the more expensive recovery costs that are inevitable. While we stress domestic production and federal regulation, the international scope of the energy picture cannot be ignored.

Both Canada and Mexico have large supplies of natural gas. The largest exporter of gas to the United States is Canada which provides about 98% of all gas imported by the United States. Algeria, Mexico, Australia, and the United Arab Emirates also export modest amounts of gas to the U.S. and total imports account for about 16% of U.S. gas supply. As with oil imports, reliance on international sources of natural gas involves concerns of national security and international politics.

Other sources of gas include liquified natural gas (LNG) and synthetic natural gas (SNG). LNG consists of natural gas that is liquified at low temperatures then shipped on specially designed tankers. Most LNG is imported from Algeria and constitutes one percent of U.S. consumption. Once delivered into the United States, the LNG is processed into its gaseous form and placed into pipelines. LNG is highly explosive, and thus it presents the threat of a catastrophic accident should a tanker be damaged, particularly while loading or unloading in port. In addition, the cost of LNG development is expensive, and current use of LNG rather than natural gas is marginally viable. A synthetic fuel is any solid, liquid, or gas that is used as a substitute for natural gas or petroleum and is produced by physical or chemical transformation of other resources such as coal. Of all synthetic fuel technologies, coal gasification technology is the most advanced. SNG created by coal gasification has the additional benefit of being a clean burning gas. The process removes heavy metals and harmful particulates including sulfur. Still, synthetic gas is not widely available to energy markets because the process is not economically feasible because traditional natural gas sources are still less expensive. Thus there exists little incentive for users to consume SNG rather than natural gas. As technology advances, synthetic gas is a hope for the future.

The first domestic natural gas well was developed in Fredonia, New York in 1821. At that time gas was produced exclusively on the East Coast. Most of the domestic natural gas production today comes from Louisiana, New Mexico, Oklahoma, Texas, and Wyoming and is recovered from onshore wells with offshore recovery accounting for about 20% of the natural gas supply as shown in Figure 1.

Figure 1. Natural Gas Gross Withdrawals by State and
Location and Gas Well Productivity, 1960-2002

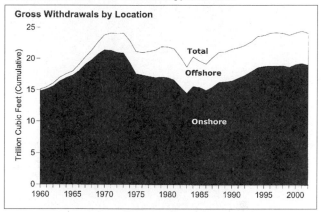

Natural gas has a variety of uses. Residential and commercial consumers use gas mostly for heating and cooking. Natural gas is also used as a dominant fuel in a wide range of industries, most notably manufacturers of pulp and paper, metals, chemicals, petroleum refining, glass production, and food processing. In addition, natural gas is used as primary feed stock for the production of fertilizers, chemicals, fabrics, pharmaceuticals, and plastics. Most significantly, natural gas is playing an increasingly important role in electricity production as you can see from the following three charts all taken from DOE Energy Information Administration, *Annual Energy Review 2002* (November 2003). Natural gas is consumed by these various sectors of the economy as follows: industries (37%); residential sources (22%); commercial sources (14%); electric utilities (24%); and transportation (2%).

Figures 2 and 3 depict the consumption of natural gas by sector over time. Please note the increase in consumption by the electricity sector. Figure 4 shows current consumption by sector.

Figure 4

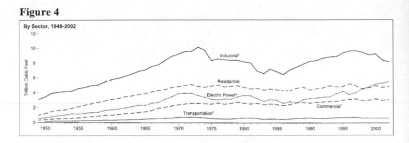

Figure 3

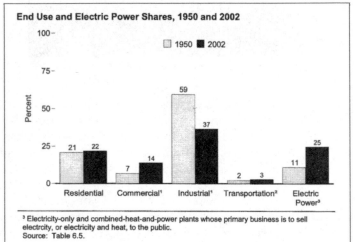

Figure 4

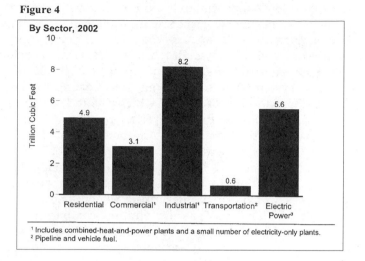

By Sector, 2002

¹ Includes combined-heat-and-power plants and a small number of electricity-only plants.
² Pipeline and vehicle fuel.

Projections are strong for an increase in the demand for natural gas and the demand must be met with supply. Estimates of current reserves indicate that the United States has an over 93–year supply of natural gas. Reserve estimates are notoriously difficult to measure and can be changed by any number of factors, including changes in demand, the development of new technologies, and the development of new sources for natural gas, such as the Alaskan wilderness or offshore deposits, both of which present environmental issues and concerns. In its 2004 Outlook, the Energy Information Agency estimates that natural gas demand would increase between 1.4% each year from 2000 to 2025 as a result of greater population, environmental protection, and greater use in electrical generation.

The industry can be divided into four primary parts: producers, pipelines, local distribution companies (LDCs) (also known as your local public utility), and end users. There are currently over 8,000 natural gas producers in the U.S. varying in size from mom and pop operations to global conglomerates. Most exploration—approximately 85% of all wells drilled—is performed by independent gas companies instead of the major, integrated companies. There are roughly two dozen "major" gas producers such as Royal Dutch Shell, British Petroleum, and El Paso Natural Gas. Pipelines play a key role in the distribution system. There are about 160 pipeline companies operating 285,000 miles of pipe of which about 180,000 miles are interstate pipelines. Pipelines offer two services—selling natural gas and transporting it. Another way of describing how a pipeline functions is to say that pipelines buy and sell gas as well as transport it. The buy-sell function puts the pipeline in a position to exercise market power in certain circumstances which will be described below. There are approximately 1200 natural gas distribution companies in the United States. Investor-owned utilities, however, enjoy a 90% to 95% share of the market. Generally, municipal gas distributors, like municipal electric companies, are much smaller.

Given the number of actors in the natural gas industry, you should get a sense that the industry, for the most part, is not vertically integrated. Production companies, however, are frequently sister companies to the exploration companies; in some instances, a firm operates as both an exploration and production company. Sometimes, but not often, producers are affiliated with pipeline companies. Producers develop, exploit, and produce the natural gas (and oil) that is discovered in the field. This cycle involves drilling and completion of new wells, recovery of natural gas, and the processing of the gas for sale to natural gas pipelines and gathering companies.

Once there are producing wells, the production company, or another entity, called a gatherer, will build a pipeline to gather natural gas from the individual wells and sell it to any one of several potential buyers. The gas may be purchased by a nearby natural gas processing plant or local industrial users. Intrastate or interstate pipelines may buy the gas for resale in another location. Or independent marketers will buy it to aggregate a supply of gas for eventual sale to intrastate or interstate pipelines.

As noted, pipelines companies usually wear two hats. As merchants of natural gas, pipelines purchase gas from producers and transport the gas from the wellhead to purchasers—either wholesale to a local distribution company (LDC) or retail to an industrial customer. This transportation and sale of gas owned by the pipelines is known as a bundled transaction, and the fee to consumers includes the cost of the natural gas and the cost of its transportation. Pipelines also act solely as transporters of natural gas. In this situation, pipelines do not buy the gas from the producer but only transmit the gas for a transportation fee, thus acting as carrier between the producer or marketer and the direct industrial or LDC buyers. Intrastate pipelines that are state regulated are known as "Hinshaw" pipelines and are exempt from NGA regulation. 15 U.S.C. § 717(c).

The distribution of natural gas to residential, commercial, and industrial customers is accomplished by LDCs, which are often privately owned local public utilities who charge the end-user a rate for the gas used at the burnertip. These rates are set by state public utility commissions. LDCs, thus, serve the traditional public utility function. They have an obligation to serve a particular territory and must set rates that are just, reasonable, and non-discriminatory. The flow of natural gas is depicted in Figure 5.

Figure 5. Natural Gas Flow, 2002

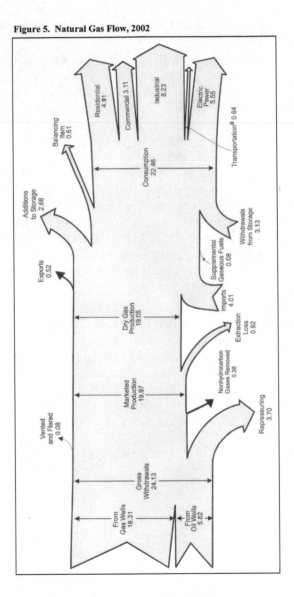

Today there are two noteworthy developments in the natural gas industry both of which are consequences of industry restructuring. The first development is the emergence of natural gas market centers and hubs. To the extent that pipelines only transport gas rather than act as merchants, market centers and hubs provide gas customers (also referred to as shippers) with support services such as interconnections with other pipelines and short-term gas balancing needs, previously provided by pipelines. Additionally, the market centers and hubs provide pricing information and trading services in support of the second development—spot markets. See, Energy Information Agency, *Natural Gas market Centers and Hubs: A 2003 Update* (October 2003).

Although natural gas spot markets have existed for some time, in a regulated environment they were not particularly active. During restructuring the industry is moving from long-term contracts to spot market sales. When the industry was heavily price regulated and was expanding, long-term contracts between producers and pipelines made economic sense. Such contracts enabled both actors to operate and plan without significant concern over price volatility. Today, however, as prices are deregulated and as access opens, spot market sales increase in importance.

B. REGULATORY OVERVIEW

The regulation of the natural gas industry tracks well with the life cycle of government regulation that we described in Chapter 1. As noted earlier, this industry is often cited as the primary example of regulatory failure. See, e.g., Paul W. MacAvoy, *The Natural Gas Market; Sixty Years of Regulation and Deregulation* (2000). This claim is not without factual support and this section describes why the industry was initially regulated; the regulatory mistakes that were made; and, the current efforts to deregulate or restructure the industry with the intent of making the industry more competitive.

1. Early Regulation

Initially, gas was produced from coal by unregulated private companies which also distributed it to nearby customers. Its primary use was lighting and was increasingly popular through the last half of the 19th century. Gas companies soon found it profitable to divide service territories among themselves and to agree to not engage in price competition. This collusion grew and evolved into gas trusts which curtailed competition over larger areas. These trusts eventually captured the attention of municipal and state regulators in the first decades of the 20th century. See Werner Troesken, *Why Regulate Utilities?: The New Institutional Economics and the Chicago Gas Industry,* 1849–1924 (1996).

About this time large oil and natural gas fields were discovered in the southwestern United States. At first, producers ignored the energy potential of natural gas and flared the gas in the fields or permitted it to escape into the atmosphere. These wasteful practices were eventually eliminated as a market for natural gas developed over time. In the 1920s and 1930s, there was more natural gas (and oil) being produced than the market could absorb because new oil and gas fields were discovered and exploited, and because the Great Depression drove down prices. As the price of natural gas (and oil) fell precipitously, natural energy producing states passed gas (and oil) conservation legislation to support these industries. See, Northcutt Ely, *The Oil and Gas Conservation Statutes* (annotated) (1933); *Oil Conservation through Interstate Agreement* (1933). See also Richard C. Maxwell, Patrick H. Martin & Bruce M. Kramer, *Oil and Gas* ch. 7 (7th ed. 2002). As the economy recovered, large pipelines were constructed to transport natural gas from the fields to refineries in other parts of the country thus creating a national gas industry.

2. Traditional Federal Regulation

The federal regulation of natural gas is grounded in the Commerce Clause of the Constitution, Art. I, sec. 8, cl. 3. Because of federalism, there is a division of authority between the state and federal governments. *Missouri v. Kansas Natural Gas Co.* (S.Ct.1924) (states cannot regulate interstate natural gas shipments); *Public Utilities Comm'n v. Attleboro Steam & Elec. Co.* (S.Ct.1927) (same as applied to electric power). Consequently, the states had authority to regulate the intrastate natural gas industry and federal regulators had authority to regulate the interstate industry. Thus, prior to 1938, the federal government did not regulate natural gas production or transportation.

Kansas Natural Gas and *Attleboro* strengthened the monopoly position of the few major interstate pipeline companies that owned much of the physical facilities used to transport natural gas throughout the country. Pipeline companies had substantial monopoly and monopsony power. Recall the dual buyer-seller function of pipelines. These pipelines had monopoly power because they were the only source of natural gas in many local areas. This meant that they could set their own sales price to LDCs and other direct consumers without state regulatory oversight. At the same time, pipelines were the only buyers of natural gas in many areas, which gave them monopsony power. A buyer has monopsony power when it is the only purchaser for a particular good or service. As the only purchaser, the buyer is in a position to dictate the purchase price to sellers, and because the sellers cannot sell their output to other buyers, the sellers must accept this price. Thus, a firm with monopsony power is in a position to pay less than a competitive price for the goods or services it purchases. A pipeline with monopsony and monopoly power paid less than competitive wholesale prices for the natural gas it purchased, and it resold the gas for more than competitive retail prices. This absence of regulation over interstate pipelines by either the state or federal government created what was called the *Attleboro* gap in both the natural gas and electric industries, *Public Utilities Comm'n of Rhode Island v. Attleboro Steam & Elec. Co.* (S.Ct.1927).

In response to complaints about the market power of interstate pipelines, the Federal Trade Commission conducted an investigation and in 1935 issued a report which found that interstate natural gas pipelines had monopoly and monopsony power which the pipelines were exercising to the economic disadvantage of consumers. As a result of the FTC report, Congress passed the Natural Gas Act of 1938 (NGA), 15 U.S.C. §§ 717 et seq. which is classic New Deal legislation and was upheld as constitutional in *FPC v. Hope Natural Gas Co.* (S.Ct.1944). The key provisions of the NGA are its jurisdictional. licensing, and ratemaking provisions.

Under the original NGA, federal jurisdiction under § 1(b) was limited to the regulation of: (1) the transportation of natural gas in interstate commerce; (2) the sale of natural gas for resale in interstate commerce; and, (3) natural gas companies engaged in such transportation or sale. James H. McGrew, *FERC: Federal Energy Regulatory Commission* 12 (2003). The intent of this section was presumably to exercise jurisdiction over interstate transportation and sales (mainly pipelines) and not over local producers and to leave retail regulation to state regulators. We will see shortly that this division between producers and pipelines did not work as well as planned.

Regarding licenses, § 7 of the NGA states:

No natural-gas company or person which will be a natural-gas company upon completion of any proposed construction or extension shall engage in the transportation or sale of natural gas, subject to the jurisdiction of the Commission, or undertake the construction or extension of any facilities therefor, or acquire or operate any such facilities or extensions thereof, unless there is in force with respect to such natural-gas company a certificate of public convenience and necessity issued by the Commission authorizing such acts or operations.

In other words, the "certificate of public convenience and necessity" is a license requirement subjecting a company to federal jurisdiction and allowing the company to operate in interstate commerce. Under this section the Commission has a wide latitude to establish natural gas policy.

In *FPC v. Transcontinental Gas Pipe Line Corp.* (S.Ct.1961), the Supreme Court was asked to review the FPC's denial of a certificate of public convenience and necessity. The FPC based its denial on the grounds of the public interest. The Transcontinental Gas Company (Transco) sought the certificate to sell natural gas to a private utility company in New York, Consolidated Edison (Con Ed), for use as a boiler fuel. Among other arguments for denying the requested certificate, FPC staff argued on "policy" grounds that boiler use was inferior to other uses such as residential and commercial heating, and that the direct sale would raise prices to other consumers. Con Ed asserted as its "policy" argument that the burning of natural gas was preferable environmentally to burning coal. The Court deferred to the Commission's reasons and decision relying on its expertise.

The final provision to which we bring your attention is NGA § 7(b) which reads:

No natural-gas company shall abandon all or any portion of its facilities subject to the jurisdiction of the Commission, or any service rendered by means of such facilities, without the permission and approval of the Commission first had and obtained, after due hearing, and a finding by the Commission that the available supply of natural gas is depleted to the extent that the continuance of service is unwarranted, or that the present or future public convenience or necessity permit such abandonment. 15 U.S.C. § 717f (b).

In other words, once gas has been dedicated to interstate commerce and federal jurisdiction has been asserted, a firm cannot withdraw (abandon) that market without Commission permission. Later in the natural gas story you will learn how this provision contributed to a domestic natural gas shortage.

Certificate proceedings require pipelines to provide data and information about the markets to be served, the financial and managerial capability of the pipeline, and the like. 18 C.F.R. § 157. This information assists investors and regulators alike in knowing that gas will serve customers and that the pipeline facilities are needed. See, *Transcontinental Gas Pipe Line Corp. v. FPC* (D.C. Cir. 1973). Further, the Commission may impose terms and conditions as the public convenience and necessity may require. *FPC v. Transcontinental Pipe Line Corp.* (S.Ct.1961).

Section 7(e) of the NGA states that the license will be granted only to entities which the Commission finds are financially able and willing to perform the proposed service *and* that the certificate is required by the public convenience and necessity. The licensing provisions of the NGA are also notable because once natural gas is "dedicated" to the interstate market the gas stays there absent federal permission to withdraw. Indeed, to protect the national market, the U.S. Supreme Court has upheld the FPC's refusal to grant a certificate of limited duration, *Sunray Mid–Continent Oil Co. v. FPC* (S.Ct.1960). During the 1960s and 1970s, the Commission did not grant abandonments frequently although, as we will see, these exit controls were later liberalized as part of industry restructuring. Further, the definition of interstate gas was expansive insofar as once domestically produced and delivered natural gas was commingled with interstate gas it fell under federal jurisdiction. *California v. Lo–Vaca Gathering Co.* (S.Ct.1965); *Louisiana Power & Light Co. v. FPC* (5th Cir. 1973).

NGA §§ 4 and 5 are as important as the licensing requirements. These sections contain the ratemaking provisions
which require that rates cannot be "unjust, unreasonable,
unduly discriminatory, or preferential." These provisions were
held to be constitutional in *FPC v. Natural Gas Pipeline Co.*
(S.Ct.1942). Additionally, the FPC is given wide latitude in
setting rates and the "end result" must satisfy these statutory
provisions. *FPC v. Hope Natural Gas Co.* (S.Ct.1944). Further,
the FPC has authority over allocating costs between a pipeline's jurisdictional and non-jurisdictional businesses. *Colorado Interstate Gas Co. v. FPC* (S.Ct.1945). As a matter of
practice, the interstate pipeline files a rate tariff which becomes effective unless a complaint is made and hearing is
held. The procedure is known as the "filed rate" and implements the *Mobile–Sierra* doctrine. See *United Gas Pipe Line
Co. v. Mobile Gas Service Corp.* (S.Ct.1956); *FPC v. Sierra
Pacific Power Co.* (S.Ct.1956). This doctrine gives weight to
contracts negotiated between pipelines and their customers.
The contract rate is in effect and is subject to review by the
Commission or upon complaint. Any rate changes must then
be in accordance with the filed contract and now standard
pipeline contracts allow for such modifications. *United Gas
Pipe Line Co. v. Memphis Light, Gas and Water Div.* (S.Ct.
1958).

The D.C. Circuit discussed these NGA requirements in
Northern Natural Gas Company v. FERC (D.C. Cir. 1987)), as
follows:

[S]ections 4, 5, and 7 of the Act reveal a single and
coherent design. Under sections 4 and 5, the Commission
determines the allowable price of natural gas services,
holding price (i.e. rate) to a "just and reasonable" standard. Under section 7, the Commission determines what
services may be provided (as well as through what facilities) reviewing them under a "public convenience and
necessity" standard. Congress' concern in regulating the
provision of services and facilities under section 7 was to

avoid "the possibilities of waste, uneconomic and uncontrolled extensions," thereby "conserving one of the country's valuable but exhaustible energy resources" as well as ensuring "the lowest possible reasonable rate consistent with the maintenance of adequate service in the public interest."

These sections of the Natural Gas Act form an integral part of the regulatory scheme creating an interstate natural gas market.

3. *Phillips Petroleum Co.*

From 1938 until 1954, the FPC asserted its jurisdiction over interstate pipelines but did not assert jurisdiction over natural gas producers. Interstate sales were defined to exclude the price that producers charged in the field (the wellhead price) to the pipeline. Naturally, the prices charged by producers to pipelines were passed through to customers by the pipelines, hence any protection afforded customers could easily be vitiated by excessive prices at the wellhead. In 1947, the Supreme Court ruled that the FPC had jurisdiction over the prices that producers charged affiliated pipelines. *Interstate Natural Gas Co. v. FPC* (S.Ct.1947). Then, in 1954, the Supreme Court expanded FPC jurisdiction to cover producer prices. *Phillips Petroleum Co. v. Wisconsin* (S.Ct.1954).

One immediate consequence of the *Phillips* decision was the imposition of a massive administrative burden on the FPC. It was estimated that the FPC could not finish its 1960 caseload until the year 2043. *Report on Regulatory Agencies to the President–Elect* 6 (1960) (known as the Landis Report). At that time, rate schedule hearings proceeded as individual adjudicatory hearings under the Administrative Procedure Act. To relieve the burden of individual adjudicatory hearings, the FPC began relying on rate-setting by gas producing regions. First, the FPC set area rates through adjudication. *Permian Basin Area Rate Cases* (S.Ct.1968); *Mobil Oil Corp. v.*

FPC (S.Ct.1974). The next development was a change from ratemaking by adjudication under the APA to ratemaking by rulemaking. Instead of individual producers and distributors having hearings, all the producers and distributors within a region were parties to a single ratemaking procedure. This regional ratemaking procedure functioned neither smoothly nor quickly. The FPC then set national area gas rates. This procedure was upheld in *Shell Oil Co. v. FPC* (5th Cir. 1976); *American Public Gas. Ass'n v. FPC* (D.C. Cir. 1977).

The exercise of jurisdiction by the FPC over interstate sales had another serious repercussion. Two natural gas markets were created—one interstate and the other intrastate. Eventually, the prices charged in these markets became nonuniform. The prices in the largely unregulated intrastate market were closer to world market prices and rose faster than those in the federally regulated interstate market because the federal rates were based on historic cost-of-service rather than being allowed to float upwards toward market levels. The price differential between the intrastate and the interstate markets had several consequences. Most notably, intrastate producers had more funds which they could use to develop new sources of natural gas. More dramatically, interstate producers reduced exploration expenditures and attempted to leave the federally regulated interstate market and participate in the intrastate market. However, because of strict abandonment rules in the federal legislation, producers with gas dedicated to interstate commerce could not move into the intrastate market without federal approval. 15 U.S.C.A. § 727(b); *United Gas Pipe Line Co. v. McCombs* (S.Ct.1979); *California v. Southland Royalty Co.* (S.Ct.1978). Thus, because of the price differential a natural gas shortage occurred.

As noted, the FPC was reluctant during this period to engage in a liberal abandonment policy. Indeed, abandonments were hard won until the FPC realized that the market distortions cut against the national interest because gas was not getting to market. The problem then became how to liberalize abandonment in light of statutory requirements. Below we will discuss the regulatory changes in more detail but two issues are worthy of note. First, the FPC could "pre-grant" abandonment as a condition of the certificate of public convenience and necessity and did so occasionally. *FPC v. Moss* (S.Ct.1976). Second, the test for abandonment changed from the needs of the specific parties to the interest of the natural gas market as a whole thus giving regulators more leeway to grant abandonment permission. *Felmont Oil Corp.* (F.E.R.C.1988).

The dual market created by federal and state natural gas regulation produced artificial shortages. The regulatory response to those shortages was that the FPC had to apportion supplies through curtailment procedures. The FPC had a choice between two basic curtailment policies—end-use and pro-rata. Pro-rata curtailment meant that each end user received its proportionate share rather than losing all supply. End-use curtailment meant that pipelines were required to sell gas according to certain priorities. Schools, hospitals, and small residential users had top priority, while large industrial customers capable of switching to other fuels would have their supplies curtailed first. *American Smelting & Refining Co. v. FPC* (D.C.Cir. 1974); *City of Willcox and Arizona Elec. Power Co-op., Inc. v. FPC* (D.C.Cir. 1977). FERC used the end-use plan under which customers were ranked according to priorities, in part such that those customers who had access to other fuels were curtailed first. These plans were upheld after judicial review. See Order No. 467, 469 FPC 85 (1973); *City of Willcox and Arizona Elec. Power Co-op., Inc. v. FPC* (D.C. Cir. 1977).

The natural gas shortage became so severe that Congress enacted the Emergency Natural Gas Act, 15 U.S.C. §§ 717x et seq. and President Carter declared a natural gas emergency under the terms of the act. The FPC, then, was authorized to order the transportation of large volumes of gas to the East Coast at prices that were similar to those in the intrastate market. Clearly price deregulation was not far behind. *Consolidated Edison v. FERC* (D.C. Cir. 1982).

As a result of the shortage a cry arose to deregulate the market prices of natural gas. The deregulation advocates argued that the industry was competitive, that the so-called natural gas shortage was artificially created by excessive and counterproductive federal regulation, and that suppressed prices prevented the development of new sources of natural gas which would relieve the "shortage." Antideregulation proponents argued that regulation was needed because the industry was not competitive, that consumers would suffer in disproportionate amounts, and that other means of exploration and development could be equally effective. These arguments failed. The reality is that two markets did exist, and they had created market distortions so that prices and allocation of gas were uneven, and new sources were needed. The result was the passage of the Natural Gas Policy Act of 1978 (NGPA).

4. The Natural Gas Policy Act of 1978 (NGPA)

The NGPA was the centerpiece of President Carter's National Energy Act. The express intent of the Act was to eliminate the dual market by setting prices for almost all "first sales" of natural gas in either the interstate or intrastate markets. Under NGPA, FERC jurisdiction was removed from all natural gas not dedicated to interstate commerce as of November 8, 1978 ("old gas") as well as other types of natural gas. The NGPA initiated four significant changes in the law. First, federal price controls were imposed on the intrastate market, 15 U.S.C.A. § 3301. Second, the NGPA created a formula for monthly increases in the wellhead price of "new" post–1978 natural gas. Third, the ceiling price on delivered "new" natural gas was pegged to the price of refined oil. Finally, the NGPA provided for the elimination of price controls starting January 1, 1985, subject to reimposition on certain natural gas sales (e.g. "new" natural gas, new onshore production wells, and certain intrastate contracts). 15 U.S.C.A. § 3331. The overall thrust of the NGPA was to begin price decontrols, stimulate production, and unify the natural gas market.

Title I began to ease the downward pressure on wellhead prices and started price decontrol. Wellhead price decontrol was set for January 1, 1993. 15 U.S.C.A. § 3301. The NGPA also created categories and vintages of natural gas with the intent of stimulating the production of some markets. The fundamental idea, also previously used with respect to oil price controls, was simple. Divide gas into "old gas," i.e. gas produced before a certain date—in this case, April 20, 1977— and "new gas" produced after that date. (There were several more categories of gas but the basic idea was the same.) Prices for "old gas" would stay regulated and "new gas" prices would be allowed to rise as a production incentive. Other incentive categories included "high-cost" gas, "deep gas," new natural gas from the outer continental shelf, and new onshore gas.

Title II of the NGPA provides for "incremental pricing." Essentially, incremental pricing is a type of marginal cost pricing, which means that the prices at which natural gas is sold reflect the additional costs of production. Instead of "rolling-in" or averaging the costs of natural gas, higher costs are charged to users as they are incurred. Title II passthrough regulations allowed the passing through of certain "incremental costs" of natural gas to industrial facilities. 15 U.S.C.A. § 3341. This means that wellhead price increases, permitted under Title I of the NGPA in an effort to deregulate the price of natural gas, were not borne wholly by high priority customers. Rather, the incremental costs were absorbed by "industrial boiler fuel facilities" as defined in the Act. The Act also provided for exemptions so that passthrough costs were not suffered by such users as existing small industrial boiler fuel facilities, agricultural users, schools, hospitals, and similar institutions. 15 U.S.C.A. § 3346. Thus, the NGPA protected certain classes of users by channeling certain increased costs to industrial customers. Such costs included: new natural gas; natural gas under particular intrastate contracts; gas from new onshore production wells; certain natural gas imports; stripper well (small producer) gas; "high-cost" gas, also defined in the Act; Alaskan natural gas; and some other identified costs, such as state severance taxes. 15 U.S.C.A. § 3343. The theory behind passthrough costs is a classical economic one: as prices increase for certain products, the supply of these products should increase. By allowing certain identified costs to be passed through, the production of those types of natural gas should be encouraged.

A fair question is raised as to whether it is unfair and perhaps even confiscatory to have industrial users absorb these costs. There should be a ceiling price above which the passthrough costs cannot go. The logical ceiling is the alternative price of replacement fuel. If the costs of natural gas rise too high, then the users subject to the passthrough will find it cheaper to buy some other fuel. Thus, the Act gives the user the option of purchasing other fuel, or limiting the amount it must pay under the incremental pricing provisions of the NGPA. This ceiling did not include the cost of coal because of a fairly uniform national policy of encouraging coal use. Thus, the incrementally priced natural gas cannot go higher than the price of alternative fuels except coal. 15 U.S.C.A. § 3344(e). Because of concerns involving the fairness of passthrough regulations, and the difficulty in identifying an appropriate ceiling, the incremental pricing provisions were repealed in May, 1987. Pub.L. No. 100–42.

5. Public Utility Regulatory Policies Act

Title III of the Public Utility Regulatory Policies Act of 1978 (PURPA), also part of the National Energy Act, applied to natural gas rate design issues. In order to conserve energy, increase the efficient use of facilities and resources, and promote equitable rates to consumers, state regulatory agencies and nonregulated gas utilities, as defined in PURPA, were required to hold hearings to consider rate design standards proposed by the Act. At the conclusion of the hearings the standards were to be adopted "if and to the extent * * * that such adoption is appropriate and is consistent with otherwise applicable state law." 15 U.S.C.A. § 3203(a)(2). These rate design provisions withstood a Tenth Amendment challenge in *FERC v. Mississippi* (S.Ct.1982).

Under PURPA, the Secretary of the DOE together with the FERC was required to conduct a gas rate design study which examined the effects of incremental pricing, marginal cost pricing, end use gas consumption taxes, wellhead natural gas pricing policies, demand rate design, declining block rates, interruptible service, seasonal rate differentials, and end user rate schedules. 15 U.S.C.A. § 3206(a). The study of these various designs was required to make reference to the effect of the design on pipeline and distribution company load factors, rates to each class of user, consumption of natural gas, change in total costs, end use of gas, and competition for alternative fuels. Rate design can be used simply for the accumulation of enough revenue to keep a responsible utility operating with a fair rate of return without gouging customers, or it can be utilized to accomplish other social policy objectives, such as conservation of resources, redistribution of wealth among classes of users, and the reallocation of various resources. After all, if a particular rate design raises the cost of natural gas to industrial consumers, for example, higher than the cost of coal, then the industrial consumer will switch to coal. A pervasive issue with rate design then becomes the purposes for which a specific design is being proposed.

The producer sales market was completely deregulated effective January 1, 1993 by Congress with the Natural Gas Wellhead Decontrol Act of 1989, Pub. L. No. 101–60, 103 Stat. 157. The Decontrol Act eliminated rate and service regulation of "first sales" of natural gas. A direct consequence of this Act is that § 7(b) NGA abandonment requirements are virtually eliminated. "First sales" are no longer regulated and with liberal pre-granted abandonments little is left of the abandonment requirement. Decontrol of wellhead prices and open access thus go hand in hand with the intent of moving cheaper gas to market more easily and more quickly, without discrimination. Note that the NGA still applies to transportation and wholesale sales by interstate pipelines.

C.   POST NGPA REGULATION

As complex as it was, the NGPA had positive effects. Most simply, it increased domestic natural gas production. Market unification and price deregulation stimulated that production. Nevertheless, the natural gas market did not function entirely as desired. As a matter of practice, pipelines entered into long-term contracts with producers to assure the pipelines' supplies. In order to assure producers of cash flow, these contracts contained "take or pay" clauses that adversely affected pipelines during the period of surplus that followed the natural gas shortage.

1.   Take-or-Pay Contracts

Take-or-pay clauses required pipelines to either take the amount of gas they contracted for, or pay up to 100% of the price of that gas. In a shortage period, this clause is desirable. The pipeline has a reliable supply and the producer has cash flow. When there is a surplus of gas, however, the clause hurts pipelines and their customers. In a period of surplus, natural gas prices decline. The long-term contracts, however, prevent the lower priced gas from getting to consumers because the pipelines must "take-or-pay" for contracted supplies, and pipelines and their customers thus overpay for the gas. By the mid–1980s, take-or-pay liability was estimated to be $9 billion. See *AGA v. FERC* (D.C. Cir. 1990).

Confronted with such a significant financial liability, pipelines tried various strategies. One strategy was to include "market-out" clauses in their contracts with producers which let pipelines suspend gas purchases when the contract price exceeded the market price. Another strategy was to reduce purchases and claim economic *force majeure* relief. This strategy was not particularly successful. Then, pipelines, mostly unsuccessfully, sought to renegotiate their take-or-pay liability. Finally, FERC help was sought. Because the flow of cheap natural gas from producers to customers was clogged, the FERC was asked to provide relief by all market actors. Pipelines sought relief from onerous contractual obligations; producers sought to capture their gains from trade; and, consumers sought access to cheaper natural gas. FERC's interest lay in restructuring the natural gas market.

2. FERC Natural Gas Initiatives

A significant market dislocation in natural gas occurred caused by dual natural gas markets, price deregulation, take-or-pay contracts, and increased supplies. The FERC responded with natural gas regulations during the 1980s which have been considered nothing short of revolutionary. Through a series of rulemaking orders, as interpreted mostly by the D.C. Circuit Court of Appeals, the natural gas industry experienced its most significant restructuring since the 1978 Natural Gas Policy Act, and that restructuring continues until today.

An early first attempt to provide relief for pipeline customers involved the variable cost portion of a pipeline's minimum bill. In Order No. 380, FERC ordered the elimination of these costs as a part of the minimum bill. This minimum charge mirrored the take-or-pay contract liability of pipelines and required customers to pay for a minimum amount of gas whether they took the gas or not. Order No. 380 was upheld in *Wisconsin Gas Co. v. FERC* (D.C. Cir. 1975).

Next, in a brief period, 1983 to 1985, FERC attempted to increase pipeline competition through "special marketing programs" (SMPs). Under a SMP, a producer and a pipeline would amend their contract to enable the producer to sell the contract gas on its own and credit the sale to its contract with the pipeline. The pipeline would be relieved of an obligation to pay and the producer would receive money from another source. The SMP was intended to relieve the pipeline's take-or-pay obligations while not injuring producers. FERC, then, would review the contract and grant the necessary abandonment.

The SMP satisfied pipelines and producers but not customers. Pipelines tried to get access to the surplus market, and producers simply wanted to get their gas to market. In effect, the SMP moved low cost gas to large industrial consumers but not to small residential consumers. Small residential consumers, thus, protested the new marketing programs that excluded them from participation. The D.C. Circuit remanded the SMP to the FERC for this reason, and then the programs expired. *Maryland People's Counsel v. FERC* (MPC I) (D.C. Cir. 1985); *MPC II* (D.C. Cir. 1985); *MPC III*, (D.C. Cir. 1985).

Other concerns of producers, pipelines, and consumers did not fall on deaf ears. The FERC reacted to requests for relief and to changing market conditions by attempting to loosen pricing and entry and exit controls for the purpose of letting gas flow more smoothly through the distribution system from producer to end-user (in industry jargon, from wellhead to burnertip). Because pipelines were the bottleneck in the natural gas fuel cycle, they were the targets of FERC regulatory efforts.

Although both Order No. 380 and FERC's SMPs ran into legal resistance, they were on the right path to industry restructuring. These regulatory schemes were aimed at getting gas to consumers who were willing to pay, and FERC, to the extent that it could, would open access to pipelines as a condition of looser abandonment rules.

In Order No. 436, FERC proposed to separate the merchant and transportation roles of pipeline companies through a process known as "unbundling" as a means of opening access for captive customers and others who found it difficult to switch fuels or supplies. Simply, under the rule, pipelines were to separate their merchant (buy-sell) and transportation services. Another way of describing this process is to say that pipelines had to allow nondiscriminatory access to transportation. The purpose of Order No. 436 was to pressure producers and pipelines to move gas to end users through easier regulation including looser entry and exit controls. The elements of Order No. 436 included:

- Open-access non-discriminatory transportation by pipelines.

- If demand is greater than capacity, then the open-access pipeline would transport natural gas on a first-come, first-served basis.

- Rate regulation to be done within a zone of reasonableness.

- Local distribution companies could switch their "contract demand" to transportation service, and had the option to reduce contract demand.

- FERC could expedite licensing for new pipeline facilities and services who choose to avail themselves of the open access provisions.

Although the D.C. Circuit generally agreed with the purposes of and upheld most of Order No. 436, the order was remanded to the FERC in *Associated Gas Distributors v. FERC* (D.C. Cir. 1987) because of the FERC's failure to adequately address the problem of take-or-pay burdens. The court upheld the FERC's jurisdiction to promulgate open access provisions as long as the provisions were nondiscriminatory, and it also sustained the order's flexible rate treatment. Additionally, customers could deal directly with producers and then request pipelines to provide transportation. This approach to ratemaking allowed pipelines to set rates within a zone of reasonableness and to give discounts rather than have the pipelines tied to a single cost-based rate. Indeed, FERC continues to experiment with alternative rate methods including market-based rates and negotiated rates. See *Alternatives to Traditional Cost-of-Service Ratemaking for Natural Gas Pipelines,* 74 FERC 61,076 (1996). More innovatively, the court upheld regulations that allowed pipeline customers to modify their contracts with pipelines unilaterally. Under certain circumstances, the customers could convert a percentage of a gas purchase obligation to contract demand gas.

NGPA and FERC efforts to correct the dual market distortion and open access were, from the consumer's standpoint, very successful insofar as now the country was experiencing an excess of supply and a "natural gas bubble." Producers, however, experienced a cash flow constriction and drilling activities declined. In order to encourage drilling, Congress pass the Natural Gas Wellhead Decontrol Act to eliminate all wellhead controls.

Take-or-pay liability continued to congest the natural gas market and regulatory relief was not forthcoming. While pipelines sought relief from take-or-pay contracts, producers did not wish to be left out in the cold and not receive their contract payments. FERC attempted to provide some relief for producers in Order No. 451 which provided some incentive pricing. The idea was that producers would get a price for "old gas" under the NGA at the highest price for "old gas" under the NGPA. Initially vacated by the Fifth Circuit, the rules were upheld by the Supreme Court in *Mobil Oil Exploration v. United Distrib. Cos.* (S.Ct.1991).

The D.C. Circuit told the FERC to look more closely at the take-or-pay issue in several cases cited above and FERC responded with Order No. 500. According to FERC Chair Martha Hesse, the underlying philosophy of Order No. 500 was "spreading the pain," with the goal of making open access "a fact of life in the gas industry." Order No. 500 in large part was a readoption of Order No. 436, with more attention paid to take-or-pay liability. Under the new order, producers had to credit the pipelines' take-or-pay liability with the volumes of gas transported under the open access provisions. Provision was also made for sharing accrued take-or-pay obligations and for avoiding future take-or-pay liability. Order No. 500 was dealt a temporary setback by the D.C. Circuit in *American Gas Ass'n v. FERC* (D.C. Cir. 1989) which remanded the order to the Commission. On subsequent review the order was affirmed for the most part in *American Gas Ass'n v. FERC* (D.C. Cir. 1990).

In promulgating Order No. 636, F.E.R.C. Stats. & Regs. ¶ 30, 939 (1992), the Commission found that, despite the legislation and its prior actions, the market still had impediments to full competition and that transactions were not as unbundled as a free market would indicate. Among other provisions, Order No. 636 contained the following:

- Mandatory unbundling of pipeline sales and transportation meaning pipelines were prohibited from selling natural gas.

- Blanket certificates, authorizing pipelines to make unbundled sales at market-based rates.

- Requirement that open access transportation services be provided "equal in quality" regardless of seller.

- Definition of transportation to include storage so as to subject storage to all open access regulations.

- Pregranted abandonment authorizing pipelines to abandon sales, interruptible transportation and short-term (one year or less) firm transportation services upon expiration or termination of a contract, and with long-term firm transportation contracts subject to existing customer's right of first refusal in response to an alternative offer.

- Policies permitting full recovery of "transition costs" incurred by pipelines in complying with the Restructuring Rule.

FERC revised Order No. 636 in Order Nos. 637, 637–A, and 637–B. FERC Stats. & Regs. ¶ 31, 091; ¶ 31,099; and, ¶ 61,202 (2002) respectively. These rules fine-tuned rate and pricing provisions as well as scheduling and reporting requirements. The rules were largely upheld in *United Distribution Cos. v. FERC* (D.C. Cir. 1996) and *Interstate Natural Gas Ass'n of America v. FERC* (D.C. Cir. 2002).

Order Nos. 436, 500, and 636 form the heart of the regulatory revolution in the natural gas industry and begin to make pipelines into common carriers. Each order attempts to pry open access to markets through pipelines, and seeks to resolve the multi-billion dollar take-or-pay liability problem. FERC has been moving toward the objective of promoting a more competitive natural gas market by focusing on pipelines. By easing entry and exit controls and by expanding price decontrols, these natural gas regulations constitute a new form of regulation. The thrust of the FERC gas initiatives is to increase competition by lightening the regulatory touch. This same philosophy is behind FERC's recent electricity regulations discussed in Chapter 8.

D.　THE FUTURE OF THE NATURAL GAS INDUSTRY AND ITS REGULATION

The Department of Energy has set out an ambitious plan for the future of natural gas. In its *Natural Gas Strategic Plan*, the DOE anticipates greater use of natural gas because of its abundance and it is seen as a clean, more affordable and reliable energy source. The largest growth in demand are anticipated to be new power plants. The DOE estimates that 90% of new power plants will be gas-fueled (which may result in much higher gas prices and a rethinking of the 90% prospect). The *Strategic Plan* also anticipates growing consumption in every sector as well as expanded transmission and delivery systems and 38,000 miles of new transmission lines.

The plan envisions enhanced domestic supplies both through deeper offshore drilling and more LNG; cleaner fuels for transportation; use of gas for small electric power production as well as fuel cells; enhanced utility infrastructure, including advanced metering; the production of clean and efficient vehicles, holdings, and industries; and, the establishment of a comprehensive national gas information system.

In March 2002, the Secretary of the Department of Energy asked the National Petroleum Council, an industry, oil, and gas group, to conduct a study of natural gas through 2025. The Council issued its report on September 25, 2003 entitled *Balancing Natural Gas Policy—Fueling the Demands of a Growing Economy*. The National Petroleum Council had conducted previous natural gas studies in 1992 and 1999 and undertook its study to examine the adequacy of natural gas supplies and the continuing demand and use of natural gas in various consuming sectors.

The NPC studied economic and environmental determinants of gas consumption and examined the relationship of gas trades between Canada and the United States. The study was sensitive to the currently higher natural gas prices as a result of a fundamental shift in supply and demand. The study was of the opinion that North America could no longer be self-reliant in meeting growing natural gas needs insofar as it felt that U.S. and Canadian production had reached a plateau. The study indicated that a solution to a responsible natural gas policy included a balance between energy efficiency and conservation, alternative energy resources for industrial consumers and power generators, including renewable gas resources from inaccessible areas of the United States, increased LNG imports, and increased gas from the Arctic.

In drafting this report, the NPC put out alternative scenarios. The study's findings included the following:

- There has been a fundamental shift in supply and demand that has resulted in higher prices and greater volatility in recent years.

- Greater energy efficiency and conservation is necessary for moderating price levels and reducing volatility.

- Power generators and industrial customers are more dependent on gas-fired equipment and less able to respond by using alternative resources.

- Gas consumption will grow.

- North American areas will produce 75% of long-term gas needs.

- There should be increased access to U.S. gas resources, including designated wilderness areas and national parks.

- Large-scale resources such as LNG and Arctic gas could meet 20–25% of the demand, but involve higher costs and could face major barriers.

- Transportation and distribution investments will need to average $8 billion per year.

The study recommends the following:

- Improve demand flexibility and efficiency through market-oriented initiatives increasing industrial and power generation capability to utilize alternative fuels.

- Increase supply diversity on mainland United States as well as enact enabling legislation for Alaska gas pipeline and process more LNG permits.

• Sustain and enhance natural gas infrastructure with quicker permitting.

• Promote efficiency of natural gas markets through transparent pricing and better gas market collection data.

Clearly, natural gas will continue to play an important and evolving role in our nation's energy picture. Regulators will continue to restructure; new technologies will develop; and, if all goes according to plan, consumer choice among suppliers and prices should expand.

CHAPTER 7

COAL

Coal can be described in two words—abundant and dirty. These two words not only describe the resource, they fairly well dictate the law and policies that affect the regulation of the industry. Briefly regarding abundance, coal accounts for 33% of the energy produced in the United States and accounts for over 50% of the electricity produced. Coal extraction, production, and use also have significant negative external effects on people and the environment. These effects have had two notable consequences. First, health and safety concerns take center stage in coal regulation and, second, the industry has invested over $50 billion in developing "clean coal" technologies in order to address domestic and global environmental consequences. We will explore each of these areas in this chapter.

Coal is our nation's most abundant source of energy. Ninety percent of the coal consumed in the United States is used as fuel for plants generating electricity. The remainder is used as primary fuel in particular industries such as steel production and glass manufacturing. Because coal is a useful substitute for other fuels such as oil, nuclear power, and natural gas, occasionally there is a movement toward having energy users convert from other resources to coal. In the case of oil, coal conversion was intended to reduce dependence on foreign oil. In the case of nuclear power, conversion of coal was intended to reduce the risk of nuclear accidents. Nevertheless, the relative abundance of this energy fuel is significantly offset by its health, environmental, and economic problems.

A. INDUSTRY OVERVIEW

Coal has played an important part in the economic development of our country and the industrial world since its inception. Barbara Freese, *Coal: A Human History* (2003). In the 18th and 19th centuries, coal fueled the Industrial Revolution and maintained its significance through the 20th century. With the discovery and development of oil, however, coal became less important in manufacturing processes and less important in the transportation sector. Where coal once powered locomotives and steamships, it was replaced with oil. In addition to the growing importance of oil, coal was perceived as a dirty burning fuel and, consequently, it was a less attractive energy source. After World War II, coal rebounded in significance with the expansion of the electric industry.

Coal is a fossil fuel and comes in the form of sedimentary, carboniferous rock. Like oil and gas, it was formed from layers of vegetation under pressure for millions of years. While different coals have different chemical compositions, all coal contains some form of carbon which, when burned, can damage the atmospheric ozone layer and can contribute to global warming.

The coal industry is large, varied, and complex. The coal fuel cycle is similar to that of oil and gas in that it encompasses mining, transportation, refining, and then combustion. There are four types of coal that differ in heat content and in sulphur content: bituminous, anthracite, sub-bituminous, and lignite. The types of coal are listed from highest heat content (bituminous) to lowest (lignite). Sub-bituminous and lignite, found mostly in the western states, have less sulphur, which is better for the environment, but they also contain less heat. Coal with the highest heat content, but which is dirtier to burn, is found in eastern states. The coal with more heat properties and a lower sulphur content is mined in the West. There is another significant distinction between eastern and western coal mining. Western coal is easily surface mined, while eastern coal is generally recovered through deep-pit mining techniques. These different techniques have led to distinct regulatory consequences.

Although we can divide coal extraction into surface mining and underground mining, there are several mining technologies within each of those two larger categories. Currently underground mining takes place approximately 200 feet below the surface and requires special machinery to cut and remove the coal. It also requires ventilation to protect miners from coal dust and methane gas. There are basically three types of underground mines. Room and pillar mines involve mining coal from a series of rooms cut into a coal bed. Ceilings of those rooms are bolted into the layers of coal above the coal that has been extracted. Pillars of unmined coal, then, are left at regular intervals to support the roof. As miners retreat from a particular bed, they remove the pillars on their way out and the roofs are permitted to fall. A second underground mining technique is known as longwall mining. Longwall mining differs from room and pillar in that there are no series of rooms. Rather, the coal is mined from one long face and the coal is extracted with a massive plow. Finally, shortwall mining differs insofar as the mined areas are smaller, but like longwall mining, the roofs are allowed to collapse to relieve pressure on underground working spaces.

Surface mining involves several different techniques as well. Common to all, however, is the feature that soil and rock are removed from coal seams which are then exposed to the surface. At that point, the coal is removed through a process of disaggregation by heavy machinery as well as through a series of detonations. Coal is then hauled from the site. The soil and rocks that are removed to uncover the coal are called the "overburden" and it is placed on the surfaces near mined areas. The overburden often contains elements which, when exposed to air and water, can damage the surrounding areas due to acid leeching.

Surface mining can take place either through contour mining in which the seam is followed along a particular line or mountaintop mining in which the mountaintop is removed and the overburden is placed in the valleys between the mines. Open pit mining is, as its name suggests, simply digging deeper and deeper into the surface.

There are an estimated 282 billion tons of recoverable coal in the United States. In other terms, at current consumption, recoverable coal resources are estimated to last at least for over 200 years and the National Coal Council estimates that U.S. coal reserves can last nearly 500 years.

In 2002, the United States produced 1,094 million short tons of coal nearly 90% of which was used for the production of electricity as shown below in Figure 1.

Figure 1 Coal Flow, 2002

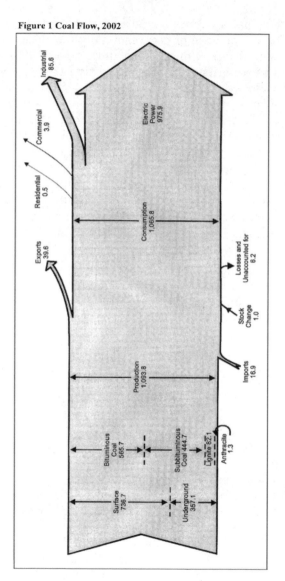

As noted, coal accounts for 50% of all electricity generated. Clearly the importance of coal, especially for electricity generation, is significant. Nonetheless, during the 1990s, the coal industry has experienced some interesting trends. At the end of the decade, coal reserves at producing mines were at the smallest level of the preceding twenty years. While coal production continued to increase throughout the decade, the number of operating mines declined by a substantial 59% from 4,424 operating mines in 1986 to 1,828 mines in 1997. Additionally, coal prices decreased by 45% during that period in real dollar terms. The figures make sense insofar as mine size increased less competitive mines shut down. Thus, through industry concentration, greater industry productivity occurred. Richard Bonskowski, *The U.S. Coal Industry in the 1990's: Low Prices and Record Production* (September 1999).

The consequence of increased production and increased mine productivity, as the laws of supply and demand would dictate, has resulted in declining prices since 1975 as demonstrated in Figure 2.

Figure 2 Coal Prices

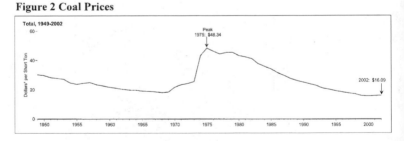

Other trends over the recent decades are also worthy of note. While coal production continued to increase as noted, in the early 1970s, surface mining overtook underground mining as the greater source of coal production as demonstrated in Figure 3. Similarly, during the same period there has been an increase in sub-bituminous coal production, a decline in anthracite production, and a fairly stable production of bituminous and lignite coals as demonstrated in Figure 4. It is also the case that coal production east of the Mississippi has remained stable, but there has been a dramatic increase of western coal production since the 1970s. Again, this is demonstrated in Figure 5.

Figure 3 Coal Production, 1949-2002 (Total)

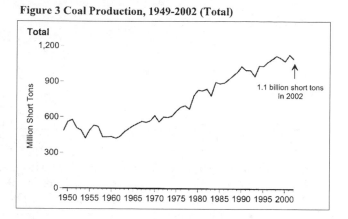

Figure 4 Coal Production, 1949-2002 (By Rank)

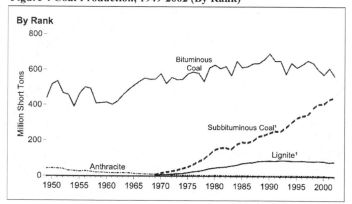

Figure 5 Coal Production, 1949-2002 (By Location)

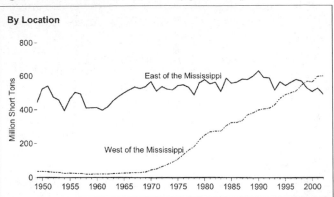

U.S. coal production has remained strong. Over the last 30 years production has doubled from 520 million tons in 1970 to over 1 billion tons in 2001. Because of its abundance, the U.S. is a net exporter of approximately 5% of its coal whereas we import 60% of our oil and 17% of our natural gas. To the extent, then, that national security is a goal of energy policy, coal continues to play an attractive role in our energy economy. Indeed, at President Bush's request, a study by the National Academy of Sciences found that, in comparison with oil, natural gas, and nuclear power, coal was the least vulnerable to terrorism and that the national security threats posed by the coal industry were so insignificant that no further protections were necessary. National Academy of Sciences, National Research Council, *Making the Nation Safer: The Role of Science and Technology in Countering Terrorism* (2002).

B.   REGULATORY OVERVIEW

1.   Federal Lands

The federal government is estimated to own approximately one-third of the nation's coal reserves. Coal on federal lands is managed by the Department of the Interior, where different aspects of coal production are handled by different agencies. The Bureau of Land Management issues leases and licenses for coal mining, pursuant to an extensive statutory and regulatory overlay. The United States Geological Survey has authority over mines; the Office of Surface Mining Reclamation and Enforcement implements the Surface Mining Control and Reclamation Act of 1977, 30 U.S.C. § 801; and the Department of Energy has acquired some jurisdiction formerly held by the Department of the Interior. The key federal statutes are the Mineral Lands Leasing Act of 1920 (MLA), 30 U.S.C. § 181; the Federal Coal Leasing Amendments Act of 1976, 30 U.S.C. §§ 201–209; the Mineral Leasing Act for Acquired Lands, 30 U.S.C. §§ 351 et. seq.; and the Federal Land Policy and Management Act of 1976 (FLPMA), 43 U.S.C. §§ 1701–1782.

The Bureau of Land Management (BLM) is chiefly responsible for leasing federal lands for coal extraction. The leases are authorized in a manner to maximize revenues through managed resource planning and to protect the environment. Coal leases are issued for a term of 20 years and may continue as long as coal is produced annually. The lessee pays the U.S. Treasury a royalty based on a percentage of the value of the coal.

Initially the MLA encouraged the development of coal on federal lands through "preference right" leases allowing people to explore for coal. Those leases could be awarded competitively or noncompetitively. The Federal Coal Leasing Amendments Act made significant changes to the 1920 Act in requiring coal leasing by competitive bids only and indexed according to fair market value. In addition, leases could only be issued after a comprehensive land use plan had been adopted. The amendments also eliminated preference right leases and prospecting permits. The amendments also added acreage limitations, although they allowed consolidation of leases based upon a demonstration of "maximum economic recovery." 30 U.S.C. §§ 201–210. In addition, the amendments provided for environmental protections and for financial returns of not less than 12 ½ percent in royalties. Additionally, the BLM requires the preparation of environmental impact statements under NEPA in reviewing lease applications.

The Federal Coal Leasing Amendments Act of 1976 and the Federal Land Management Policy Act (FLMPA) were passed to establish a more coherent federal land use policy. These acts apply not only to coal but to all federal lands and are intended to retain federal lands unless the national interest requires otherwise. In order to achieve the purposes of this legislation, the acts attempt to craft a policy which adopts the principles of multiple use-sustained yield, environmentally sound management, compensation based on fair market value, protection of areas of critical environmental concern, and recognition of the country's need to develop the use of this abundant resource. 43 U.S.C. § 1701(a). In addition, the regulations that implement these laws are intended to maintain public lands as well as to balance the conflicting needs of industrial development and environmental protection. 43 C.F.R. § 3809.1.

It should be noted that, although the federal government does not directly regulate either the price or the allocation of coal, coal prices and allocations are affected by the government's health, safety, and environmental regulations.

2. Coal Conversion

Given coal's abundance, and the realization that coal use can reduce dependence on foreign oil, conversion from oil and natural gas to coal once struck the federal government as a good idea. That legislation was a failure, but the lessons learned from that failure are useful.

It was hoped that legislation designed to increase coal consumption would reduce reliance on foreign oil and gas.

Thus, in 1974, the Congress passed the Energy Supply and Environmental Coordination Act of 1974 (ESECA), 15 U.S.C. §§ 791 et. seq. This Act authorized the then Federal Energy Administration to order powerplants and "major fuel burning installations" to substitute coal for oil or gas as their boiler fuel. In addition, the Act contained provisions to ameliorate environmental problems caused by expanded coal production. Then in December, 1975, as part of the Energy Policy and Conservation Act, 42 U.S.C. § 6201, Congress amended ESECA to extend FEA's authority to issue prohibition and construction orders relating to land conversion. Coal conversion legislation was further amended by the Powerplant and Industrial Fuel Use Act of 1978, 42 U.S.C. §§ 8301–8484 (1982).

This coal conversion legislation was largely unsuccessful. Utilities and industrial users found coal conversion too expensive and avoided costly government orders by obtaining exemptions. For example, according to one DOE report, between January 1, 1983 and December 31, 1985 *all* requested exemptions from the coal conversion legislation were granted. The ineffective and underenforced coal conversion legislation was eventually repealed.

3. Mine Health and Safety

Clearly coal mining is one of the riskiest occupations in the country. Fatalities can occur as a result of mine cave-ins, explosions, and the like. It is also the case that long-term diseases such as black lung disease are a consequence of mining. Recently, the National Mining Association indicated that there has been a decrease in mining fatalities from over 200 in 1984 to 38 in 2000 with an estimated fatality rate of 27 in 2002. Nonetheless, long-term diseases continue to be a persistent problem.

Some have described underground mining as the most hazardous occupation in the United States. Indeed, you may well recall the nation's attention focused on a small dairy farm in southwestern Pennsylvania to watch the rescue of nine coal miners trapped underground for three days in a mine rapidly filling with water. Explosions, cave-ins, flooding, and suffocation threaten lives and are responsible for the deaths of tens of thousands of miners. Coal dust threatens the long-term health of miners and can be fatal, as can working the massive machinery now employed in modern mining operations. Historically, the states were responsible for the health and safety of miners. State enforcement was inadequate because inspections were not rigorous and little attention was paid to the long-term health effects on mine workers. These inadequacies led to federal government involvement.

Federal legislation addressing the health and safety aspects of coal mining includes: the Federal Coal Mine Safety Act, 30 U.S.C. §§ 451 et seq.; the Federal Coal Mine Health and Safety Act of 1969, (codified in various provisions of U.S.C. titles 15 and 30); significant amendments to the 1969 Act in the Federal Mine Safety and Health Amendments Act of 1977, 30 U.S.C. §§ 801 et seq.; and the Black Lung Benefits Act of 1972, 30 U.S.C. §§ 901 et seq.; and the Coal Industry Retiree Health Benefits Act of 1992, 26 U.S.C. §§ 9701–9722.

In short, the federal government has attempted to provide benefits for coal miners subject to debilitating diseases through the Federal Coal Mine Health and Safety Act of 1969, as amended by the Black Lung Benefits Act of 1972. In *Usery v. Turner Elkhorn Mining Co.* (S.Ct.1976), the United States Supreme Court upheld the constitutionality and retroactive effects of those acts. This legislation established a compensation system for coal miners affected by pneumoconiosis (black lung disease), which is caused by long-term inhalation of coal dust. Still, the health benefits for coal miners appeared to be underfunded and, in response, Congress passed the Coal Industry Retiree Health Benefits Act of 1992 which apportioned liability with respect to the coal companies to fund those benefits. That act was subject to a takings challenge in *Eastern Enterprises v. Apfel* (S.Ct.1998). In that case, the Supreme

Court found portions of the Act apportioning liability to a company that had ceased mining in 1965 to be invalid. Some of the Justices found that such an imposition constituted a taking while others noted that takings cases generally dealt with specifically identifiable property that had been physically invaded whereas the Act in question was an imposition of a financial obligation on a company. Because the Justices split 4–4 on the takings issue, it remains an open matter. Significant litigation continues under the Act regarding assignments of liability, successor liability, and the like, see *Anker Energy Corp. v. Consolidated Coal Co.* (3d Cir. 1999); *National Coal Ass'n v. Chater* (11th Cir. 1996); *Holland v. New Era Coal Co.* (6th Cir. 1999); *The Pittston Co. v. United States* (4th Cir. 1999).

The issue of funding for black lung disease remains open and controversial. In 2000 the Department of Labor completed a four-year rulemaking significantly revising the rules for the black lung program, 65 Fed. Reg. 79, 920–80, 107 (Dec. 20, 2000). The new rules expanded eligibility criteria for new claimants as well as for pending benefits claims. In addition, the rules allowed for the reopening of previously denied claims and they attempted to streamline and simplify the claims process, easing the burden of proof and limiting the amount of evidence that operators could submit in opposition to a claim. The rules were challenged by mine operators and insurance companies and they were upheld in part and reversed in part in *National Mining Ass'n v. Department of Labor* (D.C. Cir. 2002).

Federal intrusion into coal miner health and safety matters is broad-based. State laws, unless they are more stringent than the federal standards, are preempted and federal inspectors have the authority to conduct warrantless searches and the power to close mines which are in violation of federal standards. *Donovan v. Dewey* (S.Ct.1981). Federal health and safety laws subject violators to civil and criminal penalties. The state must set health and safety standards at a level necessary "for the protection of life and the prevention of injuries," and it must set standards for toxic materials which appear during the mining process at levels "which most adequately assure on the basis of the best available evidence that no miner will suffer material impairment of health or functional capacity even if such miner has regular exposure to the hazards dealt with by such standard for the period of his working life." This latter test is intended to achieve the "attainment of the highest degree of health and safety protection for the miner." 30 U.S.C. § 811(a)(6)(A) (1982).

4. Land Reclamation

Costs and risks borne by workers are imposed, at least partially, on mine operators, and are to be reflected in the cost of coal. Similarly, environmental legislation involves the redistribution of the benefits and burdens of coal mining. The costs of reclaiming land after coal mining, as well as the costs of cleaning the coal before or during burning, must be imposed on someone. These costs will be reflected in the cost of a ton of coal, and they will be imposed on the coal's purchaser.

Sixty percent of the coal mined in the United States is surface or open-pit mined. In the eastern United States, about 50% of coal is surface-mined and 50% is extracted from underground mines. In the western United States, a greater percentage of coal is surface mined, and in the Great Plains nearly 100% of the coal is surface mined. Surface mining is cheaper and is less hazardous to the health and safety of mine workers than deep pit mining. However, surface mining injures the environment through soil erosion, water contamination, vegetation destruction, wildlife disruption, and aesthetic degradation.

Surface mining requires the removal of topsoil and then the removal of the layer of soil underneath the topsoil. This second layer, called the overburden, must be separated from the topsoil. If the overburden is placed above the topsoil, then rain can cause leaching which ruins the topsoil, and the accompanying runoff is acidic, which can cause damage to surrounding water systems. After the coal is extracted, the abandoned mine, with its exposed layers of acidic soil, can continue to pollute the area with acid run-off. The way to avoid these adverse environmental problems is through land reclamation.

Like miner health and safety regulations, environmental regulations to promote land reclamation were once the province of the states. Land reclamation was not rigorously enforced in part because states were protective of their coal industries. In order to combat the resulting harmful environmental effects, Congress enacted two statutes: the Resource Conservation and Recovery Act of 1976 (RCRA), 42 U.S.C. §§ 6901–6987, providing standards for disposal sites and hazardous waste treatment generally; and the Surface Mining Control and Reclamation Act of 1977 (SMCRA), 30 U.S.C. §§ 1201–1328, requiring that mined land be restored to its original condition.

The SMCRA is one of the most comprehensive federal regulations on land use. Coal mining, particularly when using "surface" or "strip" mining techniques, has a significant detrimental impact on the land and environment. Adverse environmental effects include water and soil pollution and erosion of the land. Prior to 1977, individual state regulation had proved ineffective, because state laws were under-enforced. The SMCRA was signed by President Jimmy Carter after seven years of debate in Congress. Congress believed that federal legislation was necessary to establish minimum nationwide standards, insuring that competition among coal producers would not be used to induce states to lower environmental standards or fail to enforce existing laws. Although concerns were raised over how well a uniform standard could be applied to varied regions, Congress passed the SMCRA to "assure that the coal supply essential to the Nation's energy requirements, and to its economic and social well-being is provided and strike a balance between protection of the environment and agricultural productivity and the Nation's need for coal as an essential source of energy."

Chief among Congressional concerns under the SMCRA were various agricultural and environmental interests. The Act contained four key regulations to protect these interests, including the following: (1) potential miners must submit a detailed application to commence surface coal mining; (2) coal companies must post a bond in order to ensure that reclamations costs will be covered; and, (3) highly detailed standards for reclamation must be satisfied. Finally, the Act delegated regulatory enforcement to the Secretary of the Interior and individual State regulatory agencies. In general, this Act required mining companies to restore approximate contour and use capacity of the mined land, stabilize the soil, redistribute the topsoil, and revegetate the site.

The SMCRA, administered by the Office of Surface Mining Reclamation and Enforcement of the Interior Department, is enforced through a system of permits, inspections, and fines. Not surprisingly, the Act has met with considerable resistance. Not only did private mine owners wish to avoid the costs that the Act imposed, states did not welcome federal intervention in an area that was traditionally left to local regulation. The SMCRA was challenged in the United States Supreme Court, which upheld the Act against several constitutional challenges in *Hodel v. Virginia Surface Mining & Reclamation Assn., Inc.* (S.Ct.1981), and *Hodel v. Indiana* (S.Ct.1981). Nevertheless, application of SMCRA to a particular coal property has in one case been found to be a taking by the United States Federal Circuit. *Whitney Benefits, Inc. v. United States* (Fed. Cir. 1991). Under SMCRA the Office of Surface Mining also establishes regulations for underground mining. These regulations were recently challenged and largely upheld in *National Mining Ass'n. v. Department of Interior* (D.C. Cir. 1999).

The structure of the SMCRA includes a role for state regulation. Once the state develops a reclamation plan approved by the Interior Department, then state agencies administer the plan and state courts have exclusive jurisdiction to do so. *Haydo v. Amerikohl Mining, Inc.* (3d Cir. 1987). Yet, it has not been an easy task to have states and the Interior Department develop and enforce reclamation plans. In September 1981, two environmental groups filed a lawsuit against the Secretary of the Interior and the Director of the Office of Surface Mining seeking to compel performance of these enforcement duties under the SMCRA. The plaintiffs claimed that Interior Department officials had failed (1) to assess and collect mandatory civil penalties, and (2) to take proper enforcement action against mine operators found in violation of the SMCRA. In *Save Our Cumberland Mountains, Inc. v. Watt* (D.D.C. 1982), the district court held that the Secretary of the Interior had a mandatory duty to enforce the SMCRA, and he was ordered to do so. That case was overturned on appeal due to improper venue in *Save Our Cumberland Mountains, Inc. v. Clark* (D.C. Cir. 1984). Following these developments, the parties pursued negotiations which led to a settlement of the lawsuit and to attorney's fees for the plaintiffs for their successful settlement. *Save Our Cumberland Mountains, Inc. v. Hodel* (D.C. Cir. 1987).

One of the current controversies surrounding SMCRA involves the practice of "valley fill." Valley fill is the result of a practice known as mountaintop removal mining. As its name implies, coal miners simply take the soil and rocks from the top of the mountain and deposit them in the valley so that the miners may have access to the coal. Environmentalists are primarily concerned that the valley fill stops up and pollutes rivers as well as deposits of rock and soil in valleys and they challenged that practice in *Bragg v. Robertson* (S.D. W. Va. 1999). In that case the District Court judge granted a summary judgment in favor of the plaintiffs to prohibit valley fill. Shortly after that case, the Governor of West Virginia announced a revenue shortfall and the Court stayed its permanent injunction pending appeal. In the appeal, the Fourth Circuit adjudicated the District Court's injunction and remanded with instructions to dismiss the citizens' complaint without prejudice under the doctrine of sovereign immunity as incorporated in the Eleventh Amendment, which bars citizens from bringing claims against state officials in federal court. *Bragg v. West Virginia Coal Ass'n.* (4th Cir. 2001). At the time of this writing, the Bush Administration is in the process of changing its buffer zone rules. Simply, the buffer zone rule prohibits mining within 100 feet of a stream, which has the effect of prohibiting a certain amount of groundtop removal strip mining. Groundtop removal involves the dynamiting away of mountaintops to expose coal seams and dumping the debris into valleys and streams. Some of the valley fills are hundreds of feet deep and several miles long. The proposed rule change would allow valley fills if the operators show that they are minimizing mining waste and the environmental damage caused by it. Over the last few years, mountaintop removal has become the most common form of surface mining in central Appalachia. Even though the SMCRA requires mining companies to reconfigure the hilltop, it is virtually impossible to reproduce the original landscape.

C. CLEAN AIR

Once coal reaches its destination, it is burned for its stored energy. The burning of coal presents perhaps the most sensitive and complex environmental issues of the coal fuel cycle. Coal combustion generates four main sources of pollution: sulfur oxide, nitrogen oxide, carbon dioxide, and particulate matter; all of which spoil land, water, and air. Sulfur oxide, which increases with the sulfur content of the coal, causes human health problems, crop damage, and acid rain. Nitrogen oxide contributes to the same problems and causes smog. Tons of particulate matter are emitted from coal burning facilities daily and cause property damage and health hazards. Finally, carbon dioxide causes what is known as the greenhouse effect, which is an increase in the temperature of the earth's surface. The principal form of water pollution caused by burning coal is thermal pollution.

Coal burning facilities also contribute to the problem of acid rain. Acid rain is defined broadly as the long range transport and deposit of pollutants. Acid rain begins with combustion. As coal is burned in electric powerplants, large quantities of sulphur dioxide and nitrogen oxide are released into the air. The sulfates and nitrates then combine with cloud vapor to form sulfuric and nitric acids that may be carried long distances before falling to earth. Acid rain damage is predominant in the northeastern United States and eastern Canada.

The Clean Air Act, 42 U.S.C. §§ 7401 et seq., as amended in 1990, is the basic federal law governing pollution controls for coal burning electric power plants. The law is complex and detailed. The object of the Clean Air Act is to establish standards for the emission of pollutants. The Act is administered by the states and the federal government and includes provisions that require power plants to develop and use new technologies to improve environmental quality. The Clean Air Act authorizes the EPA to set performance standards for sources of air pollution. Because electric utilities burn nearly 90% of the coal produced in this country, they are a major source of air pollution. In 1979, the EPA set restrictions on the amount of sulfur dioxide and particulate matter that can be emitted from coal-fired electric power plants. The EPA regulations were challenged by environmental groups for being too lax and by utilities for being too stringent. The District of Columbia Circuit sustained the regulations in *Sierra Club v. Costle* (D.C. Cir. 1981).

Still, the coal-fired power plant continued to present significant environmental problems. In 1998, the EPA began an industry-wide enforcement program under the heading of New Source Review (NSR). In short, plants that were to experience "major modifications" were required to install best available control technology (BACT) to reduce nitrogen oxide, oxides, sulfur dioxide, and airborne particulate matter. See *Wisconsin Electric Power Co. v. Reilly* (7th Cir. 1990) (Cudahy, J.). The New Source Review has become a hot issue in environmental struggles. The Bush Administration has proposed revising NSR regulations in order to exempt power plants from enforcement actions started under the Clinton Administration. See Robert J. Martineau, Jr. & Michael K. Stagg, *New Source Review Reform: A New Year's Eve to Remember*, NATURAL RESOURCES & ENVIRONMENT 3 (Winter 2004). As of the date of this writing, the Bush Administration's proposed rules have been stayed by the D.C. Circuit. See *New York v. EPA* (D.C. Cir., Dec. 24, 2003). Coal-fired power plants, in addition to the oxides listed above, also release airborne particulate matter which are small pieces of pollution that come in fine and coarse particles. According to an EPA study, exposure to coarse particles is primarily associated with the aggravation of respiratory conditions, such as asthma, and exposure to fine particles is most closely associated with decreased lung function, increased hospital admissions, and emergency room visits, increased respiratory symptoms and disease, and premature death. See Jonathan Martel, Janet Kester, & Elliott Zenick, *Power Plants, Particulates, and the Uncertain Science of Public Health*, NATURAL RESOURCES & ENVIRONMENT 31 (Winter 2004).

The 1990 Clean Air Act amendments also required further reductions in power plant emissions, including sulfur emissions. In order to achieve these goals, the Act introduced a market-based "cap-and-trade" system which created a finite number of "allowances," or units of pollutant emissions. Each power plant was given a certain number of allowances. If the power plant met the environmental emissions standards without using all of its allowances, that plant was permitted to sell its allowances to another power plant that cannot achieve compliance on its own. Through this system, the maximum levels of pollution emissions prescribed by the Clean Air Act were still satisfied.

In February 2002, President George W. Bush further reduced the quantity of allowable emissions as well as extended the reach of this market-based cap-and-trade system through the Clear Skies Initiative (CSI). The purpose of the Clear Skies Initiative is to "protect Americans from respiratory and cardiovascular diseases" by reducing smog, particulate matter, and haze; protecting wildlife; and reducing acid rain as well as nitrogen and mercury deposits. *The Clear Skies Initiative: Executive Summary: The Clear Skies Initiative*, available at http://www.whitehouse.gov/news/releases/2002/02/print/clear-skies.html. CSI also uses the market-based cap-and-trade system which allows power plants to trade allowances on the open market in order to achieve compliance with the emissions standards.

CSI calls for a 70% reduction in air pollution emissions from electric generators by specifically targeting sulfur dioxide, nitrogen oxides, and mercury emissions. The goals are to achieve a 73% reduction in sulfur dioxide emissions, a 67% reduction in nitrogen oxide emissions, and 69% reduction in mercury emissions by 2018. Through emissions trading, CSI is intended to encourage plant operators to develop new environmental control technologies with attendant cost savings. In addition to economic benefits to power plant operators, CSI is intended to have economic benefits for consumers as well by preventing an estimated $110 billion annually in health costs by 2020. Finally, CSI is projected to increase costs of producing electricity by only 10% in 2020.

President Bush proposed the Clear Skies Initiative on February 14, 2002. It was formally introduced into Congress as the Clear Skies Act in February 2023. Currently, the Environmental Protection Agency (EPA) oversees the progress of the Initiative. Each year, the EPA assesses its model and analysis of the Initiative, and updates the data it releases to the public. As of July 1, 2003, the EPA announced that its modeling of the Clear Skies Initiative predicted the production of even more optimistic benefits than originally anticipated. However, Congress has not enacted it into law as of this date since many have questioned the beneficial impact of this legislation.

As mentioned at the beginning of the chapter, coal production has doubled since 1970, the date of the passage of the Clean Air Act. The National Coal Council reports that since that time emissions in the form of carbon monoxide, lead, nitrogen oxide, ozone, particulate matter, and sulphur dioxide have decreased more than 35%. As part of the national energy plan, the DOE budget earmarked $330 million under its Clean Coal Power Initiative through an RFP process for private solicitations. DOE reports that since 1986 the agency has committed nearly $1.8 billion for clean coal technology in addition to this latest initiative.

Another clean coal project is the Clean Coal Technology Program which is a joint government industry venture for the purpose of developing an economically and environmentally sustainable energy system pursuant to the mission of the Department of Energy. The program has 35 active programs designed to develop new and cleaner technologies for coal burning, which are capable of satisfying existing as well as anticipated environmental regulations. Clean coal technology is also being designed for operating in a deregulated electric power market. The program is divided into four general areas. Environmental Control Devices are intended to reduce the emissions of sulphur dioxide and nitrogen oxides. The Advanced Electric Power Generation program is intended to be applied to repower existing plants as well as for the development of new plants. The Program of Coal Processing for Clean Fuels monitors the chemical and physical processes used to transform raw coal into high energy density and environmentally compliant fuels as well as the conversion of coal to methanol. A final program involves Industrial Applications which addresses environmental issues and barriers associated with coal use in industry. An example of an Industrial Application is to reduce the dependence of the steel industry on coke and the pollutant emissions inherent in coke-making as well as reduce the use by the cement industry of high sulfur coal.

D. COAL TRANSPORTATION

Railcars, barges, and trucks transport mined coal to points of distribution or consumption after it has been refined and sorted. There has been interest in the coal industry in the development of coal slurry pipelines. Slurry pipelines come into direct competition with rail transportation, and these two transportation modes are the most significant for the coal industry.

1. Rail Transportation

Railroads account for approximately two-thirds of all coal carriage. Coal, the largest single commodity carried by rail, is transported by unit trains often reaching 100 cars in length. In the eastern United States, there is a measure of competition for carriage contracts among railroads, barges, and trucks. Railroads also compete among themselves for the carriage of various commodities and passenger service. However, in the western United States, because of the great distances involved and the absence of a network of navigable waterways, the rail industry has a dominant competitive position in coal carriage.

Because rail carriage is the indispensable link between coal production at the mine and end-use by consumers such as electric utilities, railroads have what is called a "bottleneck" monopoly position, analogous to the bottlenecks created by natural gas and crude oil pipelines. Electric utilities which must depend on this monopolistic type of rail transportation are called captive shippers or captive customers. Thus, without rail transport there effectively can be no viable coal industry. Primarily for that reason, the federal government has intervened in the rail industry by requiring that rates for coal carriage be regulated.

Rail rates for coal haulage were previously set by the Interstate Commerce Commission (ICC), *Burlington Northern, Inc. v. United States* (S.Ct.1982). Historically, rail rates were based on a cost-of-service plus reasonable rate of return formula. *Northern Pacific Railway Co. v. North Dakota* (S.Ct. 1915). Electric utilities, under this formula, paid the railroad a rate which covered the railroad's transportation cost plus a percentage profit.

Because of the weakened financial condition of the railroad industry in the 1970s, Congress passed the Railroad Revitalization and Regulatory Reform Act of 1976 (4–R Act), Pub. L. No. 94–210, 90 Stat. 31. The 4–R Act was expressly intended to bolster the rail industry financially. To this end, the Act allowed the ICC to set rates so that rail carriers in competitive markets earn "adequate revenues," 49 U.S.C. § 10701(a)(b), which, in turn, was defined "to cover total operating expenses, including depreciation and obsolescence, plus a reasonable economic profit or return (or both) on capital employed in the business." 49 U.S.C. § 10704(a)(2). The 4–R Act also authorized the ICC to inquire into the reasonableness of rates charged carriers which may have dominance in their market. In other words, the ICC has authority to assess whether the rates charged by railroads are the result of their possible possession of market power.

In addition to the 4–R Act, Congress attempted to assist the rail industry by freeing it from rate hearings for every rate increase sought. In the Staggers Rail Act of 1980, 49 U.S.C. § 10101 et. seq., Congress broadened the authority of the ICC to set "rate flexibility zones." These zones allowed railroads to set their own rates within a pre-established geographical zone without formal ICC rate hearings. With the 4–R and Staggers Rail Act, the ICC moved away from a simple cost-of-service formula. In many cases, the railroads were subject to effective competition from other modes of transportation like trucks and barges. In order to help railroads stay competitive with other transporters, the ICC gave railroads the power to set a rate "zone" to avoid numerous rate hearings, and their rates may be based on comparative industry costs. The ICC was disbanded in 1995, but its functions were transferred to the Surface Transportation Board of the Department of Transportation.

2. Coal Slurry Pipelines

Coal slurry pipelines operate much like oil pipelines. Coal is mined, impurities are removed, and the coal is then crushed and mixed with water. A slurry mixture of about equal weights of water and coal is transported in the pipeline from the mouth of the mine to the point of consumption or distribution. At the end of the system, the mixture is removed from the pipeline and the coal is dewatered. Coal slurry transportation may be cheaper than rail transportation once the pipelines are built. Because coal slurry pipelines represent direct competition with rail transportation, the development of such pipelines has been opposed by railroads.

Pipeline proponents face numerous hurdles. First, rail transporters resist the construction of slurry pipelines and lobby against them because they fear that slurry transportation will reduce their market in coal transportation. Second, before a pipeline can be constructed, the project developer must acquire land or easements for the pipeline which crosses several parcels of land. This situation presents a classic holdout problem, in that even one landowner unwilling to sell the necessary fee estate or easement can "hold out" by asking exorbitant prices for the land necessary for the construction of the pipeline. *Energy Transportation Systems, Inc. v. Union Pacific Railroad Co.* (10th Cir. 1979) (railroad which owned only a surface right-of-way had to provide a right-of-way to a slurry pipeline). Because of the holdout problem, pipeline developers wishing to acquire the land at fair market value need the power of eminent domain. However, the necessary state legislation allocating that power generally has not been forthcoming.

In addition to land rights, slurry pipelines must acquire water rights. Water is a scarce, sacred, and extremely valuable resource in the western United States. So much so, that some states have passed legislation attempting to restrict the use of water, and such restrictions may preclude coal slurry pipeline development. Montana, for example, has enacted a statute which states that the "legislature finds that the use of water for the slurry transportation of coal is detrimental to the conservation and protection of the waters of the state," thus preventing slurry pipelines from acquiring necessary access to water. Mont. Code Annot. §§ 85–2–104 (1979). These state restrictions on water use are of questionable constitutionality because the states may be favoring their own citizens and impeding interstate commerce. In *Sporhase v. Nebraska* (S.Ct. 1982), the Supreme Court held that Nebraska's right to restrict the transportation of water out of the state was subject to Commerce Clause analysis. Although not directly apposite to slurry pipeline development, the *Sporhase* decision has a significant impact. If a state law restricting the out-of-state transportation of water impedes interstate commerce in coal, then the law may be unconstitutional.

In *Missouri v. Andrews* (8th Cir. 1986), the Secretary of the Department of Interior executed a contract with Energy Transportation Systems, Inc. giving a slurry pipeline company the right to withdraw 20,000 acre feet of water per year from a federal reservoir in South Dakota for forty years. (An acre foot of water is the amount of water that covers an acre to the height of one foot). Missouri, Iowa, and South Dakota contested the authority of the Secretary of the Department of the Interior to award such a contract. The states argued that the federal reservoir was governed by a series of regulations, including the Flood Control Act of 1944, and that the Secretary could not unilaterally execute a water service contract for industrial purposes to the detriment of the states. Both the United States District Court and the United States Court of Appeals for the Eighth Circuit ruled that the Secretary did not have unilateral authority to award the contract. The United States Supreme Court affirmed this holding. *Energy Transportation Systems, Inc. Pipeline Project v. Missouri,* 484 U.S. 495 (S.Ct.1988). Additionally, some states have enacted protectionist legislation to protect locally produced coal from competition from out-of-state (for example low-sulphur) coal. See *Alliance for Clean Coal v. Miller* (7th Cir. 1995).

E. GLOBAL WARMING

Global warming, also known as climate change, refers to the increase in global average temperatures. According to the National Academy of Sciences and the Environmental Protection Agency, the earth's surface temperature has risen by about 1 degree Fahrenheit in the past century, with accelerated warming during the past two decades. The 20th century's ten warmest years all occurred within the last 15 years of the century. U.S. Environmental Protection Agency, available at http://yosemite.epa.gov/oar/globalwarming.nsf/content/climate.html. The cause or causes of this temperature increase has been the subject of a good deal of debate. Although some degree of warming can be attributed to natural process and weather cycles, the real issue involves how much human activity has accelerated this warming process which, in turn, involves the amount of greenhouse gases in the atmosphere.

Greenhouse gases are the chemicals and materials present in the Earth's atmosphere that retain radiation from the sun, trapping heat within the Earth's atmosphere. While such heat retention makes life on Earth possible, the greater the concentration of atmospheric gases, the greater the amount of heat that is retained. The primary greenhouse gases are water vapor (responsible for around 90% of radiation absorption), carbon dioxide, methane, and nitrous oxide. These gases have both natural and anthropogenic (human) sources. Scientists generally believe that the combustion of fossil fuels and other human activities are the primary cause for the increase of carbon dioxide levels in the atmosphere. Since the beginning of the Industrial Revolution, atmospheric concentrations of carbon dioxide have increased by nearly 30 percent. The fossil fuel combustion burned to run cars and trucks, heat homes and businesses, and power factories and other activities comprises about 98% of U.S. carbon dioxide emissions.

In keeping with the scientific consensus that fossil fuel combustion and human activity are responsible for increased greenhouse gases in the atmosphere, in 1988 the World Meteorological Organization (WMO) and the United Nations Environment Program (UNEP) created the Intergovernmental Panel on Climate Change (IPCC) to study climate change issues. There have been domestic and international responses to this environmental issue. Internationally, in 1992, the United Nations Framework Convention on Climate Change (UNFCCC) was drafted as an international commitment to further the reduction of global warming and greenhouse gas emissions. United Nations Framework Convention, available at http://unfccc.int/resource/docs/convkp/conveng.pdf. Further, in 1997, the Kyoto Protocol was created to specifically enumerate reductions that each country had to make within certain time periods. Under Article 3 of the Kyoto Protocol, industrialized nations must reduce the emission of greenhouse gases "by at least 5 percent below 1990 levels in the commitment period 2008 to 2012." Article 3 of the Kyoto Protocol, available at http://unfccc.int/resource/docs/convkp/kpeng.pdf. Although the U.S. has ratified the more generalized UNFCCC, the U.S. has only signed, not ratified, the Kyoto Protocol. Thus, it is not legally bound to meet with the Protocol mandates. Currently, U.S. carbon dioxide emissions are 15 percent greater than they were in 1990. Natural Resources Defense Council, *Bush Administration Errs on Kyoto Global*

Warming Agreement (April 2001), available at http://www.nrdc.org/globalWarming.

The primary U.S. argument in opposition to ratifying the Kyoto Protocol is that the mandates would have a negative impact on the U.S. economy, particularly in competition with developing nations who are not subject to the same emissions reductions commitments. The "holdout" nations purport to fear the potential economic impacts of mandatory regulations in an unmonitored market. Further, some policymakers have imposed a very high bar on the amount of scientific evidence required to prove that human activities and increased carbon dioxide emissions are in fact the cause of global warming.

The U.S. position on global warming is particularly significant since the U.S. is the largest producer of greenhouse gases in the world. President Bush recently unveiled his "Kyoto alternative" plan, a plan based on the sale of pollution "credits" and advertised to reduced greenhouse gas emissions while simultaneously fostering U.S. economic growth. This alternative plan, however, faces criticism because although it aims to produce an 18% reduction in greenhouse gas "intensity" (ratio of greenhouse gas emissions to economic output) by 2012, as long as the U.S. economic output increases over the next decade, the intensity figure automatically decreases without changing the overall emission volume by the U.S. In the 1990s, the intensity level decreased by 17.4%, as the U.S. economy grew by nearly 40%, while the global warming emissions grew by 14%. Furthermore, the alternative plan uses voluntary compliance and the promise of "credits" in any future mandatory program as the enforcement mechanism, a method that has been criticized by policymakers.

Regardless of the emissions regulatory scheme, the problem of global warming is highly significant. Mandatory global emissions restrictions could have adverse effects on the coal industry; advocates for stricter emissions policies conclude that permissive maintenance of the status quo will ultimately have adverse impacts on the coal industry. If the present development of technology that will permit more efficient use of coal in a carbon-constrained world is not developed, the eventual business case for coal may be fatal.

As part of the Kyoto alternative, President Bush has introduced into Congress the Clear Skies and Global Climate Change Initiatives. Many believe that, with this introduction of these Initiatives, the United States will not ratify the Kyoto Protocol. First, the Initiatives are argued to require more reductions in carbon dioxide emissions than the Protocol. Second, the Initiatives purport to allow United States businesses to achieve such levels with less drastic effects on the energy industry and markets. Finally, the Initiatives purport to allow the United States to continue to use the energy resources most available to it and most economical to use, instead of being forced to use other resources.

On February 14, 2002, President Bush introduced his Global Climate Change Initiative (GCCI), http://www.whitehouse.gov/news/releases/2002/02/print/20020214.html. GCCI proposes to reduce greenhouse gas "intensity" by 18% over ten years by supporting research surrounding climate change. In the long term, the Initiative purports to reduce, or slow, greenhouse gas emissions over time. Finally, it will then reverse the growth of, or decrease, the "intensity" of greenhouse gases on earth.

GCCI proposes to fulfill seven goals: (1) reduce the "intensity" of greenhouse gas emissions by 18% in ten years; (2) improve the Energy Information Administration's Greenhouse Gas emission reduction registry; (3) provide transfer credits for emissions reductions; (4) review progress in 2012 and take additional action if necessary; (5) increase support from climate science and technology; (6) provide possible business tax incentives and voluntary agreements; and (7) pursue new and expanded international agreements.

While these goals may be laudable, they are only in the discussion stage and leave the United States out of the Kyoto Protocol, the world's major global warming action.

F. THE FUTURE OF COAL

Coal has played an important role in the United States for over 150 years, first fueling the Industrial Revolution and now accounting for at least half of the electricity generated in the United States. In one sense, the future of coal is problematic because of the environmental, health, and safety risks associated throughout its fuel cycle. Not only are those risks not limited to domestic production and consumption, but the contribution of coal-fired electric plants to global warming are of international concern.

Clearly such controversy continues between the coal industry and environmentalists regarding the continued or expanded use of coal-fired generation because of pollution associated with coal plants. The battleground continues to be the Clean Air Act. There is consensus that coal must be cleaner. This point is certainly recognized by the Department of Energy. DOE's Office of Fossil Energy published a report entitled *Vision 21 Program Plan: Clean Energy Plants for the 21st Century* (April 1999).

According to *Vision 21*, energy plants for the future will emphasize the elimination of environmental issues associated with utilizing fossil fuels. Pollution emissions such as sulphur dioxide, nitrogen oxides, and mercury should be reduced to essentially zero levels. In addition, emissions of carbon dioxide should be significantly reduced because of higher efficiencies. In addition to pollution reduction, the second goal of the Power Plant of the Future is to maximize efficiency. Energy efficiency will be increased through advanced technologies which might produce additional high-value chemicals as well as through generation of heat or industrial steam. In order to accomplish these ends, the Bush Administration has created resources for clean coal initiatives. See http://fossil.energy.gov/programs/powersystems/cleancoal/.

Nevertheless, environmental problems notwithstanding, coal's great abundance coupled with the country's dependence on foreign oil and the uncertain future of nuclear power means, most likely, that coal may maintain, if not increase, its importance in our energy portfolio. This growing importance is the subject of reports published by the National Coal Council which is a federal advisory committee to the Secretary of Energy. The National Coal Council (essentially a coal industry organization) exists to advise, inform, and make recommendations to the Secretary on matters relating to coal and the coal industry at the Secretary's request. The National Coal Council is comprised of members from a wide variety of interests, both public and private, but nevertheless is largely an industry organization.

In November 2000, the Secretary of Energy Bill Richardson requested the National Coal Council to conduct a study about measures to improve the availability of electricity from coal-fired power plants. His request asked the Council to address two specific areas: (1) improving technologies of coal-fired plants to produce more electricity; and, (2) reducing regulatory barriers to using those technologies. The National Coal Council responded that an additional 40,000 megawatts of increased electricity could be produced from existing plants. The additional electricity could be made available with the installation of standard improvements and clean coal technologies. Such improvements should increase energy efficiency while decreasing emissions. The study went on to say, however, that those additions could not be made without significant changes to regulatory interpretation and enforcement. In particular, the study recommended less aggressive interpretations of the Clean Air Act. The study was responding specifically to EPA enforcement proceedings against only a dozen companies under new source review sections of the Clean Air Act. The companies argued that they were performing regular maintenance which the EPA interpreted as generation which required environmental controls. The National Coal Council, *Increasing Electricity Availability from Coal–Fired Generation in the Near–Term* (May 2001). See also *Wisconsin Electric Power Co. v. Reilly, supra.*

With the change in presidential administrations, the National Coal Council was again asked to conduct a study regarding what "advanced technologies" might be available for electricity generation until 2010. The Council supported the earlier estimate of 40,000 megawatts of additional generating capacity as long as regulations, particularly new source review, were streamlined and reformed. The Council also found that between 22,000 and 65,000 megawatts of new capacity was possible again depending on government support of regulatory "reform." The Council recommended the government support and develop new technologies as well as regulatory reform. The National Coal Council, *Increasing Coal–Fired Generation Through 2010: Challenges & Opportunities* (May 2002).

CHAPTER 8

ELECTRICITY

In Chapter 1, we noted that government regulation follows a pattern or life cycle from free market to regulation and then back to the market. The electricity industry provides an excellent case study of that pattern and its history contains the merely colorful such as Thomas Alva Edison and George Westinghouse and the colorful who came to a bad end such as Samuel Insull and Kenneth Lay.[1] At the end of the 19th century, electricity generation and distribution were local, competitive, and unregulated. The industry grew, with a dedication to economies of scale and with technological innovations that enabled producers to transport electricity over longer distances, thus serving larger markets. The developments, in turn, encouraged firms to consolidate. Those developments also led to corporate abuse and to state and federal regulation of prices and profits for most of last century. Over the last decade or more, however, both state and federal regulators have been actively discussing and implementing deregulation or restructuring policies. These efforts have been difficult, complex, and messy with major setbacks caused by the California electricity crisis of the summer of 2000, the collapse of Enron and its accounting firm Arthur Anderson, and the largest blackout in history in August 2003. As a result, deregulation efforts have slowed. Nevertheless, the core concept of moving the industry from command-and-control

1. For a comparison see the three-part article Richard D. Cudahy, *Insull and Enron: Is There a Parallel?* 42 INFRASTRUCTURE 3 (Spring 2003); 42 INFRASTRUCTURE 1 (Summer 2003); and, 42 INFRASTRUCTURE 7 (Fall 2003). INFRASTRUCTURE is the newsletter of the ABA Section of Public Utility, Communications and Transportation Law.

price regulation to pricing through market competition is generally sound although the complete absence of regulation is not in the foreseeable future as explained in this chapter.

A. INDUSTRY OVERVIEW

Although static electricity can trace its roots back to ancient Greeks playing with amber, the modern history of the electricity industry began on September 4, 1882 when Edison flipped a switch at the Pearl Street Station and 400 incandescent bulbs softly glowed in lower Manhattan. See Jill Jonnes, *Empire of Light* (2003). With that glow, years of hard work and substantial capital investment began to pay off for Edison and his investors as the electric industry was born. Today the electric industry is valued at over $300 billion in annual revenues.

In one sense, the idea behind electricity is simple. The movement of electrons generates light and heat. Nevertheless, two physical laws make electricity unique and, consequently, make its regulation difficult. First, electrons do not move in any predictable path over a grid. Therefore, when you turn on your computer, there is no way of knowing who produced that electricity. Second, electricity cannot be stored effectively. Think of the size and weight of a battery, for example, and its useful life. Additionally, electricity supply must be ready and available. Think of keeping beer cold in your refrigerator. In short, the industry must have sufficient and reliable capacity to serve that demand instantaneously.

Electricity is not a natural resource; it is the product of electric generators. Energy resources such as oil, natural gas, coal, uranium, hydropower, and alternative resources, are used to create steam which turns a turbine shaft, which rotates coils of wire within stationary magnets, which then generate electricity. The electricity fuel cycle, then, consists of an energy resource being converted into electricity; the electricity is then transmitted from the source of production directly to end users or to local public utilities for distribution.

Figure 1 depicts the amount of electricity produced and consumed in 2002 in BTUs. Notice on the left hand side of the graph the several resources used to produce electricity and on the right hand side the sectors that consume the product. Also notice that more than one-half of the electricity produced is "lost" in the conversion process reflecting the Second Law of Thermodynamics. Much energy is lost as heat, and is not converted into usable electricity.

Figure 1. Electricity Flow, 2002

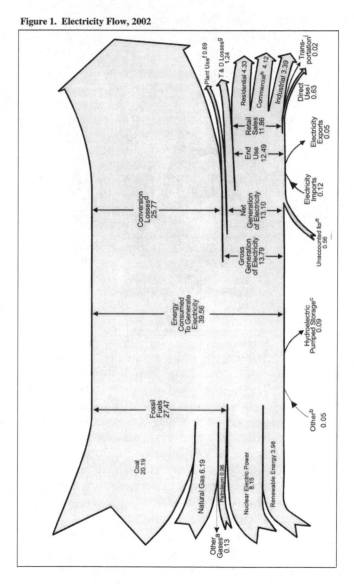

The next graph shows the percentages of resources used to generate that electricity.

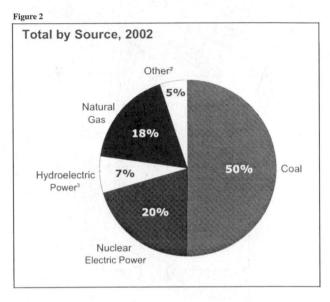

Figure 2

Total by Source, 2002

Other[2] 5%

Natural Gas 18%

Hydroelectric Power[3] 7%

Coal 50%

Nuclear Electric Power 20%

To deliver electricity, the industry has several actors. Not so many years ago, and to a large extent today, the dominant electricity provider in the United States has been the local public utility. Commonwealth Edison, Pacific Gas and Electric, and New Jersey Power & Light are all examples of local public utilities, which are also known as investor-owned utilities (IOUs). IOUs are privately owned and, most often, vertically integrated, which is to say that these companies generate, transmit, and distribute electricity to the end users. According to the Edison Electric Institute, there are 217 IOUs distributing electricity in the United States

In addition to privately owned IOUs, there are numerous state (22), local (1,857), and federally-owned public utilities (12) and, over the last two decades, there has been an increase in firms that generate electricity but do not own or operate transmission facilities. These firms are known as non-utility generators (NUGs). NUGs resulted from two federal statutes that will be described in more detail below—the Public Utility Regulatory Policy Act and the Energy Policy Act of 1992. Again according to the Edison Electric Institute there are non-IOUs units also generating electricity. Nevertheless the IOUs serve approximately 74% of the market. Edison Electric Institute, *Key Facts: A Look At the Electric Power Industry* 5 (available www.eia.org last reviewed January 7, 2004).

Historically, the electricity industry has enjoyed tremendous growth along with the economy as Figure 3 shows:

Figure 3*

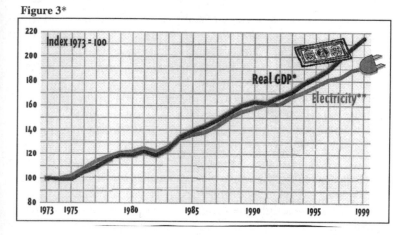

*This graphic has been modified from its original which can be found at http://www.eei.org/industry_issues/industry_over-view_and_statistics/nonav_key_facts/section1.pdf

For most of the last century utility companies continuously expanded the size of their plants, and power generation became more cost and energy efficient. That is, the per unit costs of electricity decreased, and the ratio of the amount of the energy used to the amount generated increased. Thus, utilities were able to provide more electricity to more people for more uses at lower costs. Declining unit costs for electricity continued until the late 1960s and the early 1970s. This cost trend translated into predictable growth at 7% per annum from the end of World War II until that time. After that time, costs rose due to slowing technical advances, inflation, rising capital costs, more rigorous environmental requirements, and high fuel costs. Since then, the industry and its regulators have been trying to address the changed nature of the industry. This linkage between energy and the economy has been a fundamental assumption of the country's energy policy as noted in Chapter 2. That linkage has also been questioned by critics promoting alternative policies that we will discuss in Chapter 11.

The electricity industry is comprised of three segments— generation, transmission, and distribution. The generation segment has three basic forms. "Base-load" generators are operated continuously to meet customer demand. These units have high capital costs but the lowest operating costs. Base-load plants are most often nuclear powered or coal-fired. "Intermediate load" plants, such as oil fired plants, are used as demand rises. When demand is highest, "peak-load" generators (with low capital costs and high operating costs) are brought into operation. These various generators must be kept in balance to meet demand. The difficult part of the balance is to have enough base-load generation for constant and assured demand, and enough peaking capacity to meet demand increases without having too much excess capacity, i.e., unused generating capacity at the peak. To promote economy and reliability, electric utilities interconnect with each other and transfer their output as demands vary.

Once generated, electricity must be transmitted to an end user or to a local distributor through high voltage lines ranging from 69 kilovolts (kv) to 745 kv. Transmission lines perform an additional function, they form an interconnected grid to attain an industry-wide scale economy. To further attain those economies, utilities entered into voluntary arrangements known as power pools. The first major power pool was the Pennsylvania, New Jersey, Maryland Interconnection (PJM) which served to balance load, realize operating economies, save capital investment and enhance system reliability. Power pools extend throughout the country to form three interconnections east and west of the Rocky Mountains and one in Texas. These grids are further subdivided into regional "electric reliability councils" which also operate on a voluntary basis.

Overall the reliability of the power grid in the United States is the responsibility of a voluntary organization known as the North American Electric Reliability Council (NERC) which includes the three interconnected pools and the Hydro–Quebec System. This is an organization of utilities which was formed in 1968 in reaction to a power failure in the Northeast United States which resulted in blackouts in New York City and other major disruptions. NERC has responsibility for setting reliability standards and for planning coordination of the interconnected power system. Today, as the industry proceeds to restructure, the NERC's effectiveness is being questioned insofar as voluntary operation of the various grids may well not adequately serve the needs of consumers and of society in general and may not provide sufficient reliability for the future.

The distribution segment provides retail delivery of power to customer premises and is in the hands primarily of IOUs, electric cooperatives and municipal utilities. These utilities distribute electricity to three customer classes: residential; commercial, and industrial, each consuming approximately 1 trillion kwh annually. The residential sector generally uses electricity for heating, air conditioning, lighting, refrigeration, and entertainment. The commercial sector includes non-manufacturing businesses, such as hotels, restaurants, retail stores, and the like and has needs similar to the residential sector. Finally, the industrial sector includes construction, manufacturing, mining, agriculture, and the like and this sector consumes electricity not only for heating, lighting, and refrigeration, but also as a primary input into manufacturing processes such as work performed by electric furnaces in steel plants.

B. REGULATORY OVERVIEW[2]

The regulatory history of the electricity industry is the story of how a commodity or service in the public interest is promoted in a mixed market economy. Thus, both private investors and public policymakers are interested in developing the product albeit for perhaps different reasons, i.e. for profit and for political popularity respectively. The story of electricity regulation is complicated by our federal system and the presence of state as well as federal regulators. For the most part, states regulate retail electricity sales and federal regulators address wholesale and interstate sales with courts giving wide berth to federal jurisdiction. See, *FPC v. Southern California Edison Co.* (S.Ct.1964); *FPC v. Conway Corp.* (S.Ct. 1976). However, the relatively neat division of authority between state and federal regulators is changing as restructuring proceeds. See *Mississippi Power & Light Co. v. Mississippi* (S.Ct.1988); *Nantahala Power & Light Co. v. Thornburg* (S.Ct. 1986); *Entergy Louisiana, Inc. v. Louisiana Pub. Serv. Comm'n.* (S.Ct.2003).

The regulatory history of the electric utility industry addresses two sets of interrelated milestones. The first set involves industry events such as a blackout, some form of corporate activity, or a significant economic shift. The second set involves the regulatory responses to such events either in the form of new legislation or new regulation. Indeed, you can best follow this history by paying attention to a handful of statutes, cases, and regulations and by asking what event gave rise to those laws.

2. From Joseph P. Tomain, *Electricity Restructuring: A Case Study for Government Regulation*, 33 Tulsa L.J. 827 (1998). See this article for additional references.

1. Competition 1882–1905

On September 4, 1882, when Thomas Edison switched on the country's first electric generation and distribution project (central station), 85 consumers were able to light their homes and businesses with electric lights rather than by natural or coal gases. Like any start-up industry with a promising technology, growth was vigorous at the start. However, by 1910 Samuel Insull had consolidated the electric industry in Chicago. By 1922, there were 3,774 privately owned electric utilities. In the early stages of the industry, power stations were constrained by existing technologies and did not exceed 10 MW. By contrast, it is not unusual today to have a 1000 MW power plant. With increasing demand for the product, more producers proliferated and the market contained a multiplicity of electric generation stations and distribution plants. Thus, duplication was inevitable. With that duplication came technical problems of incompatibility, excess cost, and reliability, which posed a challenge for the industry and spurred further innovation.

A firm faced with growing demand and vigorous competition naturally tends to seek greater market share through technological innovation, corporate merger, or both. The electric industry did both. The major early technological innovation was the change from direct current to alternating current, a change fostered by George Westinghouse and unsuccessfully, and unwisely, resisted by Edison, which enabled large generating plants to transmit power over longer distances. Coincidentally, the corporate structure changed as firms vertically integrated and expanded generation and distribution capacities in order to capture economies of scale and greater market share. The larger firms also sought to capture economies of scope by building generators, ground conductors, electric fixtures, and even light bulbs. In Edison's own case, several companies merged to become the General Electric Company, today the world's largest corporation. With such vigorous competition in a technologically advancing industry, it was not unlikely that economies of scale would be realized and that concentration would occur.

2. Concentration: 1920–1935

From 1922 to 1927, over 1600 privately-owned electric systems were eliminated as the industry concentrated. To facilitate that concentration, entrepreneurs like Samuel Insull and Henry Villard created holding companies so that by the mid–1920's, 16 holding companies controlled 85 percent of the nation's electric industry. These holding companies helped advance the capture of scale economies but at a real cost to consumers. The power trusts, like the oil trusts before them, were susceptible to stock manipulation and shareholder abuses. And, as with the oil industry, the public reacted sharply to the power trusts as the electricity industry came under scrutiny by state and federal politicians and regulators. At the state level, government was drawn to retail ratesetting in order to protect consumers, and at the federal level government was drawn to curbing trust abuses and making electric service universally available.

3. Regulation: 1935–1965

The federal government entered the field of electricity regulation first with the passage of the Federal Power Act Part I in 1920, 16 U.S.C. §§ 791a–823c. This act regulated hydroelectric power and continues to operate today as amended. We examine hydroelectricity in Chapter 10.

The specific legislative reaction to the abuse of power trusts was the Public Utility Holding Company Act of 1935 (PUHCA). 15 U.S.C. § 79. Even though utilities are, in theory, subject to the antitrust laws, *Otter Tail Power Co. v. United States* (S.Ct.1973), additional legislation was needed. Fundamentally, PUHCA is a registration act requiring holding companies, whose subsidiaries are engaged in either the electric utility business or in the business of the retail distribution of natural or manufactured gas, to register with the Securities and Exchange Commission. A holding company is defined as a company that controls, directly or indirectly, ten percent or more of the voting securities of a public utility. Under the Act, the SEC was authorized to examine the corporate and operational structures of the holding company and to simplify and integrate operations for the purpose of avoiding shareholder abuses. The SEC also has the authority to order divestiture where utility and non-utility operations pose the potential for financial abuse or where electric utility operations are not integrated.

The federal government became more heavily involved with the industry in 1935 with the passage of Part II of the Federal Power Act, 16 U.S.C. §§ 824–824m. This legislation greatly affected the regulation of the industry and was passed in part as a response to the industry's only partial regulation by the states. State regulators had authority over intrastate sales and retail rates. Interstate sales and transmission had been left unregulated and the new statute regulated interstate whole-sales of electric power, thus closing what had come to be known as the *Attleboro Gap* in the regulation of electricity, *Public Utilities Comm'n of Rhode Island v. Attleboro Steam & Elec. Co.* (S.Ct.1927). *Attleboro* had held that states were precluded from regulating the interstate sales of electricity and were limited to retail sales. Today, *Attleboro* has been slightly modified giving states some authority over wholesale transactions. *FERC v. Mississippi* (S.Ct.1982); *Arkansas Elec. Co-op Corp. v. Arkansas Pub. Serv. Comm'n* (S.Ct.1983). Part II of the FPA gave what was then known as the Federal Power Commission the authority to regulate those interstate sales through ratemaking and otherwise. In other words, the heart of the national electric utility industry, interstate generation and transmission, came under federal authority in the form of command-and-control price setting.

The intellectual backbone of federal regulation of the electric industry, as with the regulation of the natural gas industry three years later, was twofold. First, electricity was a product that was deemed to be in the public interest and was highly desirable as a consumer product. The idea that the federal government should promote consumption was a dramatic shift in economic thinking which emanated from the New Deal. Prior to the New Deal, laissez-faire reigned as courts, most notably the United States Supreme Court, see *Lochner v. New York* (S.Ct.1905), maintained a hands-off stance towards private industry. The New Deal dramatically changed that stance and its economic program was based upon the idea that government had a role to play, not only of national economic stability, but of positive growth while encouraging product availability. Thus government assumed an active role in promoting the use and development of certain resources and the promotion of growth of the electric industry as well as the consumption of electric power became central to the New Deal regulatory program.

The second idea that drove electricity regulation was based on the economic notion that natural monopolies had to be regulated in order to keep prices competitive and to avoid economic waste. Better to promote one firm than to have wasteful competition from a multiplicity of firms. In such a market, government regulation is necessary and was advocated by Samuel Insull in 1898. If unchecked, the strongest natural monopoly firm will consolidate until it has monopoly market power and can then visit the sins of monopoly on consumers. See *Jersey Central Power & Light Co. v. FERC* (D.C. Cir. 1987).

Earlier we discussed ratemaking in Chapter 4. The FPC set rates for electricity sold wholesale and interstate using the traditional rate formula which provided utilities with the opportunity to earn profits and invest capital in expansion.

Under Section 205 of the Federal Power Act, tariffs are filed and the rates in those tariffs must be just and reasonable. If a customer believes the rates to be unjust or unreasonable, he (she) may file a complaint and demand a hearing by the Commission to review those rates. The Commission may overturn the rates within five months. Otherwise the rates go into effect subject to rebate. In fact, filed rates are presumed to reflect good faith bargaining. See *United Gas Pipe Line Co. v. Mobile Gas Serv. Corp.* (S.Ct.1956); *FPC v. Sierra Pacific Power Co.* (S.Ct.1956).

During this period, the traditional formula served the industry well. In fact, this period has been called the "golden age" of the electric industry, see Leonard S., Andrew S. & Robert C. Hyman, *America's Electric Utilities: Past, Present and Future* ch. 18 (7th ed. 2000). For privately owned, vertically integrated utilities (IOUs), economies of scale continued as the size of generation units grew. Growth and demand for electricity also grew steadily, doubling every ten years at a rate of roughly seven percent annually. Continued technological advances, together with reliable and predictable growth, caused the average cost of production to stay relatively flat or to decline for this period of time and rates fell continuously. Thus, state public utility commission (PUC) hearings were non-controversial and PUCs had little work to do aside from the occasional rate decrease. Utilities were content because they continued to grow and earn more money. Shareholders were pleased because their stock portfolios were stable. Consumers were satisfied because their rates were modest and generally declining. Indeed, from 1945 to 1965, the price of residential electricity fell 34%. Id at 58. And legislators and regulators were content because there were no political costs associated with electricity regulation. Once technological advances subsided, this complacency changed.

4. Regulatory Failure: 1965–1980

The regulatory compact, establishing a government protected monopoly operating essentially under a cost plus rate formula, works well in an expanding economy with accompanying technological advances. Under such circumstances, industry growth occurs while prices stabilize or fall. However, when economies of scale and technological advances subside, then the cost of doing business increases. An increased cost of doing business can have negative effects on any business. It can have disastrous effects on a regulated business whose activities are constrained because of regulations.

In economic terms, starting approximately in 1965, the marginal costs of utility operations began to exceed its average costs resulting in a profitability squeeze. This economic situation is disastrous for a regulated firm whose earnings are calculated on prudently incurred historic costs. The traditional rate formula is based on historic (average) costs. As a firm continues to take advantage of economies of scale, its average costs decline and the firm can expand its capital investment, thus earning a reasonable rate of return on that investment. However, when marginal costs exceed average costs, then profits fall until rates are set at marginal cost. Further, just as microeconomic theory predicts, increased costs bring higher prices and higher prices mean declining demand.

This change in the financial circumstances of electric utilities came at a particularly inopportune time because utilities were investing billions of dollars in nuclear plants because nuclear power promised to be cleaner and cheaper than coal for electricity generation. For many utilities, their nuclear investments turned sour as those plants resulted in enormous cost overruns and plant cancellations. Those expenditures had to be covered either by shareholders or ratepayers and, as we explain in Chapter 9, federal and state regulators apportioned those losses.

During this period, electric utilities, with the rest of the economy, faced inflation, rising labor costs, the collapse of the nuclear power industry, and the OPEC and Arab Oil Embargoes. These economic events put great pressure on utilities to raise prices at an unprecedented pace, causing rate shock among consumers and dramatic political repercussions for state regulatory commissions. Rising prices also revealed that there was more price elasticity of demand for electricity than previously assumed. As utilities overexpanded and tried to capture their high fixed costs, electricity rates rose and consumers, contrary to expectations, consumed less electricity than predicted.

5. PURPA's Surprise: Increased Competition

The combined effects of the political and economic events in the late 1960s and early 1970s raised general public concern about the country's energy future and raised particular concern, as noted, in the White House. PURPA was the surprising part of President Carter's National Energy Act. PURPA encouraged states to move away from declining block ratemaking because it promoted consumption; toward marginal cost pricing because it was more efficient; and, encouraged independent power production through co-generation and small power generation (80 megawatts or less) as energy sources alternative to large public utilities. See *FERC v. Mississippi* (S.Ct.1982). These smaller sources of generation were known as qualifying facilities (QF's) and PURPA was more successful than people imagined. Not only did QF's conserve power, QF's also became new (and cheaper) generation sources.

The Federal Energy Regulatory Commission (FERC), the renamed Federal Power Commission under the Department of Energy Organization Act, further assisted the development of new generation sources by requiring that local public utilities buy excess power generated by QF's at the "full avoided cost." See *American Paper Inst., Inc. v. American Elec. Power Serv.*

Corp. (S.Ct.1983). The local utility, in other words, had to connect with cogenerators and small power producers and purchase any excess electricity generated by the QF at the *utility's* "full avoided cost" which was the utility's marginal cost of electricity. Utilities which had over-expanded their facilities had to buy a competitor's electricity not at the prevailing market value, but at the utility's own higher cost of producing electricity. Needless to say, new producers found this market attractive. If you are an entrepreneur selling a low cost product to a guaranteed purchaser, what do you do other than produce as much of that lower cost product as possible particularly if you can sell at a guaranteed higher price? PURPA, unintentionally, discovered a new generation market.

It should be apparent that the stage for competition was then set. Traditional, rate-regulated utilities (IOUs) followed the rules, earned favorable, stable returns but overbuilt. The overbuilds and capacity built at excess cost raised the utilities' fixed costs. These utilities needed to recover their fixed costs but consumers balked for two reasons. First, in some instances consumers were asked to pay for capital expenditures that generated little or no electricity. Consumers did not want to pay something for nothing. Second, consumers, especially large industrial, fuel-switchable firms, saw the availability of cheaper electricity and they wanted to purchase that product. The question then became: How do consumers get to the cheaper electricity?

Non-utility generators (NUGs) of various sorts, including QFs, were perceived as being able to generate electricity at a lower cost than traditional public utilities. Consequently, consumers wanted to take advantage of new sources of cheaper electricity, and free market advocates of deregulation thought this was a good idea. What surprised everyone was how much new non-utility generated electricity was available and how eager new generators were to enter the market. The success of PURPA revealed that traditional regulation had run its course. Generating units, with then existing technologies, could not continue to get bigger and commercial nuclear power was not "too cheap to meter." In microeconomic terms, the traditional, regulated electric industry had reached the end of its scale economies. In other words, unregulated producers existed that were willing to supply the market with electricity priced lower than the electricity being supplied by incumbent regulated utilities and the new entrants profited by doing so with a little help from government.

It is at this point in the regulatory story that transmission becomes important and regulators, especially FERC, begin to rethink its regulation. While QFs could sell their power to the local utility, they did not have access to the utility's transmission lines to "wheel" their power to any other utility or end user. Consequently, the creation of QFs had two dramatic effects. First, their existence marked the formal introduction of competition into generation. Second, the purchase requirement began to force open the transmission access door.

Electricity transmission is known as a bottleneck, i.e. electricity must go through a few privately owned high voltage transmission lines to get from generator to distributor. Because these transmission lines are privately owned, they are not common carriers available for use by anyone willing to pay for the transportation service. Instead, private owners are motivated to favor their affiliates with low prices and disfavor their competitors with high ones. If the emerging market was to work, transmission access had to open.

PURPA raised questions about the natural monopoly rationale for regulating the electric industry because of apparent competition in generation. See Peter Z. Grossman & Daniel H. Cole (eds.), *The End of Natural Monopoly: Deregulation and Competition in the Electric Power Industry* (2003). Transmission, however, was and is still a natural monopoly bottleneck which is pivotal for the operation of the electric industry. Id. at ch. 6. Transmission must also maintain an adequate and reliable flow of electricity through the system. Consequently, the transmission segment must have adequate *capacity*, maintain *reliability*, avoid *congestion*, and do so at *reasonable* prices with *no discrimination*.

PURPA, thus, caused a rethinking of regulation at both ends of the fuel cycle. At the generation end, the market was competitive. See Richard D. Cudahy, *PURPA: The Intersection of Competition and Regulatory Policy*, 16 ENERGY L.J. 419 (1995). At the buyers' end, consumers wanted to purchase the cheaper electricity. Unfortunately, a full-scale move to market rates was problematic not only because of the transmission problem, but also because market rates had uneven effects on consumers. All consumers are not similarly situated. Large consumers have more leverage to bargain for discounts because they buy larger quantities of electricity and they can switch fuels more easily. Further, often small users are cross-subsidized and market prices may not be favorable to them. This situation poses several challenges for regulators including: (1) encouraging new entrants; (2) not saddling incumbents with stranded costs; (3) maintaining affordable rates for small consumers; and (4) assuring reliability.

C. THE CURRENT SITUATION IN THE ELECTRIC INDUSTRY

The history of the electric industry demonstrates that regulation enabled the country to build an electric infrastructure and provide universal service. It is also the case that today the traditional regulatory scheme has satisfied its purpose and that the industry and its regulation must find a more competitive form. Two large issues loom before that more competitive environment takes shape—transmission must be transformed and a new market must be designed. Over the last three years both issues have been seriously challenged.

Transmission owners have no obligation to serve all customers. Even though transmission is an essential facility, historically it has not had common carrier status. In other words, absent regulation to the contrary, owners of transmission facilities can price discriminate; they can also favor themselves and their affiliates. Additionally, competition exists between public and private electricity providers. The key impediment to an open and competitive market is that because the transmission segment is privately owned, its managers have a fiduciary duty to their shareholders to maximize value. Private owners will raise prices to what the market can bear. There is little incentive to give up either ownership or operation.

Conceptually, the current problem facing the electric industry is simple. Allow access to transmission systems so that cheaper sources of supply can get to consumers willing to buy. In this way competition is promoted and prices should decline. However, an industry that has been heavily regulated for nearly a century finds the access idea hard to accept because capital investments in transmission must be recovered. Regulators must now do two things: First, develop a system of open access to transmission systems; and, second, deal with those costs incurred under traditional utility regulation. These problems of wheeling and stranded costs, respectively, are issues that currently confront federal and state regulators and are the subject of new federal and state regulation.

1. The Energy Policy Act of 1992

By the early 1990s, PURPA made two things clear. First, alternative power producers wanted to get into the market. Second, the market was not as robust as it could be because transmission access was not open because of two limiting factors. Non-utility generators, other than QFs, found it difficult to enter the market because they had to follow PUHCA requirements. These generators were particularly desirable because they could provide new generation at a lower cost. The second constraint was FERC's lack of a workable authority to mandate wheeling over transmission lines. PURPA in

1978 had provided wheeling authority (§§ 211–212), but it was saddled with unworkable conditions.

In 1992, Congress passed the Energy Policy Act (EPAct), Pub. L. No. 102–486, 106 Stat. 2776, and partially eliminated both constraints. EPAct advanced restructuring by authorizing firms exclusively in the business of selling electric energy at wholesale, called exempt wholesale generators (EWGs), to be exempt from PUHCA's ownership restrictions 15 U.S.C. § 79z–5a. This exemption set the stage for the development of a more competitive, and unregulated, wholesale market. Second, EPAct authorized FERC to order utilities that owned transmission facilities to transmit wholesale power over their systems. The Act gave FERC broad authority subject to a public interest standard to order transmission owning entities to wheel power for wholesale transactions at the request of a broad range of potential applicants involved in wholesale power transactions. However, EPAct prohibited FERC from ordering access to transmission for retail power. 15 U.S.C. § 79z–5b. See also, Richard D. Cudahy, *Retail Wheeling: Is This Revolution Necessary?*, 15 ENERGY L.J. 351 (1994). EPAct advanced the restructuring ball by promoting EWGs and by opening transmission access. It remained for FERC to implement the Act.

2. FERC Initiatives

FERC implemented EPAct with Order No. 888, 18 C.F.R. pts. 35, 385, and Order No. 889, 18 C.F.R. pt. 37. Order No. 888 requires public utilities that own or operate transmission facilities in interstate commerce to file open access non-discriminatory transmission tariffs that contain minimum terms and conditions for non-discriminatory service. Order 888 also requires utilities to "functionally unbundle" their transmission service from their generation and power marketing functions, and to provide unbundled ancillary transmission services. The unbundling was intended to reduce or eliminate opportunities for self-dealing by utilities owning both generation and transmission facilities. Functional unbundling means that the activities are treated separately within the corporation without necessarily being put into separate corporate entities. In short, utilities were being required to separate their generation and transmission functions.

Utilities were required to file separate tariffs with separate rates, terms, and conditions for wholesale generation service, transmission service, and any ancillary services, 61 Fed. Reg. 21, 540–01, 21,552 (May 10, 1996). Ancillary services include activities taken to affect transmission such as scheduling and dispatching, and services necessary to maintain the integrity of the transmission system. To ensure that a utility does not favor itself with its own transmission facilities, the order required utilities to take transmission service and ancillary services for all of its new wholesale sales and purchases of electricity under the same tariff that applies to outside users of its transmission.

Open transmission on a non-discriminatory basis is needed to create a more robust competitive market in wholesale power by allowing generation access to more customers. FERC estimated that open access transmission would save U.S. electric consumers between $3.8 and $5.4 billion a year as well as encourage more technical innovation in the industry. 61 Fed. Reg. at 21, 540–01, 21,675 (May 10, 1996). To help assure reliability, the order provided utilities with a fair opportunity to recover prudently incurred regulatory costs as well as the costs of making the transition to a competitive wholesale market.

Order No. 889 established an electronic information system to promote competition. This system, called OASIS (open access same-time information system), provides existing and potential transmission users the same access to transmission information that the transmission owner enjoys. Order No. 889 also requires public utilities to comply with standards of conduct intended to preclude anticompetitive behavior by transmission owners, such as favoring affiliated generators or power marketers with transmission services.

At the wholesale level, Orders 888 and 889 had a dramatic impact on the industry and Order No. 888 has been largely upheld in *New York v. FERC* (S.Ct.2002). Since their inception, the industry has experienced significant changes including the development of retail competition in the states; the divestiture of generating units by traditional utilities; an increase in energy company mergers; a notable increase in the number of power marketers and independent generators; and, the establishment of independent system operators to manage transmission. Those orders, however, did not address either retail wheeling or the appropriate organizational form for a transmission facility.

To this point, interregional coordination has proceeded on a voluntary basis. FERC believes that the voluntary coordination that previously existed is no longer effective because the volunteer groups are "not vested with the broad decision-making authority needed to address larger issues that affect an entire region, including managing congestion, planning and investing in new transmission facilities, pancaking transmission access charges, the absence of secondary markets in transmission services, and the possible disincentives created by the level and structure of transmission rates." To facilitate greater coordination and greater access in transmission, FERC has been promoting the use of regional transmission organizations (RTOs).

To further industry restructuring, FERC proposed and adopted Order No. 2000, 18 C.F.R. pts. 34–35, designed to formalize the formation of independent transmission organizations under the name Regional Transmission Organizations (RTOs). RTOs are independent of the owners of generation facilities either through a physical separation or through separate corporate entities. RTOs manage the transmission systems either for profit as owners or as not-for-profit operators. Since the inception of the RTO order, FERC has proposed various regional markets. Today, however, FERC is moving toward the development of a nation-wide seamless, transparent, and competitive market. See Joseph P. Tomain, *The Persistence of Natural Monopoly*, 16 NAT. RESOURCES & ENV'T 242 (Spring 2002); Lisa G. Dowden, *The RTO in Your Future: What Should Your Clients Know?*, 16 NAT. RESOURCES & ENV'T, 247 (Spring 2002).

In FERC's opinion, Order 2000 was necessary because the market was insufficiently competitive due to engineering and economic inefficiencies, and continued opportunities for discrimination. Regarding engineering and economic inefficiencies, FERC found that:

- The reliability of the bulk power system was being stressed;
- There were increasing difficulties in computing transmission capacity;
- Regional coordination was desirable for congestion management;
- There was increased uncertainty with transmission planning and expansion; and,
- Pancaked rates hindered market development.

Regarding undue discrimination, FERC was concerned both with self-dealing and the appearance of self-dealing because both retarded the development of competitive markets. Overt self-dealing occurs when a utility owning transmission and generation charges itself a transmission charge lower than that charged to other customers, giving itself a competitive edge. The appearance of self-dealing raises the transaction costs of doing business because the market is not seen as reliable, thus reducing efficiency gains from competition.

Order 2000 describes two fundamental approaches to creating RTOs—the non-profit independent system operator (ISO) and the for profit independent transmission company (transco). FERC Order 2000 establishes the parameters for any

RTO which may take either form or some hybrid. FERC set four minimum standards for any RTO. An RTO must have:

- Independence from market participants
- Regional scope of operations
- Authority to plan and expand
- An "open architecture" policy to allow structural modifications

The Order also sets out the minimum functions that an RTO must perform including:

- Tariff administration and design
- Congestion management
- OASIS participation
- Market monitoring
- Planning and expansion
- Interregional coordination

FERC continues to take the position that an RTO can be an ISO or a Transco although most RTOs are non-profit ISOs. In addition, FERC has attempted to set RTO conditions, some of which have not survived judicial scrutiny. *Atlantic City Elec. Co. v. FERC* (D.C. Cir. 2002) (FERC did not have authority to require utility to give up rate filing rights under FPA or to require FERC permission to leave RTO); *Atlantic City Elec. Co. v. FERC* (D.C. Cir. 2003) (same).

The central force behind the non-profit ISO form of RTO is as an operator of the transmission system. As such, the ISO owns no facilities. Rather, it operates transmission facilities that are made available to it by generating units. The ISO exists to serve the public interest in having available for consumers reasonably priced, reliable electricity. The situation of a non-profit as a non-owner operator of transmission units presents certain complications. The first complication is its relationship with the generators. The ISO is to be "independent" of a generator, specifically to avoid self-dealing. At what point does an independent board have adequate understanding of the industry and sufficient influence with generators such that it can encourage generators to invest in maintenance and expansion of transmission facilities? The Board of Directors of the ISO will have a fiduciary duty running either to the state or to the federal government, whoever gives the ISO its charter. Consequently, they have some motivation to act independently and they have motivation to keep the ISO in business, which is to say to keep electricity running through the system.

Not surprisingly, most industry arguments are made in favor of the for-profit Transco. The arguments against the ISO generally focus on insufficient incentives. The insufficient incentives come from hypotheses about profit motivation. Critics argue, for example, that while an ISO may have an incentive to maintain the short-term reliability of the system, its distance from ownership of facilities gives it little incentive or control over long-term reliability. Following this analysis, critics argue that the ISO has little ability or incentive to make capital investments in plant, innovate through the use of new technologies, or engage in cost-setting for management efficiencies.

The arguments critical of ISOs mirror the arguments in favor of Transcos. Again, the central variable for the Transco is that it is a for-profit company which both owns and operates transmission assets. Its for-profit motivation is designed to maximize the value of the company and to return income and value to shareholders. Shareholders, of course, elect the Board of Directors and, presumably, conflict of interest rules will prevent unfair advantages going to generators. Similarly, the incentives for the Transco mirror the disincentives for the ISO. Because the Transco is profit-motivated, it must necessarily invest in plant maintenance and innovation. It must also maintain short-term and long-term reliability. The arguments in favor of the Transco, given its profit motivation, however, should not be taken too far. It is also the case that a profit-driven Transco may pay more attention to short-term gains; may cut costs in a way that affects reliability; and, may price discriminate where it is economically wise to do so.

The non-profit nature of the ISO presents problems as does the for-profit nature of the Transco. There are, however, alternatives available. One alternative is to engage in a transitional movement starting with an ISO moving to a Transco. The other alternative is to create an ISO or a Transco and apply performance-based rates that allow a sharing of profits between ratepayers and shareholders. Regardless of form, however, Transcos and ISOs must achieve five goals. Every RTO must have sufficient capacity; provide reliable service; manage congestion; not discriminate; and, offer reasonable prices.

In theory, the RTO order makes sense, i.e. access is needed to make the electricity market competitive. However, three impediments have prevented FERC from achieving its goal of having all utilities in an RTO by the initial target date of December 15, 2001. This goal has been stymied by the voluntary nature of the order, the desire by utilities to continue to control their private property, and federalism.

Because the electricity industry is dually regulated, restructuring must proceed on both federal and state levels. While a regulatory bright line can be drawn between interstate wholesale sales of electricity and retail sales, that bright line is one of political convenience only, not physical reality. Historically, the federal government limited its reach to interstate wholesale sales and left retail regulation to the states. Regulatory restructuring has continued to follow this division between state and federal regulation. This continued allegiance to dual regulation may have made political sense at one time. It does not make good economic sense today. Unfortunately, federal-state coordination remains elusive.

Regarding federalism, the idea that utilities would restructure and join ranks for the purpose of freeing transmission access has not taken hold as utilities jockey for position. So too state regulators have not been eager to cede power to the FERC or to newly formed RTOs even to the point of imposing barriers to utilities seeking to join RTOs. FERC decided to slow down and assess the RTO process through a series of public hearings. On November 21, 2001, FERC issued an order entitled *Electricity Market Design and Structure*, Docket No. RM01–12–000 reaffirming its commitment to the RTO process by more fully defining required RTO services; engaging state regulators; performing an RTO cost-benefit study; and, developing a standard market design including proposed tariffs and interconnection agreements. Interconnection agreements are separately addressed in Docket No. RM02–1–000. This docket is also known as Standard Market Design (SMD).

FERC's major SMD Notice of Proposed Rulemaking (NOPR) was issued on July 31, 2002 in Docket No. RM01–12–000. The SMD NOPR has yet to be finalized and together with Order Nos. 888 and 2000 comprises the bulk of a new national electricity market through an attempt to "bring the industry within a single set of rules governing FERC's regulation of the wholesale side of the industry." James H. McGrew, *FERC: Federal Energy Regulatory Commission* 183 (2003).

FERC's most recent SMD plans are set out in a white paper entitled "Wholesale Power Market Platform" (April 28, 2003) available as are all statutes, rules, regulations, and reports at www.ferc.gov. In that document FERC declares its goals for a standardized national electricity market:

> Our goals continue to be reliable, reasonably priced electric service for all customers; sufficient electric infrastructure; transparent markets with fair rules for all market participants; stability and regulatory certainty for customers, the electric power industry, and investors; technological innovation; and efficient use of the nation's resources. Further, providing regulatory certainty for the

industry and investors in order to build needed infrastructure is a critical need facing the energy industry and requires Commission action. *Id* at 1.

According to FERC, "Healthy and well-functioning wholesale power markets are central to the national economy, and we believe that regional, independent operation of the transmission systems, with proven market rules in place is the critical platform for the future success of electric markets." *Id.* at 2.

FERC proposes to accomplish this goal by, among other things:

- Requiring all FERC jurisdictional utilities to join an RTO.
- All RTOs, together with state regulators and market participants, will conduct regional transmission expansion studies.
- Costs for transmission facilities will be fairly allocated without pancaked rates.
- Each RTO will establish an independent market monitor and establish market power mitigation measures.
- Adopt a transparent and efficient transmission congestion management system.

Congress requested FERC to conduct an independent cost-benefit study assessing the impact of the SMD NOPR. The results were reported in *Impacts of the Federal Energy Regulatory Commission's Proposal for Standard Market Design* (April 30, 2003) (DOE/S–0138), which findings include:

- SMD would facilitate competitive markets in electricity.
- Total consumer savings (after SMD costs) are estimated at $700 million to $1 billion per year.
- Retail prices should decline 1%; wholesale prices should decline between 1% and 2%.
- SMD should improve safety and reliability.

In short, the design and construction of a nationally integrated market will require a fully interconnected grid that maintains the reliable provision of electricity at competitive prices. This goal is ambitious and necessary if the restructuring efforts are to be successful.

D. AN INDUSTRY IN CRISIS

It is at this point in the developing history of the electricity industry and its regulation that two new words, and one old one, enter our vocabulary. California and Enron are the new words and blackout is the old one. Since the summer of 2000, the California electricity crisis and the Enron debacle appear to demonstrate the failure of electricity restructuring. That appearance is misleading even though the restructuring movement has been slowed. As of January, 2004 five states have delayed restructuring activities, California has suspended action, 17 states and the District of Columbia are active, and 27 states are listed as inactive. See http://www.eia.doe.gov/cneaf/electricity/chg_str/regmap.html. Both the California restructuring effort and Enron's energy trading *modus operandi* were the products of design failure and faulty factual assumptions. They were not necessarily the result of faulty theoretical assumptions about making the market more competitive. Indeed, although both were failed attempts, California's electricity restructuring and Enron's energy trading point to the future of the electric industry.

1. California

There is no shortage of analyses of the California electricity crisis. See e.g., James L. Sweeney, THE CALIFORNIA ELECTRICITY CRISIS (2002); Severin Borenstein et al., *Measuring Market Inefficiencies in California's Restructured Wholesale Electricity Market* (Univ. of Calif. Energy Inst., CSEM WP 102, June 2002); Paul L. Joskow, *California's Electricity Crisis*, 17 OX-FORD REV. OF ECON. POLICY (December 2001). The crisis resulted in prices beyond any previously recognized level and in a bankruptcy filing by Pacific Gas & Electric, one of California's Big Three utilities. These market disruptions were created by poor predictions about demand, a hot summer, a dry Northwest, high natural gas prices, miscalculations about supply, air quality requirements in the Los Angeles basin, no new generation, a poor regulatory design, and, perhaps most significantly, market manipulation.

Although the California crisis has passed, and prices have lowered and blackouts, rolling or otherwise, are not on the horizon, there are lessons to be learned from the California experience. See Richard D. Cudahy, *Electricity Deregulation After California: Down But Not Out*, 54 ADMIN. L. REV. 333 (2002). Chief among these lessons involves regulatory design, the crux of which was an inflexible market for buying, selling, and pricing electricity which enabled market manipulation. There are three notable aspects to this design, one of which was certainly fatal. First, the major public utilities in California divested many of their generating units while maintaining an obligation to serve their customers. As long as costs are passed through to consumers, the obligation to serve does not present a severe problem because the utilities earn money to pay their bills. This pass-through was not allowed in the California restructuring scheme. Second, two new regulatory entities were established, the California Power Exchange (PX) which set prices, and the California Independent System Operator (ISO) which directed the movement of electricity through the system. The PX was the market mechanism intended to make the industry competitive. The PX and the ISO are perfectly appropriate entities, if properly designed.

The third and fatal flaw design element was the price restrictions. Price restrictions were the medicine intended to help the consumers but killed the restructuring. Utilities had to buy wholesale energy at market price from the PX in no more than day-ahead or hour-ahead markets which meant that they could not enter long-term contracts. These spot-market wholesale purchases were subject to a great deal of volatility and the highest bid set the price. At the same time, retail prices to consumers were capped until the utility recovered its stranded costs. San Diego Gas & Electric was able to capture its stranded costs and be relieved of the price cap. This situation, however, caused prices to rise significantly for San Diego's customers who launched vehement protests and the Legislature reimposed a price cap. The problem was that the utilities bought in the spot-market at extraordinarily high prices and sold in a lower priced capped retail market, thus putting themselves in a credit crunch with high profits for outside producers, high prices to some consumers, and a political crisis for the Governor. The market distortion was aggravated by the fact that the retail cap sent consumers the wrong price signals. They had little incentive to conserve and, to aggravate matters, California had stopped bringing power plants on-line.

There are several culprits to blame for the California energy crisis of 2000. Governor Gray Davis blames the owners of power production as "out-of-state profiteers" for allegedly withholding power from California utilities in an attempt to drive up prices. His suspicions were correct. Consumer groups blamed the same energy companies as well as California politicians willing to bail out the California power retailers, such as SoCal Edison, Pacific Gas and Electric (PG & E), and San Diego Gas and Electric (SDG & E). The out-of-state owners of energy production, Dynegy, Duke Energy, and Enron criticized the California politicians and bureaucrats that crafted a system that allowed the generators to capitalize on the circumstances that led to the problems in California. And, state regulators blamed FERC for its failure to act expeditiously.

By December 2000, the crisis had not eased. Early that month, the ISO declared Stage 2 power alerts. At this point, federal intervention was needed. The ISO needed FERC to cap a limit on wholesale energy rates and Energy Secretary Bill Richardson ordered out-of-state suppliers to send their electricity to California under threat of federal intervention by way of price setting. Additionally, the utilities' credit was threatened. Chase Manhattan Bank led a consortium to oppose a $5 billion credit line extended to SoCal Edison based on fears that the loan would not be repaid and Standard and Poor's lowered SoCal Edison's and PG & E's credit ratings.

Events were so problematic that drastic steps, including state ownership, were openly discussed. Governor Davis and others called for a regional price cap, long-term contracts for purchasing power, and the creation of a state power authority that would issue bonds to help the utilities to pay their bills, and to take over the transmission system owned by the Big Three utilities. The leading consumer group in California, the Foundation for Taxpayer and Consumer Rights'; proposed to end deregulation immediately fearing that long-term contracts would lead to higher prices. Consumers were opposed to a bailout of privately owned utilities for the same reason.

Governor Davis asked the California Legislature for more authority to finance power plant construction, take over ownership, and borrow money for investigators to determine whether power plants that are shutting down for "unscheduled maintenance" actually need to be fixed, and repeal the law requiring the Big Three utilities to sell their remaining plants, thus keeping out-of-state generators from buying the plants.

By January, 2001, bankruptcy threatened as utilities had difficulty meeting their bills to purchase power and out-of-state suppliers had become hesitant to supply power because bills were not being paid. On January 17, California imposed statewide rolling blackouts for the first time. The next day, Governor Davis declared a State of Emergency over the power crisis and asked the legislature to authorize emergency funds to keep electricity on for the next seven to ten days. The utilities agreed not to go to court if the Legislature passed a bill allowing the utilities to enter into long-term contracts with suppliers, which would then be resold to consumers at a cost set by the state plus a modest charge. On January 18, the legislature approved spending hundreds of millions of dollars to keep power flowing in California and Governor Davis signed legislation making the Department of Water Resources the main buyer of power.

By the middle of February, Governor Davis announced that the state would buy the utilities' transmission system, the utilities' parent companies would provide them with cash to pay off their debts, the utilities would keep the power they produced at their own plants for ten years, and the utilities would drop all lawsuits against the state. The winners in deregulation were out-of-state owners of generating plants who were able to take advantage of a poorly-crafted law for their own benefit.

Although the failure of California's deregulation effort frightened many other states considering similar ideas, other states have enjoyed success. Pennsylvania, for example, has deregulated but with an entirely different approach, the success of which is not clear. Utilities are allowed to keep their generating plants, and the phasing in of market prices is over a ten-year period. Utilities that could buy power for less would make a profit, those that could not make a profit would have to absorb the loss. Any utilities that sold their generating plants were forced to enter long-term contracts with suppliers. Perhaps the most remarkable turn of events is that FERC did step in with price caps, and other investigations, and the crisis passed by 2001.

2. Enron

Enron's role as power marketer and energy trader is exactly what a deregulated electricity market needs. Unfortunately, its bankruptcy and ensuing civil and criminal investigations prevent Enron from fulfilling that role. Because demand requires instantaneous supply (i.e., reliability), there must be some mechanism to assure that supply. In the traditional regulated environment, the local utility maintained adequate reserves to satisfy demand. In unregulated or deregulated markets, consumers protect themselves either with contracts for futures or with back-up power. Enron bought and sold futures contracts and helped make a market in electricity, and other products and services. Enron was the industry leader in taking advantage of deregulation and restructuring. It was estimated that Enron controlled about one-quarter of the country's energy trading.

Enron was a small traditional natural gas pipeline firm that went on to become a huge company with market capitalization of $60–70 billion. It also transformed its business from a stodgy enterprise to a high flying trader which traded in electricity futures, bandwidth, advertising space, and even weather features. In the end, Enron became less an energy company than it did a hedge fund. It had a difficult enough time explaining its business even to its CEO, ultimately collapsing into bankruptcy. Nevertheless, energy futures can be an effective way to provide reliable sources of electricity, supplement the reserve margins held by traditional utilities, and control price uncertainty. Futures, then, can work with either power exchanges or ISOs to stabilize electricity markets.

Enron's collapse, however, has little to say about energy markets in general or even hedge funds in particular. Nor should its collapse have much to do with a change in direction for energy deregulation. As Congress, the Justice Department, and the Securities Exchange Commission continue investigation into Enron, the deregulation of the energy industry continues as Enron sells off assets and settles lawsuits and other companies take up futures trading where Enron left off.

Enron played into the design flaw in California's restructuring by enabling it and other companies to manipulate the wholesale and retail markets to the tune of hundreds of millions of dollars. See Jacqueline Lang Weaver, *Can Energy Markets Be Trusted? The Effect of the Rise and Fall of Enron on Energy Markets*, HOUSTON BUSINESS AND TAX LAW J. 1 (2004) (available www.hbtlj.com). In fact, investigations indicate that this was the case together with a number of other market manipulation practices neatly set out in internal Enron documents. See, news.findlaw.com/wp/docs/enron/specinv020102rpt1.pdf, www.ferc.gov/Electric/bulkpower/PA02–2/pa02–2.htm.

The most frequent market abuse was the practice of round-tripping of energy, also known as "wash trades." FERC defined wash trades as the sale of electricity "to another company together with a simultaneous purchase of the same product at the same price." The round-trip starts with one energy-trading company selling electricity to another. Simultaneously, the second firm sells the same electricity, at the same price, back to the first company. There are two effects of wash trades. First, there is the appearance of doing business and of market activity. Second, these trades push up the numbers on a company's books making the company look more healthy financially than it is. Both effects are empty of any financial substance.

Although the Securities and Exchange Commission (SEC) has been prosecuting brokers using wash trades in securities, the practice was apparently not illegal in the unregulated market. This trading activity inflated electricity prices because demand appeared to increase. According to one energy company, CMS Energy, the round-trip trades were done solely to boost trading volumes for marketing to try and attract new business. If there is a determination by FERC that prices were driven up as the result of round-tripping, the likely lawsuits would lead to situations similar to that of Enron.

Enron used four other schemes in order to capitalize on the inadequacies of the California deregulation laws. The first strategy, known as "Death Star," involved Enron receiving payments for relieving congestion by transporting energy away from congested areas to out-of-state locations. When the transmission paths became too congested in certain areas of

California, Enron would be paid to generate power or to send power in another direction. The power was then imported back into the state, with the effect that Enron was paid for relieving congestion without actually moving any energy or relieving congestion because these trades were simply paper sales.

The next strategy was known to Enron officials as "Fat Boy." In the day-ahead ISO market, Enron would schedule an artificially high number of megawatts to be delivered to one of its subsidiaries thus threatening congestion. The subsidiary would receive the energy, but only use a fraction of the energy. Under the California rules, Enron had to be paid a percentage. However, while Enron was paid for power it did not need to produce, its actions actually had the effect of counteracting other energy companies, which frequently kept their plants from running at full capacity in order to raise prices thus creating an electricity shortage.

Another strategy used by Enron was known as "Get Shorty." Enron agreed to provide ancillary services in the day-ahead market and then provided these services through buying them at a lower price in the hour-ahead market. At no time, however, did Enron actually have the services to sell on the day-ahead market, so Enron provided falsified information to identify ancillary services sources.

The final strategy used by Enron negatively affected people inside California and in other Western power markets as well. Dubbed "Ricochet," Enron would buy wholesale power on the California market at $250/MWh, which was the capped rate. Enron would then sell the power in other deregulated power markets that were also suffering from shortages, such as Washington. Since rates were not capped in other states, Enron was able to sell the power purchased in California at a higher rate, sometimes reaching $1,200/MWh. By exporting the power out of California, Enron was also contributing to the power shortages in California by decreasing the amount of power available on the market.

While much of the publicity regarding market manipulation focused on Enron, that company was not alone in its fraudulent trading. Dynergy paid a $3 million fine to the SEC and a $5 million fine to the Commodity Futures Trading Commission, and the Williams Cos. settled a suit with California for $150 million. All in all what appeared to be a $300 billion industry collapsed with investors losing billions of dollars. Further, deregulatory efforts have slowed as questions arise not so much about whether to have energy trading but how to do it. Trading will be necessary for reliable supplies in a competitive market. The difficult question is how much regulation of energy trading will be necessary.

FERC staff issued its Final Report on Price Manipulation in Western Markets (Galinas Report) on March 26, 2003 http://www.ferc/gov/industries/electric/indus-act/wem/pa02–2/orders.asp. The Galinas Report found that market design helped facilitate market manipulation and that Enron and other firms engaged in gaming practices. As a result of the findings, FERC ordered show cause orders to over 40 power trading companies alleged to have engaged in the manipulation.

These companies will appear in trial-type hearings to determine whether or not they did so engage. If so, they can be asked to disgorge profits and FERC may withdraw market-based rate authority in certain instances. Additionally, the Galinas Report and other investigations have resulted in settlements with energy traders. See e.g. Dockets No. EL02–113–000 et al.; EL03–17–000 et al.; Investigation of Certain Enron–Affiliated *QFs*, 104 FERC ¶ 61,126 (2003).

In an associated proceeding, FERC issued final orders regarding market-based rate behavior. Order Amending Market–Based Tariffs and Authorizations, 105 FERC ¶ 61,218 (2003). The purpose of the order is to curtail the market manipulations used during the California energy crisis by Enron and others. The new behavior rules prohibit certain conduct including the following:

- Generating units must follow a set of established rules and regulations.

- Behaviors "without a legitimate business purpose" such as wash trades or transactions based on false data, collusion with trading partners, or taking units out of service are prohibited.

- All information provided to FERC, RTOs, ISOs, or like entities must be factual, accurate, and complete.

- Reports to publishers of price indices must be accurate and factual and not knowingly false, misleading, or incomplete.

- Price records and reports to index publishers must be maintained for three years.

- Sellers must comply with FERC's code of conduct and cannot collude with others to violate that code.

We thus find ourselves in the anomalous position of wanting to move to the market to allow free trading and, at the same time, trying to prevent collusion and manipulation. Investigations by FERC, the SEC, Congress, and others, as well as new rules for market behavior should uncover anomalies in the market. It remains to be seen whether or not a workable market for trading can be designed.

3. Blackout

On August 14, 2003, the United States and portions of Canada experienced the largest blackout in history with dramatic effects on eight states and two Canadian provinces. According to DOE officials, the blackout caused three deaths, forced 12 airport closures, and sporadic looting. The blackout also affected over 50 million people with over $6 trillion in lost economic activity. The blackout began at 4:00 in the afternoon on the East Coast, and power was not restored for two days in some parts of the country. On August 15, President Bush and

Prime Minister John Crétien created a joint task force which issued its report, *Final Report on the August 14, 2003 Blackout in the United States and Canada* (April 2004). The finding that the utility First Energy in Ohio, as well as the regional agency that was to oversee it, the Midwest Independent System Operator (MISO), failed to respond in a timely manner to signals of problems in the transmission grid. The immediate problem seemed to be untrimmed tree limbs affecting First Energy power lines. Nevertheless, the MISO oversight agency should have been able to redirect power and prevent the blackout.

The report has been criticized, not surprisingly, by First Energy. It is more likely the case that a whole series of cascading events caused the widespread blackout. Regardless of initial blame or fault, the blackout does underscore the fragility of the existing grid and the need for more uniform and stronger reliability standards and oversight.

In addition to the joint U.S.–Canadian report, other agencies including FERC and the U.S. General Accounting Office are engaged in studying what happened. FERC has established Docket No. RMO4–2–000 which considered power grid reliability legislation and the GAO has published a report, *Electricity Restructuring: 2003 Blackout Identifies Crisis and Opportunity for the Electricity Center* (November, 2003) (GAO–04–204). For some time, Congress has been considering adopting mandatory reliability standards like those developed by the North American Electrical Reliability Council (NERC).

Recall that NERC is a voluntary organization which has published reliability standards. Proposed legislation addresses reliability along the following lines:

- Make NERC reliability standards mandatory.

- Create an independent, industry-led reliability organization.

- Monitor and enforce the standards.

Each of these goals are intended to make the industry more competitive as well as reliable.

E. THE ELECTRICITY FUTURE

The Enron collapse had good news as well as bad. The billions of dollars lost, the lives ruined, the disintegration of Arthur Andersen needless to say were all bad. So too was the blatant market manipulation. The good news was that energy trading market absorbed the loss of Enron quickly and futures trading continued.

The central concept behind electric industry restructuring is to move the industry to more competitive pricing but with strong reliability standards. Because, however, electricity is a vital product, a reliable supply is needed. Under the traditional command-and-control scheme, reliability was provided by a public utility's "reserve margin," that is, an excess of supply over and above average daily requirements. The utility was able to recapture those costs through the rate formula.

The major attraction of restructuring is competition. Consumers should benefit by price competition and more choice; producers should benefit by higher profits through more efficient service. The competitive environment requires trading either on the spot market or in the future. Unfortunately, restructuring was dealt two severe blows, both of which demonstrated that trading markets were manipulated rather than competitive.

In a non-regulated world, products are traded in open markets as supply satisfies demand. Products can be purchased in spot markets for use now or in the immediate future or they can be stored for future use. With sensitive commodities such as food stuffs and currencies, futures contracts allow sellers and buyers to anticipate supply and demand. Because electricity cannot be stored efficiently, it can be traded on either spot or future markets. Thus, electricity futures contracts can, theoretically, take the place of reserve margins. In short, for competition to occur, energy trading, retail and wholesale competition must be available, and markets must be designed and monitored. In other words, the future will be shared by government and industry.

CHAPTER 9

NUCLEAR POWER

Nuclear power once promised to be the safe, clean, cheap and abundant energy source for the future. Today none of those claims are accurate. Health and safety issues have arisen regarding plant operation and waste disposal. Construction costs have made nuclear power more expensive than anticipated, and uranium also became costly to process. However, commercial nuclear power plants are less costly than coal plants to operate. Consequently, they continue to play an important role as a source of energy.

The history and regulation of nuclear power can be divided into three stages. The first stage begins in the late 1930s as scientists attempted to harness the power contained in the nucleus of the atom. As we know, the first application of nuclear energy was in the atomic bombs dropped on Hiroshima and Nagasaki, Japan in World War II. See Richard Rhodes, *The Making of the Atomic Bomb* (1986). This stage lasted until the mid–1950s when authority over nuclear power was transferred from military to civilian hands for the express purpose of developing commercial uses particularly for electricity generation.

The transfer from military control began with the passage of the Atomic Energy Act of 1946, Laws of 1946, ch. 724, 60 Stat. 755, establishing the civilian Atomic Energy Commission (AEC) to regulate and control military use and to promote commercial development. The 1946 Act, however, precluded private ownership. The passage of the Atomic Energy Act of 1954 begins the second stage in the history of nuclear power because now private ownership was permitted and commercial nuclear power gained in popularity only to come to a screeching halt in the 1970s.

The country is now in the third stage of its nuclear power history since the nuclear collapse as we address this most significant question: What is the role of nuclear power in our energy future? This chapter attempts to answer that question as we take you through the nuclear fuel cycle and explain the regulatory history of this energy source.

A.   INDUSTRY OVERVIEW

Nuclear power can be obtained either by fission or fusion. Fission is a chain reaction which splits the uranium nucleus and results in the release of energy (heat). Nuclear fusion also produces energy, but it uses an opposite process through which a reaction and consequent heat are obtained by combining nuclei. Although fusion produces a great deal more energy than fission, fusion is both technologically and financially prohibitive at this time.

Nuclear fission is used in all commercial nuclear power reactors today. The first nuclear reactor in the United States, intended for weapons production, was operated in 1942 by a group of scientists led by Enrico Fermi and Leo Szilard to counter the perceived threat of Germany's building and using an atomic bomb. Nuclear power's first public appearance resulted in the desolation of two Japanese cities, the end of World War II, and the dawn of the Nuclear Age. The destructive force of the atom became known before the public was aware that the power could be tamed for peaceful purposes. The end of the war ended the military's near-exclusive control of nuclear technology.

The United States is the world's largest supplier of commercial nuclear power. There are 104 nuclear power plants operating in the United States, and these plants produce about 20% of the nation's electricity. Nuclear reactors are in effect large expensive tea kettles that heat water to generate electricity. There are two basic types of U.S. nuclear reactors: 69 units are pressurized water reactors (PWRs) and 35 units are boiling water reactors (BWRs). PWRs and BWRs operate similarly. In the PWR, the reactor core creates heat and pressurized water carries that heat to the steam generator where the pressurized water is vaporized to drive the turbine; then the vapor is released. In the BWR, the heated water is returned to the reactor core to cool thus forming a closed loop.

The uranium used in the nuclear power fuel cycle, as originally conceived, was also to be part of a closed system. The ore would be mined, processed, used by reactors, and then reused by reactors. Then the used, or "spent," nuclear fuel would be reprocessed. In such a closed system, uranium becomes a nearly inexhaustible energy source because the reprocessing creates plutonium which is a fuel that can be used in fast "breeder" reactors. Fast breeder reactors create more fuel than they consume. However, plutonium has a higher toxicity and longer life than any element now known; therefore safety concerns over its development and use run high. In *Westinghouse Elec. Corp. v. NRC* (3d Cir. 1979), the Third Circuit upheld a Nuclear Regulatory Commission (NRC) order suspending its decisionmaking processes regarding the recycling of spent nuclear fuel because that process produced plutonium which can be used in weapons thus posing national security risks. As a consequence, the U.S. does not reprocess spent nuclear fuel. Instead, spent fuel must be disposed.

The various steps in the fuel cycle raise safety and environmental issues, which are addressed through regulation. The first step in the fuel cycle involves locating and mining uranium ore. Once the ore has been mined, it is milled into uranium oxide, a substance which is commonly referred to as "yellow cake." The "yellow cake" is then converted into gaseous uranium hexaflouride. This gas is then subjected to an enrichment process which raises the concentration of uranium from U_{238}, a nonfissionable substance, to U_{235}, a uranium enriched isotope which is capable of causing a chain reaction.

After enrichment, the enriched gas is returned to a solid state and is fashioned into pellets about the size of pencil erasers which are then fashioned into the fuel rods used in reactors to create nuclear fission. These steps constitute the front end of the fuel cycle.

The back-end of the fuel cycle involves many issues such as facilities decommissioning, plant cancellations, emergency planning, transportation, and spent fuel storage and disposal, each of which are subject to regulation.

The first nuclear reactor to be connected to an electric distribution system in the United States began operating in late 1957 at Shippingport, Pennsylvania. Its sixty-megawatt capacity was the largest at that time. Over the next three to four years, larger and larger plants were built as part of the nuclear power experiment. The public and the electric utilities were becoming comfortable with the nuclear idea. This market was vigorous and the support for nuclear power by investors was strong. The market, however, was also short lived. The energy and economic crises of the 1970s, together with events peculiar to nuclear power, such as the accident at Three Mile Island, were disastrous for the industry. Today, nuclear plant construction and licensing is at a near standstill. Since 1951, 259 plants have been ordered of which 104 remain in operation, 124 have been canceled, 28 shut down, and 3 license applications are pending.

B.　REGULATORY OVERVIEW

1.　Legislation

The federal government has been pivotal in the development, regulation, and promotion of nuclear technology since its inception. After World War II, the shift from the military to the commercial use of nuclear power did not remove the federal government from the regulatory process. In fact, the federal government steered the course of this technology through its infancy. The Atomic Energy Act of 1946 created two regulatory bodies: the civilian five-member Atomic Energy Commission (AEC) was the primary administrative agency. The chief functions of the AEC were to encourage research and promote development of the technology for peaceful uses. The act also created an eighteen-member Congressional Joint Committee on Atomic Energy (JCAE). This watchdog committee was comprised of members from each legislative chamber.

Very little development of commercial nuclear power occurred during the period 1946–1954. The physicists involved with regulation, naturally, were more interested in scientific problem solving than with commercialization. In the late 1940s and early 1950s, the AEC together with the JCAE shifted nuclear policy to producing electricity for the public's use on a larger scale. A small "breeder" reactor first produced electricity in 1951, but the major breakthrough came when the Navy's submarine Therman Reactor I began producing electricity in 1953. Under Admiral Rickover's direction, the groundwork was laid for the prototype of the present-day reactor, designed as part of the U.S. Navy's submarine program.

While the AEC and JCAE looked to the eventual commercialization of nuclear power, the Atomic Energy Act of 1946 restricted ownership of reactors and fuels to the government. By 1953, the Eisenhower administration, under pressure from scientists, business leaders, and diplomats, revised the nation's atomic energy policy and encouraged private commercial development through passage of the Atomic Energy Act of 1954, 42 U.S.C. §§ 2001 et seq. The 1954 Act ended the federal government's monopoly over nonmilitary uses of atomic energy. It allowed for private ownership of reactors under an AEC licensing procedure. The purpose of the new law specifically regarding private participation was to provide for "a program to encourage widespread participation in the development and utilization of atomic energy for peaceful purposes to the maximum extent consistent with the common defense and security and with the health and safety of the public." 42 U.S.C. § 2013.

The 1954 Act, much of which governs today, set the tone and the goals for commercial nuclear energy. At the time, utilities believed that nuclear-generated electricity would be "too cheap to meter," that costs would be so low that they would not need to bother billing customers. The peaceful use of such destructive resources would help absolve the guilt of Hiroshima and Nagasaki while keeping the United States in the forefront of the development and control of nuclear technology. This approach rallied public opinion behind nuclear power.

Lewis Strauss, chairman of the AEC, interpreted the policy behind the 1954 act as a mandate to rely principally on private industry, principally private utilities, to develop civilian reactor technology. The first step, the Power Reactor Demonstration Program of 1955, was an attempt to involve private industry in a competitive program whereby five separate reactor technologies would be tested. Government and private industry were to develop reactors jointly. Once the reactors were developed, government was to step out of the project, and privately owned utilities were to assume fiscal responsibility for the success of commercialization as well as for liability for accidents. Private industry was not receptive to bearing the financial burden and was unenthusiastic about this program.

Officials of General Electric, one of the major reactor builders, threatened withdrawal from nuclear development activity, stating that GE would not proceed "with a cloud of bankruptcy hanging over its head." In reaction, Congress passed the Price–Anderson Act of 1957, 42 U.S.C. §§ 2210 *et seq.* limiting industry liability while assuring some compensation for the public in the event of a nuclear accident. Congressional hearings on the Price–Anderson Act reveal that there would be no commercial nuclear power plants built by the private sector without a financial safety net provided by the government.

Basically, the act limits a public utility's financial exposure in the event of a nuclear incident. *Duke Power Co. v. Carolina Environmental Study Group, Inc.* (1978) (Price–Anderson Act held constitutional). The ceiling for liability was set at $560 million in the original act. This amount consisted of all the private insurance the utilities could raise at the time which from 1957 to 1967 amounted to $60 million, with the government standing good for the remainder. Every ten years the act comes up for renewal. Under the 1975 amendments to the Act, industry was assessed $5 million per reactor to place in an insurance pool. Price–Anderson was again amended in 1988 (Pub. L. No. 100–408). Under those amendments, the premium for which each licensee would be liable in the event of an accident increased from $5 million per incident to $63 million per incident. Further, that figure is to be inflated in line with the Consumer Price Index every five years. The corresponding limit for liability thus increased from about $700 million to about $7.1 billion.

Currently each nuclear power plant operator must maintain as much private insurance as is available. Today, that is about $200 million. Each large reactor licensee must also participate in a plan of secondary insurance coverage. This secondary coverage plan assesses a retrospective premium of nearly $90 million payable over a period of years following a major nuclear accident. Further, the Nuclear Regulatory Commission, successor agency to AEC, is authorized to enter into indemnity contracts with each licensee, covering public liability arising from nuclear incidents (for the difference, if any, between the licensee's private insurance and a $560 million cap). Because these insurance premiums and coverage are pooled, the total liability coverage is over $9.1 billion.

At the time of the publication of this book, the Price–Anderson Act's limitations of coverage for new facilities have lapsed. Nevertheless, Congress continues to negotiate an extension of coverage. This problem is less immediate than it might appear given the fact that there are no facilities about to come on line. The only major claim asserted under the Price–Anderson Act resulted from the accident at Three Mile Island in 1979 discussed below.

Until Congress passed the National Environmental Policy Act of 1969 (NEPA), 42 U.S.C.A. §§ 4321–70, requiring environmental impact statements for all major federal activities, the AEC had no formal environmental assessment mechanism. In *Calvert Cliffs' Coordinating Committee, Inc. v. United States AEC* (D.C. Cir. 1971), the appeals court held that NEPA's provisions applied to the AEC, which subsequently drafted its own environmental provisions. NEPA continues to limit NRC actions. *Limerick Ecology Action, Inc. v. United States NRC* (3d Cir. 1989) (NRC policy statement addressing severe accident mitigation did not satisfy NEPA).

In the 1970s, public attitudes toward nuclear power changed. People were no longer complacent about nuclear safety, nor convinced by environmental claims made by industry and government. Throughout the 1960's and into the early 1970s, the demand for electricity was growing at a steady rate and coal burning facilities were an environmentally unattractive alternative. With the staggering oil price hikes of the mid–1970's, nuclear power not only remained economically desirable, it was also given a prominent position in national energy plans. Still, a rift in the government-industry partnership started to develop which would first manifest itself in a bureaucratic realignment.

The AEC had conflicting functions: promoting the use of nuclear technology and, at the same time, insuring that the technology was applied safely. In 1974, realizing the cross purposes of both promotion and safety oversight, Congress split the AEC. It created the Nuclear Regulatory Commission (NRC), an independent agency responsible for safety and licensing, and formed the Energy Research and Development Administration (ERDA), later absorbed by the Department of Energy, responsible for promotion and development of nuclear power. Energy Reorganization Act of 1974, P.L. 93–438, 88

Stat. 1233 (1974) (codified as amended at 42 U.S.C.A. §§ 5801–79). This alignment did not completely remove a fundamental regulatory anomaly for the NRC. The NRC had the responsibility both for licensing plants and for safety oversight. If the NRC too vigorously exercises its safety role, then the attendant compliance costs could act as a disincentive to invest in nuclear plants.

The Energy Policy Act of 1992, Pub. L. No. 102–486, 106 Stat. 2776, contained several provisions affecting nuclear power including streamlining the licensing process, supporting research regarding new reactor technologies, and addressing permanent high-level waste storage.

2. Nuclear Power and the Courts

The Supreme Court first spoke about nuclear power in 1961 in a case contesting the Atomic Energy Commission's grant of a construction license for a breeder reactor plant. The precise legal question was whether the Atomic Energy Commission must make the same definitive finding of safety before granting a construction license, the first in a two-step procedure, that it must make before granting an operating license in the second step. The commission issued the construction license with a safety analysis less detailed than that required by the commission's own regulations and by Congress's statutory standard for the operation license. The federal Court of Appeals for the District of Columbia Circuit held that both safety analyses had to be of comparable quality. The United States Supreme Court, in an opinion by Justice Brennan, reversed the lower court by deferring in favor of the AEC. *Power Reactor Development Co. v. International Union of Elec., Radio & Mach. Workers* (S.Ct.1961).

The constitutionality of a Minnesota statute was at issue in *Northern States Power Co. v. Minnesota* (8th Cir. 1971). The statute imposed more stringent requirements for the release of radioactive waste from a nuclear power plant than AEC regulations. In broad language, the federal appeals court held that:

> [T]he federal government has exclusive authority under the doctrine of pre-emption to regulate the construction and operation of nuclear power plants, which necessarily includes regulation of the levels of radioactive effluents discharged from the plant.

The United States Supreme Court affirmed *Northern States Power* without opinion.

The Court addressed licensing again in *Vermont Yankee Nuclear Power Corp. v. NRDC* (S.Ct.1978) in which it was asked to review the procedures for a construction permit and an operating license. At issue in the case was whether the procedures used in those instances by the NRC satisfied constitutional due process. The Court ruled that absent "extremely compelling circumstances the administrative agencies should be free to fashion their own rules of procedure...." The Court again deferred to the NRC in *Baltimore Gas & Electric v. NRDC* (S.Ct.1983) sustaining a ruling that allowed licensing decisions to be made without a specific waste disposal assessment in the environmental impact statement because waste issues were considered in the licensing process. See also, *Metropolitan Edison v. People Against Nuclear Energy* (S.Ct. 1983).

Thus, the Supreme Court adopted the practice of deference to a centralized nuclear agency—that is, until *Pacific Gas & Electric Co. v. State Energy Resources Conserv. & Develop. Comm'n* (S.Ct.1983). In *Pacific Gas & Electric*, California's legislative response to nuclear waste was to impose a moratorium on new nuclear plants until a disposal method was found. The Pacific Gas and Electric Company, a utility building nuclear plants, brought suit alleging that sections of the state legislation were preempted by the Atomic Energy Act because the state-imposed moratorium frustrated the federal effort to develop and promote the use of nuclear power. The district court agreed with the utility. The court of appeals reversed reasoning that the Atomic Energy Act constitutes a congressional authorization for states to regulate nuclear power plants "for purposes other than protection against radiation hazards."

The United States Supreme Court, for the first time, ruled explicitly that decisions regarding nuclear power are not within the exclusive province of the federal government. Significant decisions (involving the need for power) about this most controversial of natural resources are also to be made by individual states. *Pacific Gas & Electric* signifies an important departure from previous nuclear regulation and announced a period of shared decision making between federal and state governments.

The bow to cooperative federalism, and therefore decentralization, was repeated in *Silkwood v. Kerr–McGee Corp.* (S.Ct. 1984) where the Court held that a state's punitive damage award for radiation exposure was not preempted by federal law. See also, *Goodyear Atomic Corp. v. Miller* (S.Ct.1988); *English v. General Electric Co.* (S.Ct.1990).

C. LICENSING

The NRC's primary regulatory function is licensing. Reactor licensing is a two-step process. One license is required for construction and another for operation. *Vermont Yankee Nuclear Power Corp. v. Natural Resources Defense Council, Inc.* (S.Ct.1978); *San Luis Obispo Mothers for Peace v. NRC* (9th Cir. 1986); *Power Reactor Development Co. v. International Union of Elec., Radio and Machine Workers* (S.Ct.1961). The NRC also issues licenses for the use of nuclear materials, for transportation, the export and import of nuclear materials, facilities, and components, and for production facilities that produce nuclear material that may be used for weapons which can affect public health and safety. Licenses will be granted to persons who conform to NRC regulations and standards. No license will be issued unless the NRC judges that the license is not inimical to the common defense and security or to the public health and safety. 42 U.S.C. § 2133(d); *Power Reactor Development Co. v. International Union of Elec., Radio & Machine Workers* (S.Ct.1961). The NRC also has the power to renew licenses—a jurisdiction that assumes an increasingly important role given the aging of nuclear power plants.

As part of the reactor licensing process, the NRC undertakes an extensive site evaluation assessing such matters as seismology, geology, hydrology, and the like, and no license will be granted unless there is "reasonable assurance" that the nuclear power reactor can be constructed and operated without undue risk to public health and safety. *North Anna Environmental Coalition v. NRC* (D.C.Cir. 1976); *Northern Indiana Pub. Serv. Co. v. Porter County Chapter of the Izaak Walton League, Inc.* (S.Ct.1975). In addition, licensees are required to show that they have the financial wherewithal to decommission as well as to operate a facility. The NRC licensing regulations are extensive, examining financial, safety, and environmental data. 10 C.F.R. Part 50.

As noted, licenses are required for construction and operation. The construction license can be converted into an operation license upon completion of the facility and upon a demonstration of conformity with the requirements established by the NRC.

In 1989, the Commission drafted regulations for a combined license in an effort to streamline the process and those regulations were upheld in *Nuclear Information Resource Service v. NRC* (D.C. Cir. 1990). Regulations also provided for early site permits and standard design certifications—again to streamline the process, which has taken more than a dozen years in the past. 10 C.F.R. Part 52. The standard design process can proceed by rulemaking rather than adjudicatory hearing. 10 C.F.R. § 52.51.

In a further attempt to streamline licensing procedures, the NRC may amend operating licenses without a hearing upon a finding of "no significant hazard." In *Sholly v. NRC* (D.C. Cir. 1980), the Court held that a statutory hearing was required when requested. Congress, however, responded to *Sholly* and now allows license amendments without hearing upon the specified finding. 42 U.S.C. § 2139(a)(2).

Operating licenses are initially issued for a 40 year period. This means that nuclear plants will soon require relicensing. According to the NRC, the first operating license will expire in the year 2006. Approximately 10% of the licenses will expire by the end of 2010. Forty percent will expire by 2015.

Licensees can seek a renewal for an additional 20 years based upon an NRC determination that plants continue to maintain adequate levels of safety. In 1991, the NRC published safety requirements for such renewals. 10 C.F.R. Part 54. The renewal process looks at safety issues as well as environmental issues, and the licensee must address plant aging as well as the potential impact on the environment for the additional 20 years of useful plant life. These license renewals will be subject to public hearing.

D.   REACTOR SAFETY

Safety issues surrounding nuclear power fall into two main categories: reactor accidents, which are discussed in this section and exposure to radioactivity, discussed in the next. Reactor safety presents the quintessential example of a low-probability/high-risk event. Clearly, the potential consequences of a reactor core meltdown are staggering. Additionally, regulators must do everything feasible to minimize the probability of such an occurrence. Reactor safety is, thus, a primary concern of the Nuclear Regulatory Commission which states that its strategic goal is to "prevent radiation-related deaths and illnesses, promote the common defense and security, and protect the environment and the use of civilian nuclear reactors." *NRC Strategic Plan: Appendix, Fiscal Year 2000– Fiscal Year 2005.*

Although it remains with the private licensee to design, construct, and operate reactors, reactor safety standards are set by the NRC under very strict, conservative principles including: (1) no nuclear reactor accidents; (2) no deaths resulting from acute radiation exposure from nuclear reactors; (3) no events of nuclear reactors resulting in significant radiation exposure; (4) no radiological sabotages at nuclear reactors; and, (5) no events that result in releases of radioactive material from nuclear reactors causing adverse impact on the environment.

Clearly a zero tolerance policy is impossible to maintain and the NRC promulgated a safety policy goal in 1986 which adopts an acceptable level of risk from nuclear power plant operations. The NRC has stated that fatalities from a nuclear reactor accident should not exceed 1/10 of 1% of the sum of accident risks of comparable accidents and that cancer fatalities from power plant operations should not exceed 1/10 of 1% of cancer fatality risks to which other members of the U.S. population are generally exposed. 10 C.F.R. Part 50.

There are two basic ways to determine risk—experience and modeling. In the United States the single most serious reactor safety experience occurred in Pennsylvania at Three Mile Island in 1979. A few seconds after 4 o'clock on the morning of March 28, 1979, pumps supplying feedwater to steam generators in the containment building of General Public Utility's Unit No. 2 near Harrisburg, Pennsylvania, closed down. Automatically, emergency feedwater pumps kicked in, but a closed valve in each line prevented water from reaching the generators. The closed valves were not noticed by plant operators. As a result, another critical valve, the PORV, thought by plant operators to have closed after thirteen seconds, stuck open, sending critically needed coolant to the containment building floor rather than to the reactor core. As the steam generators boiled dry, the reactor coolant heated and expanded. Two large pumps automatically began pouring coolant into the reactor chamber while pressure dropped. As a result of further operator errors, known anomalously as common-mode failures, these pumping system, designated to send cooling water into the reactor vessel to reduce pressure and heat, were manually shut down. For critical hours, as water boiled into steam, the reactor failed to cool and began to disintegrate. The fuel rods crumbled, and gases within the rods escaped into the coolant water. After two hours and twenty-two minutes, a blocked valve was closed, stopping the flow of over 32,000 gallons of contaminated coolant into the containment building. Then thousands of gallons of deadly radioactive water were negligently pumped into an adjoining building. These events and those that followed are commonly referred to as the accident at Three mile Island. TMI, a milestone in the history of commercial nuclear power, marks the end of its development period and, most likely, its development for some time to come. See Daniel Ford, *Three Mile Island: Thirty Minutes to Meltdown,* 16–34 (1982); *Report of the President's Commission on the Accident at Three Mile Island* (October 1979) (Kemeny Commission Report).

Prior to TMI, the popular conception of a nuclear catastrophe was a core meltdown. A meltdown, colloquially referred to as the China Syndrome, is a nightmarish phenomenon in which the molten reactor core melts through thousands of tons of concrete and steel encasing the fuel rods and burns its way into the ground, emitting massive amounts of radioactive gas on its way to contaminating underground water tables. The radioactivity released into the atmosphere and the water system is predicted to cause thousands of prompt fatalities, and billions of dollars of economic losses.

TMI is the most notorious nuclear reactor accident. The Kemeny Commission concluded that "the fundamental cause of the accident was 'operator error.' " *Report of the President's Commission on the Accident at Three Mile Island, The Need for Change: The Legacy of Three Mile Island* (1979). More specifically the Kemeny Commission noted four factors that significantly contributed to operator confusion. First, the training of the operators was "greatly deficient." The training may have been adequate for normal operations but it was deficient for serious accidents. Second, the specific operating procedures were confusing, and could and did lead operators to take incorrect action. Third, lessons from previous reactor accidents did not lead to remedial instructions. Finally, the design of the control room was confusing and seriously deficient under accident conditions.

The Kemeny Commission also concluded that in spite of serious damage to the plant, most of the radiation was contained and the amount released was expected to have a negligible impact on human physical health. However, the mental stress caused by the accident was quite severe and this was found to be the most serious health effect. In addition to direct risks to human health, the accident at TMI also contaminated air and water in the plant that had to be disposed of. The threat of air and water pollution has naturally enough engendered litigation, see *Susquehanna Val. Alliance v. TMI Nuclear Reactor* (3d Cir. 1980). Class action suits were also instituted under the Price–Anderson Act.

Under the Price–Anderson Act, payments were made for living expenses of families with pregnant women and pre-school-age children who had to evacuate a five mile area around the plant. Those claims totaled $1.4 million for living expenses and lost wages. In addition, there were numerous suits filed against the owner of TMI claiming economic loss. Those suits were settled for about $20 million. In addition, another $5 million settlement was reached on behalf of individuals who felt they needed medical monitoring. Additional claims were brought alleging conditions due to the exposure to radiation, some of which were upheld as stating a viable cause of action. In re *TMI Litigation* (3d Cir. 1999).

While TMI is the most notable nuclear event on which to base risk assessments, we have had other nuclear experiences.

Less well-known, there have been a number of reactor events that reactors like the Davis–Bess reactor experienced in March 2002 during a reactor shutdown. The inspection disclosed a large cavity in the vessel next to one of the reactor control rod mechanisms causing a boric acid leakage and corrosion. That cavity seriously jeopardized reactor vessel integrity, and it was discovered before the restart of the reactor. Such events are required to be reported to the NRC, 10 C.F.R. § 50.72 and can be viewed at the NRC web site www.nrc.gov/what-we-do/regulatory/event-assess.html.

The Three Mile Island accident substantially changed the character of analysis of severe accidents by the NRC. Major investigations resulted in recommendations that probabilistic risk assessment (PRA), the second method of measuring risk, be more widely used. *Kemeny Commission Report*; *Rogovin Report* (NRC Inquiry Group, *TMI Report to the Commissioners and to the Public* (1980)) (NUREG/CR–1250). In 1991, the NRC published NUREG–1150 (Severe Accident Risks: An Assessment for Five U.S. Nuclear Power Plants) which used improved PRA techniques to assess risk. See also *NRC–Risk Informed Regulation Implementation Plan* (September 2003).

Based on historic experience, we might conclude that nuclear accidents are infrequent occurrences. Are they infrequent enough? Since 1957, more than one hundred nuclear power plants have been built and operated in the United States with over 2,700 reactor years of experience. During this time, there has been one reactor core accident at Three Mile Island. Therefore, based on historic experience, there was one reactor accident every 2,700 reactor years.

Probabilistic risk assessment, however, looks at possible failures caused by any number of events through a risk assessment model. Using PRA, the best estimate of core damage frequency appears to be once in 10,000 reactor years, rather than once in 2,700 years. Clearly, there is a discrepancy between experience and model. A recent MIT Study argued that a ten-fold reduction in the likelihood of a serious reactor accident is a desirable goal, which would mean core damage in one out of 100,000 reactor years. *The Future of Nuclear Power: An Interdisciplinary MIT Study* (2003). See also *Reactor Safety Study*, WASH–1400 (October 1975); *Severe Accident Risks*, Nureg–1150 (December 1990); and *Individual Plant Examination Program*, Nureg–1560 (December 1997).

It should come as no surprise that risk assessments are not free from criticism. Indeed, the Union of Concerned Scientists, a watchdog group on many environmental and energy issues, argue that NRC's attempts to limit risk increase rather than reduce the threat to the American public. Union of Concerned Scientists, *Nuclear Plant Risk Studies: Failing the Grade* at http://www.uscusa.org/clean_energy/nuclear_safety/.

After the 1979 Three Mile Island (TMI) accident, the NRC increased safety inspections, stepped up enforcement, and developed retrofitting and emergency preparedness rules. See *Union of Concerned Scientists v. United States NRC* (D.C. Cir. 1987). Off-site emergency preparedness did not become an issue until after TMI. *Suffolk County v. Long Island Lighting Co.* (2d Cir. 1984).

E. RADIOACTIVITY

The nuclear fuel cycle, from mining through reprocessing, produces four major types of waste: high level, low level, mill tailings, and gaseous effluents. Mill tailings are the residues from uranium mining and milling operations. High level wastes, a classification based primarily on heat and radiation emission rates, derive from spent nuclear fuel rods generated in the processing of the fuel and the fabrication of plutonium. These wastes are highly toxic and remain so for hundreds of thousands of years.

1. Low–Level Waste

Low level nuclear waste constitutes items that have been contaminated: radioactive material, or materials that have become radioactive through exposure to neutron radiation. Such wastes includes contaminated clothing, wiping rags, and other cleaning equipment, reactor water treatment residues, equipment and tools, medical waste, and other laboratory waste. The amount of radioactivity can range from the background levels found in nature to very high radioactivity such as that contained in parts inside the reactor vessel of the nuclear power plant. Low-level waste is typically stored on site by licensees until it has either decayed or can be disposed of as ordinary trash or until it is shipped to low level waste disposal sites.

Low level waste storage requires a license from the NRC or by a state. Thus, the responsibility for low level waste is split between the federal and state governments. See Low–Level Radioactive Waste Policy Amendments Act of 1985, 42 U.S.C. §§ 2021(b)–2021(j). The licenses impose regulations which require the waste to be stored in a manner which keeps the radiation below NRC standards. The waste is packaged in containers, sometimes protected with lead, concrete, or other materials. Currently, storage is available at one of the three operating low level waste facilities in the country in Barnwell, South Carolina; Richland, Washington; and Clive, Utah. Other waste disposal sites have been closed and no longer accept wastes. Disposal facilities must be designed, constructed, and operated to meet safety standards. See 10 C.F.R. Part 61. The Low–Level Radioactive Waste Policy Act was designed to regulate low-level waste on a regional basis and allowed states to enter into compacts in order to deal with low-level waste. Today, most states have entered compacts, but only the three-mentioned disposal sites remain available.

The United States Supreme Court has restricted the reach of the Low–Level Radioactive Waste Policy Act in the case of *New York v. United States* (S.Ct.1992). The Amendments Act of 1985 imposed upon states an obligation to enter into regional compacts with other states to provide for the disposal of waste generated within their borders. The Act provided certain incentives, including allowing states to impose a surcharge on waste received from other states, and under which the Secretary of Energy can collect a portion of the surcharge to be place in an escrow account. States that have satisfied the requirements of the Act can receive a portion of those funds. Additional incentives allowed states to increase the cost of access to their sites and even deny access altogether to waste generated in states that did not meet federal guidelines. The third and final incentive was that states that failed to provide for the disposal of internally generated waste must take title to the waste and become liable for all damages suffered by the generator or owner. In *New York v. United States* the United States Supreme Court held that the monetary incentives and access provisions were constitutional. However, the Court ruled that the take-title provisions were unconstitutional and coercive.

2. Uranium Mill Tailings

Uranium mill tailings result from mining uranium ore and are regulated by the Uranium Mill Tailings and Radioactive Control Act of 1978 (Mill Tailings Act), 42 U.S.C. §§ 7901–12. The detailed regulations are contained in 10 C.F.R. pt. 40. See also *American Mining Congress v. NRC* (10th Cir. 1990). Additionally, in the early 1980s as the price of uranium fell, many uranium mills were shut down or had their operation scaled back. As a result, many mills are in the process of cleaning up waste residue. The waste is constituted primarily of mill tailings, which presents a potential hazard to public health and safety. Uranium mill tailings contain the radioactive element radium which produces radon, a radioactive gas. This radium will not decay entirely for thousands of years.

The Mill Tailings Act is directed to provide for the disposal, long-term stabilization, and control of these mill tailings in a safe and environmentally sound manner. The Act also addresses efforts to minimize or eliminate radiation hazards to the public. The Act operates through two programs.

The Title I program establishes a joint federal-state funded program for remedial action at abandoned mill tailing sites. These sites generated tailings largely as a result of production of weapons-grade uranium. While the Department of Energy is responsible for the clean-up and remediation of these sites, the NRC is required to evaluate DOE's design and implementation and to assess whether or not the site meets Environmental Protection Agency standards. The Act also covers site decommissioning of land and structure as well as groundwater protection and radon emission monitoring programs.

The second program under the Mill Tailings Act is directed at uranium mill sites licensed after 1978. The Act directs the NRC to control radiological and non-radiological hazards; directs the EPA to set generally applicable standards for both sets of hazards; and arranges for the eventual state or federal ownership of disposal sites.

3. High–Level Waste

While the effects of low level radiation on humans are still largely unknown, exposure to high level doses may be lethal or may induce a variety of somatic effects, including leukemia, other forms of cancer, and genetic mutations. Thus, wherever radioactive materials accumulate there are sensitive health problems.

High level wastes are comprised of either spent reactor fuel or waste materials remaining after processing. Spent fuel is the used fuel from a reactor that is no longer useful in creating electricity and it is highly radioactive. Until a permanent disposal repository is built for accepting wastes, licensees must store the fuel on the reactor site. There is also significant high level radioactive waste produced at defense reprocessing plants which are regulated by the Department of Energy, not by the NRC.

Currently there are two storage methods for spent fuel. Some of the spent fuel rods are stored in designated pools at the individual reactor sites. Spent fuel pools involve storing fuel rods under at least 20 feet of water and the rods are moved into those pools directly from the reactor. Those rods are changed every 12–18 months. If pool capacity is reached, then licensees may move towards the use of above-ground dry storage casks. Dry cask storage allows the spent fuel that has already been cooled to be encased, and there is inert gas inside steel cylinders called casks which are then bolted closed. The cylinders are surrounded additionally by steel, concrete, or other material. The casks are then transported to a number of power plant sites around the country.

Most radioactive waste is stored on reactor sites. When spent fuel rods and other waste products occupy the storage capacity at utility plants, plants have to expand their storage capacity, or permanent off-site storage areas must be established. Expansion of on-site capacity is a delicate temporary solution viewed in the light of the uncertainties surrounding the development and implementation of safe methods for the ultimate disposal or even long-term storage of wastes. Ultimately, what will be required is the shipment of nuclear wastes offsite. This solution will entail extensive transportation of wastes to some central repository.

4. Transportation

As noted, all spent fuel cannot be stored at the reactor site and must be transported to designated and licensed facilities around the country. Such fuel must be shipped in containers that shield and contain the radioactivity as well as dissipate the heat contained in spent fuel rods.

The NRC estimates that around 3 million packages of radioactive materials are shipped each year either by highway, rail, air, or water. Safety requirements for those shipments are the joint responsibility of the NRC and the Department of Transportation. The NRC establishes requirements for the design and manufacture of the packages for the material and the Department of Transportation regulates the shipments while they are in transit.

Transportation presents several issues, including public health and safety as well as national security. It is also a matter of great concern for the citizens of particular states through which the material is being transported as well as the states that are to receive such materials.

Transportation of nuclear materials poses problems similar to those of waste disposal. Transportation occurs at both the front and back ends of the fuel cycle, but it is the back end transport that raises issues of most concern. If radioactive material escapes, health risks are extreme. States will want to forbid movement of nuclear wastes through the state. However, state laws prohibiting such transport are preempted.

5. Nuclear Waste Policy Act

The National Academy of Sciences began looking for disposal sites in the mid–1950s. Preliminary screening identified four large potentially promising regions containing either salt domes or bedded salt mines. These formations offer relatively safe space for nuclear waste because they restrict the flow of water that can spread radioactivity. However, even today, there is no consensus that these depositories are acceptably safe.

In 1970 the Atomic Energy Commission identified specific disposal sites, and in the late 1970s, the National Waste Terminal Storage Program helped develop the technology necessary for repository licensing, construction, operation, and closure. In 1980 the Department of Energy, after engaging in an environmental impact statement process, selected mined geologic repositories as the preferred storage space for spent commercial nuclear fuel. All of those efforts culminated in the Nuclear Waste Policy Act (NWPA) of 1982 P.L. 97–425, 96 Stat. 2201.

The NWPA was the first comprehensive program governing the disposal of nuclear waste, and the Act requires the DOE to dispose of the waste safely and with environmentally acceptable methods with the intent of underground burial. Under the original 1982 Act, the Secretary of the Department of Energy was to nominate several potential sites for nuclear waste disposal. On May 28, 1986, the Secretary nominated five sites: Richton Dome, Mississippi; Yucca Mountain, Nevada; Deaf Smith, Texas; David Canyon, Utah; and Hanford, Washington. Of these five sites, the Secretary recommended and the President approved for site characterization studies the three sites in Nevada, Texas, and Washington.

Although the federal government has the primary responsibility for permanent disposal of such waste, the costs of disposal are intended to be the responsibility of generators and owners of the waste and spent fuel. The Act also recognizes an important role for public and state participation. The reason for the broad participation of other public bodies is that repositories must be located somewhere and choosing a site is, as expected, controversial. Thus, the statute involves the Secretary of Energy, the president, Congress, the states, Indian tribes, and the general public in the site selection process.

Since the passage of the NWPA, the siting program has faced a number of challenges, including legislative mandates, regulatory modification, fluctuating funding levels, and the evolving and often conflicting needs and expectations of various and diverse interest groups. The challenges from scientists, citizens, legislators, and governors all complicated the process, generating increased Congressional dissatisfaction. In 1983 the Department of Energy located nine sites in six states as potential repository sites. Based on initial studies, the president approved three sites at Hannaford, Washington, Defsmith County, Texas, and Yucca Mountain, Nevada.

In 1987 Congress amended the Nuclear Waste Policy Act, Pub. L. No. 100–203, directing the Department of Energy to study only Yucca Mountain, which is now the designated site awaiting NRC approval. The selection of Yucca Mountain has not been without controversy. In *Nevada v. Watkins* (9th Cir. 1990), the United States Court of Appeals for the Ninth Circuit rejected the state's challenge to legislative authority for this decision. If this site satisfies DOE, NRC, and EPA standards, it will begin receiving nuclear waste by the early part of the 21st Century. *County of Esmeralda, Nevada v. United States DOE* (9th Cir. 1991) (prior to designation of this Nevada site, DOE must consider the potential for groundwater contamination, and the risks associated with various transportation routes). If Nevada is selected as the host state of a high level nuclear waste repository, it may receive up to $50 million per year in benefit payments pursuant to the amended Nuclear Waste Policy Act. Also pursuant to NWPA, Nevada exercised a veto over site selection, and that veto was overridden by both houses of Congress.

Since then, in 1997 Congress directed the DOE to complete a "viability assessment" of the Yucca Mountain site. The viability assessment was codified into law by the Energy and Water Development Appropriations Act, which directed that no later than September 3, 1998, the Secretary of Energy provide to the president and Congress a viability assessment of the Yucca Mountain site. The viability assessment had to include: (1) preliminary design concept of the repository and waste package; (2) total system performance assessment describing the probable behavior of the repository relative to overall system performance; (3) plan and cost estimates for remaining work required to retain a license; and, (4) an estimate of costs to construct and operate the repository.

The NWPA envisioned that site selection would be completed in 1998 and that a facility would then be available to accept waste. That date, of course, has passed. The site characterization process and the politics involved have become increasingly complex. In 1987 the DOE announced an opening date in

2003, a date that also was not met. In 1989 a further delay was announced by the Department of Energy to 2010.

In December 1998 the DOE submitted its assessment to the president and Congress. The viability assessment indicated that the site required further study, although it supported a recommendation of the site to the president. The Department of Energy now seeks final authorization from the Nuclear Regulatory Commission to develop the site as a repository. Consequently, Yucca Mountain is currently earmarked for receipt of waste pending Nuclear Regulatory Commission approval.

Nuclear wastes are currently located in 129 sites in 39 different states, which include 72 commercial nuclear reactor sites, a commercial storage site, 43 research sites, and 10 Department of Energy sites. Once the major disposal site is finally designated, the Secretary of Energy is authorized to enter into contracts with owners and generators of spent nuclear fuel for storage. In addition, transportation plans must be developed to guarantee an environmentally safe and sound transit. Although the commercial nuclear power market has been stagnant for nearly two decades, nuclear waste disposal issues continue to be an important part of the nation's energy planning.

At the time of this writing, the fate of the Yucca Mountain storage facility is still uncertain. In January, 2004, the D.C. Circuit U.S. Court of Appeals heard arguments on how long the proposed repository should have to retain the waste. At issue was the EPA claim that DOE need be concerned about radioactivity for the first 10,000 years. The National Academy of Sciences, however, asserted that radioactive hazards would come hundreds of thousands of years later. A decision is expected by Spring, 2004.

6. Decommissioning

The cost of dismantling spent nuclear plants will likely be enormous. By the year 2025, over 100 nuclear reactor licenses are scheduled to expire. The decommissioning of the plants will entail removing most radioactive elements within the plant's nuclear reactor, and then razing the entire plant. The cost, per plant, will be over one billion dollars, to be paid by the utility customers in their rates.

F. PLANT CANCELLATIONS AND ABANDONMENTS

Even prior to TMI, the nuclear power industry was experiencing economic difficulties. The cost of plants escalated beyond even liberal estimates, doubling, tripling, and even quintupling. The Shoreham Nuclear Power Plant on Long Island, New York, was estimated to cost $265 million in 1967. Before it was canceled, the estimated price of the plant was $4.2 billion. Shoreham may be the most dramatic example, but not by much. In 1968, the Zimmer Nuclear Power Plant, just outside of Cincinnati, Ohio, was anticipated to cost $240 million. When construction stopped, costs were targeted at $1.7 billion and it would cost another $1.8 billion to convert the plant to a coal operated facility. The nuclear industry is indeed moribund. No new plant has been ordered since 1978 and all plants ordered after 1974 have been canceled or converted.

Plant cancellations and conversions present a staggering amount of investment in the billions of dollars. This presents a stark, simple, and important question: Who pays? See Joseph P. Tomain, *Nuclear Power Transformation* (1987); Richard J. Pierce, Jr., *The Regulatory Treatment of Mistakes in Retrospect: Canceled Plants and Excess Capacity*, 132 U. PENN. L. REV. 497 (1984).

Federal and state utility regulators were confronted with the question of who pays and they had two rules from which to draw that we discussed briefly in chapter 4. The first rule is the prudent investment standard which, as its name implies, means that investments that were prudently made should be included in the rate base. The consequence of rate base inclusion is that shareholders earn a return on their investment and that the costs are paid by consumers. The second rule is the used and useful standard which, also as its name implies, means that costs associated with plant cancellations or conversions or excess capacity, can not be included in the rate base because they are not used and useful in furnishing public utility devices. Consumers should not have to pay for investments that did not in fact generate electricity. The consequence of the used and useful rule is that consumers are protected against paying for those investments, but shareholders are not, even when those investments were prudent when made.

Utilities naturally did what they could to avoid saddling shareholders with hundreds of millions and, in some instances, billions of dollars in costs and sought regulatory relief. State agencies and FERC were presented with dozens of cases along these lines. An illustrative case, and one that is noteworthy for its extended discussion of the issue of plant cancellation is *Jersey Central Power & Light Co. v. FERC* (D.C. Cir. 1987). *Jersey Central* was an en banc opinion for which Judge Bork wrote the majority opinion with Judge Starr concurring and Judge Mikva dissenting. Each of these opinions is worth reading to understand the depth of the problem, particularly reflecting the tension between the used and useful test and the prudent investment test.

At issue in *Jersey Central* was an investment of $397 million in the canceled Forked River nuclear power plant. The Federal Energy Regulatory Commission (FERC) allowed Jersey Central Power and Light Company to amortize its $397 million investment over a fifteen-year period. However, Jersey Central was not allowed to put the unamortized balance in the rate base, because the plant was not "used and useful." The effect of this treatment means that the interest costs are charged to shareholders while the principal costs are charged to ratepayers over a fifteen-year period.

Rate amortization is a method for sharing cancellation costs between ratepayers and shareholders. Assume that an investment in a canceled nuclear plant was $397 million. Under a fifteen-year amortization scheme, a public utility commission would allow the utility to charge its customers approximately $26.5 million per year ($397 million divided by 15) as an operating expense for 15 years, thus recouping its entire principal of $397 million after 15 years. But what about the time value of money (interest)? After the first year, the utility receives its first $26.5 million amortization payment from the ratepayers and has $370.5 million yet to recover. Therefore, the utility is losing the use of $370.5 million in the first year. By comparison, if the regulator had put the remaining $370.5 million into the rate base, the utility would have been earning a return on that investment. FERC, and state commissions, chose to split the costs of the canceled plant by letting the shareholders recover their principal investment over the amortization period, but not interest for the use of the money, by disallowing the unamortized portion from being included in the rate base.

Jersey Central argued that such a cost allocation threatened its financial integrity. FERC responded that this approach was its usual practice and it did not give the utility a hearing on whether or not the amortization treatment constituted a Fifth Amendment taking. Judge Bork, writing for a majority of the D.C. Circuit, sitting en banc, held that FERC must hold an evidentiary hearing to examine whether the failure to include a prudent investment in the rate base resulted in unreasonable rate of return. Judge Starr concurred and Judge Mikva dissented, joined by four other judges.

After *Jersey Central*, it appeared that the stage was set for Supreme Court review of the *Hope* (end result) test, particularly as it applies to canceled nuclear plants. The Court seemed poised to review the problem after having accepted two such cases.

In *Kansas Gas and Electric Company v. State Corporation Commission* (Kan. 1986), the utility challenged the state commission's disallowances of (1) $183 million as an imprudent investment to be treated as an expense; (2) a return on $944 million to be included in the rate base because of excess capacity; and (3) a return of $266 million also to be included in the rate base on excess economic capacity. The appeal to the Supreme Court was withdrawn as part of a settlement between the state and the utility. The Court then accepted another plant cancellation case, *Duquesne Light Co. v. Barasch* (S.Ct.1989).

At issue in *Duquesne* was the treatment for ratemaking purposes by Duquesne Light Co. of an approximately $35 million investment in a canceled nuclear power project. The Pennsylvania Public Utility Commission found that the investment was prudent when made and authorized an amortization of the expenditures over a ten-year period. The Pennsylvania Office of Consumer Advocate challenged the amortization in the state supreme court, based on a state statute that imposed the "used and useful" test. In other words, a Pennsylvania statute prohibited that canceled investment from being included in the rate base or otherwise salvaged for the stockholders. The court reasoned that, since no electricity was generated by the project, the ratepayers should not be required to absorb the loss and reversed the PUC. The utility appealed to the Supreme Court.

In *Duquesne*, the Court observed:

Today we reaffirm these teaching of *Hope Natural Gas*: "[I]t is not theory but the impact of the rate order which counts. If the total effect of the rate order cannot be said to be unreasonable, judicial inquiry ... is at an end. The fact that the method employed to reach that result may contain infirmities is not then important." This language, of course, does not dispense with all of the constitutional difficulties when a utility raises a claim that the rate which it is permitted to charge is so low as to be confiscatory: whether a particular rate is "unjust" or "unreasonable" will depend to some extent on what is a fair rate of return given the risks under a particular rate-setting system, and on the amount of capital upon which the investors are entitled to earn that return. At the margins, these questions have constitutional overtones.

One wonders what the Court would have done if the disallowance was $350 million, rather than $35 million? A $350 million disallowance would significantly raise the risk of investment in Duquesne Light Company, or even threaten bankruptcy.

In addition to plant cancellations, conversions, and excess capacity, regulators have been confronted by a similar problem during the construction process. Regulators could choose again from two standards. The first standard was known as Allowance for Funds Used During Construction (AFUDC). Under this method, the costs of construction, including interest, were kept in a separate account and when the plant went on-line, were included in the rate base. The utility then depreciated the total amount over the useful life of the plant but nevertheless made a return on that investment. The problem came as construction times extended five or six years or a decade or more with huge amounts of money piling up on a utility's books.

These long construction times created serious cash flow problems for utilities and commissions were asked to include some of those monies in the rate base during construction. This practice was known as Construction Work In Progress (CWIP). Commissions varied on how much and when they would allow inclusion in the rate base and under what circumstances. Some states allowed a percentage. Others have prohibited its inclusion at all. Regardless, AFUDC and CWIP present the same problem as to who pays when. AFUDC methodology can result in a major rate shock as the plant and accumulated interest comes on line.

G. THE FUTURE OF NUCLEAR POWER

For now, and for some time to come, nuclear power is not a financially attractive investment. The transitional period has been earlier characterized by two phenomena, the shift in concern from safety to financial problem and the decentralization of decision-making power and authority. These difficulties provide the subject of the regulatory reforms needed to spread costs fairly and efficiently and that will provide a basis for a prospective nuclear policy. How the legal system allocates costs will be reflected in monthly utility bills and will have an important impact upon the viability, structure, and design of the electric industry and, consequently, upon the country's energy program.

The United States is every bit as dependent on an electricity-based economy as it is on an oil economy. The assertion about the impact of nuclear financing on energy policy is not intended to be a hyperbolic proposition in the sense than an uninformed or wrong solution will bring energy or economic chaos. But recall, nuclear power accounts for about 20 percent of the electric supply. Indeed, can the country afford to scrap nuclear power entirely and replace it with coal-fired plants, alternative sources, conservation measures, or some combination of the three? At this point, alternative sources provide too little electricity and coal has major environmental problems. Even with the costs associated with nuclear power, the nonuclear option is unrealistic. Too much time, money, and effort has been committed to nuclear technology over the last five decades by the public and the private sectors, domestically and internationally, to make retreat from nuclear power economically or politically feasible.

In short, nuclear generated electricity can be more environmentally sensitive than fossil fuel alternatives, particularly coal. In addition, nuclear can also reduce our dependence on oil. The challenge then remains how to make nuclear power safe, clean, and more economical. In the MIT study, referred to earlier entitled *The Future of Nuclear Power*, the economics of nuclear power were analyzed and it was found that the baseline costs of nuclear power are greater than those of electricity generated by either coal or natural gas. If, however, costs are assigned to carbon emissions with their impact on global warming, then nuclear power could become economically competitive. To those costs must be factored in the costs of financial risks inherent in large-scale investment in a nuclear power plants, in which case some type of government assistance would seem necessary. The back end of the fuel cycle continues to be problematic with respect to the long-term and temporary storage of nuclear waste.

The MIT study states that nuclear power can make an important contribution to meeting the world's energy needs but non-proliferation, safety, economic, and waste issues must be addressed. One advantage that nuclear power has is environment. According to the study, over the next fifty years, unless patterns change dramatically, energy production and use will continue to contribute to global warming through large-scale greenhouse gas emissions. Nuclear power can contribute to reducing greenhouse gases as well as meeting needs for a growing electricity supply. The study finds the following:

- Nuclear power is not cost competitive with coal and natural gas.

- The cost gap can be reduced by plausible reductions in capital costs and operations.

- Reactor designs can achieve a very low risk of serious accidents.

- Long-term disposal is technically feasible, but not demonstrated.

- Current international safeguards are inadequate to meet security challenges.

Clearly, the country has not given up on nuclear power. Still, economic, environmental, safety, and national security issues remain to be addressed before we witness a resurgence of the nuclear power industry.

The Cheney Energy Plan includes strong support for nuclear power and the construction of nearly 2,000 new power plants over the next 20 years. That estimate seems significantly optimistic. This is particularly true given the fact that non-utility generators are building smaller plants (mainly gas turbines) in increasing numbers. In short, the trick is to figure out exactly the proper mix of baseload electric generating units. Coal is dirty, gas can get expensive, renewables may be economically challenging and may be available only in small amounts, and nuclear remains a potential factor. It is still the case that while nuclear plants have significantly high capital costs, they have generally lower operating costs than fossil fuel plants.

The Bush Department of Energy believes nuclear power to be safe, clean, and economical and the proposed Energy Policy Act of 2003 had several nuclear provisions including extending the Price Anderson Act until 2023. The bill proposed to keep the Price Anderson Act's structure by requiring each nuclear plant operator to purchase all of the private insurance that is available (currently $300 million) as a primary level. The secondary level would be proposed to be raised from $63 million to $95.8 million per reactor, a raise from $10 million to $15 million per annual payout. The proposed act also contains several adjustments to licensing and decommissioning as well as research and development investments, about $2.7 billion over the next five years.

CHAPTER 10

HYDROPOWER

Hydropower, the energy derived from falling water, has long been an energy resource in the United States. It was first used to provide mechanical energy to grind grain and operate local machinery. In the 20th century, hydropower has been used almost exclusively to generate electricity.

Because hydropower is essentially free, the electricity produced from it is less costly than electricity produced from other sources. Hydropower, however, is not a completely reliable source of energy, which presents challenges for energy planning. In the sections below, we describe the trade-offs to be made between cost and reliability and we discuss the environmental issues surrounding this energy source.

A. INDUSTRY OVERVIEW

The first hydroelectric facility was built on the Fox River at Appleton, Wisconsin in 1882. Most of the hydropower development in the United States began in the early part of the 20th century with the installations of the Hoover Dam on the Colorado River and large power plants on the Tennessee and Columbia Rivers. There are over 2,300 licensed hydroelectric facilities in the United States. Forty-four percent are federally owned; thirty-five percent are privately owned and the remaining facilities are owned by non-federal public entities such as municipalities, and irrigation and water districts.

Dams, which are the core component of hydropower projects, are built for various purposes including irrigation, flood control, navigation, and recreation, as well as for power generation. Key federal actors in dam construction are the Bureau of Reclamation of the Department of Interior and the Army Corps of Engineers.

Hydroelectricity is produced by the passage of water through a turbine contained in the hydroelectric facility, the design of which has various consequences. Hydroelectric facilities are comprised of a dam to back up the water; a channel to move the water to where it will be used; a powerhouse to generate the electricity; and a conduit to return the water to the stream. The dam may in fact be large enough to back up water and create a significant lake that can be used for recreation and other purposes. The water can then be returned to the stream. Plants which return water to the stream immediately are known as run-of-river plants; these pass all the water directly through the dam to generate electricity. The other dam configuration is known as store-and-release; this backs up the water, usually in a manmade lake and draws down the water when needed to generate electricity.

The amount of hydroelectricity that can be derived from a plant is proportional to the energy delivered to the turbine, which in turn depends on the speed and amount of water flowing through it. Generally speaking, the broader and higher the dam, the more energy that can be generated. The energy is transferred to a generator which converts the energy to electricity.

Hydroelectricity is an attractive energy resource for a number of reasons. First, the cost to produce electricity by hydropower is less than the cost to produce electricity from either fossil fuel or nuclear power plants because the "fuel"—moving water—is relatively costless. Second, the price charged for hydroelectric power is generally stable and does not fluctuate with changes in the price or availability of fuel. This is because the large capital costs of dam construction are sunk and operating costs are low. The availability of hydropower does, however, depend on the amount of water in the stream or river. Third, hydroelectric facilities do not present the environmental concerns that fossil fuel and nuclear power plants arouse, such as acid rain or hazardous waste disposal. Yet hydropower does have environmental consequences, primarily associated with the construction of dams and the consequent changes in the surrounding area. Also, changing the flow of streams and constructing hydroelectric facilities may adversely affect fish and other wildlife in the area. Federal agencies, such as the Environmental Protection Agency and the Army Corps. of Engineers, will deny a permit or license if there is thought to be too much environmental risk to the surrounding area.

While the total amount of hydroelectric energy generated in the United States has increased in recent years, its share of the total energy used by consumers in this country has declined. In the 1940s and 1950s, hydropower provided 40% of the nation's electric energy. By the 1990's, that amount has dropped to 6% of the country's electricity and approximately 4% of all energy. Hydroelectricity accounts for 96% of renewable energy in the United States and hydropower generates 310 billion kilowatt hours of electricity, which are the equivalent of over 530 million barrels of oil per year. Today the expansion of hydroelectric facilities is limited by the small number of sites on which new dams may be located, and by the limits that streams and rivers themselves impose on facility size and output.

Finally, hydroelectric use varies among regions of the country. Hydroelectricity provides a major source of electricity in the Pacific Northwest, where appropriate water sources are especially abundant, and in the Southeast, where the Tennessee Valley Authority operates in the Tennessee and Mississippi River Basins. In order to distribute that power in various regions of the country, the United States has created six regional power marketing agencies. Power marketers include the Bonneville Power Administration, the Southeastern Power Administration, the Southwestern Power Administration, and the Western Area Power Administration. A sixth federal marketer, the Alaska Power Administration, was sold to the State of Alaska in 1995. These administrations are power marketers for different regions of the country.

B. REGULATORY OVERVIEW

Water rights constitute a complex set of legal relationships which have developed through common law doctrine, state statutes, and federal legislation. The key variable in shaping water law has been the availability of water. On the East Coast of the United States, for example, water is abundant and the common law doctrine of riparian rights exists to apportion water rights. Riparian rights simply mean that an owner whose land borders flowing water has a right to use a particular river or stream. Such rights can conflict, of course, with those of downstream or upstream owners who have equal rights. Where water is abundant, a regime based on riparian rights works well.

In western states, however, water is less abundant and states have adopted laws of prior appropriation under which, as the phrase implies, the first user can divert flowing water for its use and can maintain that right as long as the use continues. These state water rights were developed under the common law and codified by statute. Thus electricity derived from water power was initially considered to be under the jurisdiction of state and local governments because the electricity produced by hydropower was confined to local use. But, with the growth of interstate commerce, the need arose for uniform controls at the federal level.

Our federal system means, of course, that federal law, under appropriate circumstances, can come into play and it does so in the arena of water rights. Under the Commerce Clause of the United States Constitution, the federal government exercises regulatory authority over navigation for national defense, as well as for interstate and foreign commerce and also regulates energy production. *Gibbons v. Ogden* (S.Ct.1824).

Federal hydropower development is also significant because of the expanse of major federal lands holdings, particularly in the western half of the United States. Although individual states are naturally protective of their own resources, federal legislation exists to protect federal rights and these sets of rights can conflict. The River and Harbor Act of 1884, 46 U.S.C. § 330, for example, authorized the then Secretary of War to remove unauthorized obstructions including public and private bridges from navigable waters. In 1896, further legislation authorized the federal government to provide free rights of way through federal lands for electricity generation and transmission thus opening the door for private hydroelectricity development. Federal Land Policy and Management Act, 43 U.S.C. § 957.

Early federal legislation also authorized the Secretary of the Interior, under the Yosemite National Parks Act of 1901 (codified as amended at 16 U.S.C.A. § 79 and 43 U.S.C.A. § 959) and under the General Dam Act of 1906 (codified as amended at 33 U.S.C.A. § 491), to grant rights-of-way and leases for energy production at hydroelectric facilities. The General Dam Act also provided for a municipal preference for federal hydropower and, as significantly amended in 1910, incorporated provisions for monetary charges to be imposed on private development, a fifty-year permit limitation on privately owned dams, and recovery of privileges by the federal government at the conclusion of a private project. Even with substantial amendments, the General Dam Act had not successfully coordinated hydroelectric planning.

The earlier acts did not have the effect of promoting any hydroelectricity projects, even though private power interests were interested in pursuing hydroelectricity. To that end, with Congressional support, the Omnibus Water Power Bill of 1912 was introduced in Congress. The bill would have authorized 17 private power projects. While that bill was being considered, President Taft vetoed a special act providing for a private power project and this veto indicated his unwillingness to sign the Omnibus Bill. Thereafter, several other bills to allow private power projects were introduced in Congress and all were defeated on the issue of whether or not the federal government had the right to impose a charge for developing such projects. Finally, hydropower development was stimulated during World War I as the country experienced shortages of coal and oil.

Hydroelectricity development began in earnest in 1920 when Congress passed the Federal Water Power Act of 1920, 16 U.S.C.A. § 791 et seq. Known today as the Federal Power Act (FPA), this 1920 legislation, although amended significantly in 1935 and in 1986, remains the fundamental law governing hydroelectricity. The purpose of the FPA was to assert jurisdiction over widespread waterpower sources, to begin comprehensive planning for national water power, and to create the Federal Power Commission (FPC), now the Federal Energy Regulatory Commission (FERC). Passage of the FPA was partly the result of efforts by conservationists who fought to ensure a comprehensive nationwide water power plan against pro-development interests. One objective of the legislation was to reconcile and accommodate conflicting uses such as navigation, recreation, hydropower, and wildlife preservation within one framework.

Federal jurisdiction over hydroprojects is most frequently based on the fact that hydroelectric plants use water from navigable waterways that fall within the federal domain. Federal jurisdiction is also based on the Commerce Clause of the U.S. Constitution, Art. I, sec. 8, cl. 3. Under the FPA, the FPC has authority to issue licenses for 50 years, and the federal government has the authority to recapture the power at the end of the license. These powers now reside in the FERC.

In 1935, Congress passed Part II of the Federal Power Act, 16 U.S.C.A. § 824 et seq., which extended the Federal Power Commission's authority to include ratemaking and licensing power over hydroelectric facilities. Under Part II, the FPC had jurisdiction over the transmission of electric energy in interstate commerce, and over the sale of such energy at wholesale in interstate commerce. Today, FERC has authority to issue licenses to citizens, corporations, or to state and municipal governments to construct and operate hydroelectric plants.

In 1968, the FPC realized that the first set of 50 year licenses were about to expire and sought methods for relicensing. Congress passed the appropriate legislation, 16 U.S.C. § 807(a) and § 808(b) for license renewal. Additional legislation affecting hydropower includes the Public Utility Regulatory Policy Act and the aforementioned Electric Consumers Protection Act of 1986, both of which will be discussed in more detail below. Most recently the Energy Policy Act of 1992 effected various changes in FERC's regulation of hydroelectric facilities. EPAct authorizes FERC to assess charges on licensees to recover the administrative costs of operating fish and wildlife agencies as well as others. EPAct also effected changes on licensing requirements more generally.

C. FEDERAL JURISDICTION[1]

FERC has the authority to license hydroelectric projects consistent with certain guidelines. The hydroelectricity guidelines state that the project must (1) be within the United States; (2) be located on navigable waters; (3) use water or waterpower from a government dam; and (4) affect interstate commerce. Whether a potential site is subject to FERC jurisdiction has been the subject of much litigation.

Although federal hydropower authority under the above enabling legislation is intended to result in comprehensive water power planning, it is to some extent limited. In *First Iowa Hydro–Electric Cooperative v. FPC* (S.Ct.1946), a hydropower cooperative had been granted a license by the FPC to

1. A recent and comprehensive review of hydroelectricity regulation can be found in Michael A. Swiger, Jonathan D. Simon & Charles R. Sensiba, *Hydroelectric Power* in 2 ENERGY LAW & TRANSACTION ch. 53 (David J. Muchow & William A. Mogel eds. 2003).

build a dam on a tributary of the Iowa River, although the dam would significantly impede the flow of the river and compliance with Iowa law was virtually impossible to obtain. The Supreme Court read FPC jurisdiction broadly and allowed the dam to be built, holding that section 9(b) of the Federal Power Act, which required a showing of compliance with state law, was merely informational and that the Commission's decision must be binding in order to allow the FPC to provide for comprehensive nationwide planning.

Most often, federal authority will preempt state authority. For example, states explicitly retain their proprietary rights over water resources under § 27 of the Federal Power Act, 16 U.S.C.A. § 821, but they cannot impose conditions on dam permits for federal projects. See also *California v. FERC* (S.Ct.1990) (FPA vests sole authority to set flow rates of hydropower projects in FERC).

In determining the extent of early federal jurisdiction, the critical issue was the navigability of waters for a proposed hydroelectric plant site. In *United States v. Appalachian Electric Power Co.* (S.Ct.1940), contrary to the findings of the lower district and circuit courts, the United States Supreme Court held that part of the New River in West Virginia was "navigable" and subject to FPC jurisdiction. The Court admitted that there was no definitive test for navigability, but found that the waterway was suited for "use of the public for purposes of transportation and commerce," and as such was considered "navigable" for purposes of the Federal Power Act. Federal preemption of hydroprojects also extends to the waters on United States reservations. *FPC v. Oregon* (S.Ct.1955).

Later, expanding federal jurisdiction, the Supreme Court held that FERC has jurisdiction over a pumped storage facility located on a non-navigable tributary of a navigable waterway because the hydropower derived from the tributary would be used in interstate commerce. *FPC v. Union Elec. Co.* (S.Ct. 1965). The Supreme Court found that the facility could affect navigability downstream because the proposed "pumped storage" facility—by which water would be pumped to a high reservoir, stored, and then released to generate power during periods of peak demand—could affect navigability downstream. The nexus with interstate commerce as supporting federal jurisdiction was expanded in *Fairfax County Water Authority* (FERC 1988) to include a project owner's power consumption. See also, *Habersham Mills v. FERC* (11th Cir. 1992) (upholding *Fairfax*).

Another problem arises when a hydroelectric plant is erected on a waterway contained completely within the borders of one state and whose electricity is used only within that state. In *City of Centralia v. FERC* (9th Cir. 1981), a court held that the FERC did not have jurisdiction in the circumstances of that case because any effect on interstate commerce was insubstantial. Subsequently, that same court upheld FERC jurisdiction over the same project based on a finding of navigability rather than effect on interstate commerce. *City of Centralia v. FERC* (9th Cir. 1988).

The FERC does not, however, have exclusive authority over hydropower facilities. Local, state, and federal agencies also have statutory powers to regulate hydroelectric projects, as long as state or local regulations do not impede the exercise of federal authority. Under the Clean Water Act § 401, 33 U.S.C.A. § 1341(d), for example, states may set water quality standards for hydropower projects. Also, the federal government may not preempt state tort law. *South Carolina Public Service Authority v. FERC* (D.C. Cir. 1988). Further, under the FPA, states may not set minimum water flow requirements for fish preservation if the requirements conflict with the provisions of a FERC licensee. *California v. FERC* (S.Ct. 1990). States may establish a water use plan when the Federal Bureau of Reclamation is the regulating authority. *California v. United States* (S.Ct.1978).

D. LICENSING

1. Federal Power Act

Once the question of jurisdiction is settled, the next step is the licensing of a hydroproject. FERC can authorize preliminary permits, licenses, new licenses, annual licenses, and exemptions. Applicants must satisfy the requirements of the Federal Water Power Act of 1920. In addition, applicants must follow the requirements of the Federal Water Pollution Control Act amendments of 1972, Pub. L. No. 92–500, 86 Stat. 816 (1972); Clean Water Act, 33 U.S.C. § 1341(a)(1), and 33 U.S.C. § 1342(a)(1); the Wild and Scenic Rivers Act, 16 U.S.C. §§ 1271–1287; the Energy Security Act, 16 U.S.C. §§ 2705, 2708; and the Endangered Species Act, 16 U.S.C. §§ 1531–1544, among others, and the most important of which are the National Environmental Policy Act of 1969, 42 U.S.C. §§ 4321 et seq.

Section 10(a) of the FPA requires the FERC to choose the project "best adapted" to improve or develop a waterway for interstate or foreign commerce or hydropower development. Under the Electric Consumers Protection Act of 1986, the "best adapted" requirement demands that a license must be judged by FERC to be "best adapted to a comprehensive plan for improving or developing a waterway ... for the use or benefit of interstate or foreign commerce, for the improvement and utilization of water-power development, for the adequate protection, mitigation, and enhancement of fish and wildlife ... , and for other beneficial public uses.... " 16 U.S.C. § 803(a)(1). In making this determination, FERC also must consider comprehensive plans developed by other state and federal entities and Indian tribes. *Scenic Hudson Preservation Conference v. FPC* (2d Cir. 1965). In short, the license should be based on a comprehensive review.

If no applicant can demonstrate a specific project's superiority under these criteria, then section 7(a) of the Act states that preference be given to state or municipal applicants over private developers. This so-called "municipal" preference is valuable because of the low cost of hydroelectricity relative to electricity generated from coal-fired, oil-fueled, or nuclear powered plants. Because there often is a strong public interest in granting licenses to public applicants, if a private developer's application is more comprehensive than that of a public entity, the FERC must allow time for the public developer to revise the application to equal that of the private applicant. Finally, the FERC may deny an application by nonfederal developers if the Commission decides that, for the benefit of the public, the facility should be constructed and maintained by the United States itself.

Generally, however a license must be granted to an applicant who satisfies the review of the proposed project: (1) is located along or across any navigable waters; (2) occupies any part of the public lands of the United States; (3) utilizes surplus water or water power from a government dam; or (4) affects interstate or foreign commerce.

Hydropower licensees hold different sets of rights due to the statutory history of water power licensing. Hydropower projects are treated differently depending upon whether they were developed before 1920, after 1935, and after 1986, those dates corresponding to major water power legislation.

Licenses are granted for periods of up to 50 years before relicensing is required and the date of institution of the project is important. The FERC may grant licenses to voluntary applicants for projects built on nonnavigable streams before 1935 under the jurisdictional grant of § 4(e) of the 1920 Act. 16 U.S.C.A. § 797(e); *Cooley v. FERC* (D.C.Cir. 1988). In *Farmington River Power Co. v. FPC* (2d Cir. 1972), the court held that § 23(b) of the 1935 Amendments required a license of any project constructed on a navigable waterway built between 1920 and 1935. *Puget Sound Power & Light Co. v. FPC* (9th Cir. 1977). FERC authorization is also required for substantial reconstruction of projects built before 1920.

Minnesota Power & Light Co. v. FPC (8th Cir. 1965); *Northwest Paper Co. v. FPC* (8th Cir. 1965). Compare *Aquenergy Systems, Inc. v. FERC* (4th Cir. 1988) (permit required for major post–1935 reconstruction by new owner on nonnavigable stream), with *Washington Water Power Co. v. FERC*, (D.C. Cir. 1985) (no license needed for project completed in 1911); *Puget Sound Power & Light Co. v. FPC, supra* (no permit required to repair damaged pre–1935 project); *Thomas Hodgson & Sons, Inc. v. FERC* (1st Cir. 1995) (12 year shutdown not an abandonment and the resumption of power plant production does not require a license). The dates and terminology of these cases are important for knowing the rights attendant on a particular license.

Conflicts over licenses became a major problem in the mid–1960s when licenses, which had been granted for a fifty year period, began to expire. Private license holders sought renewal of their licenses in opposition to municipal or state bodies that wished to take over the facilities. Given less costly hydropower, it is not surprising that private developers objected to the preference given to public entities in licensing.

This tension between private projects and municipal preferences in the relicensing context was discussed in an important FERC opinion. In re *City of Bountiful, Utah* (FERC 1980). In that case, private developers argued that the preference clause for municipalities pertained only to applications for original licenses, not relicensing. The FERC held that "new licensee" referred to any license, and that therefore public bodies were meant to receive preference in relicensing of hydro facilities, as well as for original licenses. The controversy regarding the continuation of preferences on relicensing was addressed by Congress in the Electric Consumers Protection Act of 1986, 16 U.S.C.A. § 800(a), which eliminated the preference. *Kamargo Corp. v. FERC* (D.C. Cir. 1988). Courts have held that the preference applies only to original licenses, not to relicensing. *Alabama Power Co. v. FERC* (11th Cir. 1982); *Clark–Cowlitz Joint Operating Agency v. FERC* (D.C. Circ. 1987). Still, new licenses are to be granted to applicants whose plans are best adapted to serve the public interest, and license transfers will not be made for "insignificant differences." 16 U.S.C.A. § 808(a)(2). Thus, incumbents are still favored, even though the preference has been eliminated.

As the above discussion indicates, the traditional licensing process began to meet with resistance. In response, FERC developed an alternative licensing process. The alternative licensing process, 18 C.F.R. § 4.34(i), complemented the traditional licensing process but responded to the need for licensing reform. The alternative process was transitional. Starting in 1998, FERC together with the Departments of the Interior, Commerce, Agriculture, and Energy, as well as the Council on Environmental Quality and the Environmental Protection Agency, formed an interagency task force to improve hydroelectric licensing processes. The task force reported its findings to Congress in January 2001, after which event Congress directed FERC to submit a comprehensive report on hydropower licensing. As a result of all of those efforts, FERC issued a Notice of Proposed Rulemaking for the integrated licensing process.

Regardless of whether applicants pursue traditional, alternative, or integrated licenses, the process is lengthy, as well as costly. Applications for licenses include the submission of significant data including maps, plans, specifications, cost estimates, and evidence of compliance with other laws. The FERC rulemaking was intended to streamline hydroelectric licensing. The final rule was issued on July 23, 2003. 104 FERC ¶ 61, 109 (July 23, 2003).

The new rule creates what is now known as an integrated licensing process (ILP), in which the applicant can have a prefiling consultation with FERC and undertake its National Environmental Policy Act review while concurrently seeking the hydroelectric license.

The ILP process includes:

- greater coordination with FERC as well as with other federal and state agencies.

- increased assistance by FERC staff for the applicant and other stakeholders.

- increased public participation.

- comprehensive environmental assessment.

- establishment of a plan, schedules, and deadlines for all participants.

- commission of a FERC-approved study plan for dispute resolution procedures via ILP, which provides an alternative to the traditional licensing process and the alternative licensing process already established by FERC.

Although it is too early to tell whether the ILP has achieved its goals, the reform has been responsive to concerns expressed about the traditional licensing process.

2. Environmental Laws

Environmental concerns began to play a part in the licensing procedures of hydroelectric projects beginning in the 1960s. As a precursor to NEPA requirements, in 1965, environmental groups won a ruling that the FPA required that Consolidated Edison's request to build a pumped storage facility on the Hudson River should include an examination of the environmental value of preserving that area of the river in its then present condition. *Scenic Hudson Preservation Conference v. FPC* (2d Cir. 1965). See also *Udall v. FPC* (S.Ct.1967); *Platte River Whooping Crane Critical Habitat Maintenance Trust v. FERC* (D.C. Cir. 1989). Thus, prior to NEPA, several federal court cases required FERC's predecessor, the Federal Power Commission, to consider and assess environmental impacts before issuing a license.

In *Scenic Hudson*, the Second Circuit required the FPA to determine what environmental conditions the projects were best adapted for the comprehensive use of the waterway. In *Udall*, the United States Supreme Court held that the FPC must consider the environmental effects of its proposed action regarding the construction of a hydroelectric project on the Snake River. In that case, the Secretary of the Interior asked the FPC to postpone consideration until it had an opportunity to review fish protection measures. The FPC issued the license without addressing the Secretary's concerns and the Supreme Court overturned the FPC's decision.

Hydropower licenses are also subject to NEPA, most notably the environmental impact statement requirement. NEPA requires that FERC prepare an environmental impact statement for any "major" project that will "significantly" affect the quality of the human environment including federal hydropower projects. The agency must act reasonably in these circumstances and cannot fail to file the EIS. The environmental impact statement is required for licenses, *La Flamme v. FERC* (9th Cir. 1988) and for relicenses, *Confederated Tribes and Bands of Yakima Indian Nation v. FERC* (9th Cir. 1984).

Nevertheless, FERC has excluded some projects and actions from the review, including: issuance of preliminary permits; transfers of project licenses or exemptions; withdrawals of applications, permits, licenses, or exemptions; small conduit hydroelectric facility exemptions; and requests for gas or electric lines, among others.

In addition to NEPA, applicants may be subject to other environmental legislation, such as the Clean Water Act, 33 U.S.C.A. § 1251 et seq., and the Wild and Scenic Rivers Act, 16 U.S.C.A. §§ 1271–87.

In *La Flamme v.* FERC, supra, the court held that an EIS was required for a license. The scope of that decision, however, has been called into question. Under *National Wildlife Federation v. FERC* (D.C. Cir. 1990), *La Flamme* may be restricted to the 9th Circuit because it seems to be in conflict with *National Wildlife*. In the latter case, the D.C. Circuit rejected claims of petitioner *National Wildlife Federation* that FERC improperly issued a license without full consideration of the "comprehensive plan" for the project. In that case, prior to issuing a license, an environmental impact statement had been prepared but this did not look at the environmental consequences of an expansion of the project. The Court held that FERC's actions did not violate NEPA. In effect, FERC can compare and analyze alternatives without necessarily filing a NEPA-required environmental impact statement.

Environmental considerations have also been highlighted in the Electric Consumers Protection Act of 1986 (ECPA), 16 U.S.C.A. § 808. The ECPA amends FPA § 4(e) by requiring the FERC to make licensing decisions which give "equal consideration" to environmental matters in relation to power production.

Under the ECPA, FERC must give equal consideration to such things as "energy conservation, the protection, mitigation of damage to, and enhancement of, fish and wildlife (including related spawning grounds and habitat), the protection of recreational opportunities, and the preservation of other aspects of environmental quality." 16 U.S.C. § 797(e). Although "equal consideration" does not require "equal treatment," the examination must be substantial. *California v. FERC* (9th Cir. 1992). In this way, NEPA and ECPA are complementary acts.

As attractive as hydroelectric power is because of its low costs, the environmental issues surrounding construction have been significant. Perhaps the most noteworthy case in this area was the Supreme Court decision in *Tennessee Valley Authority v. Hill* (S.Ct.1978). *Tennessee Valley* involved NEPA as well as the Endangered Species Act and resulted in a court's blocking the nearly completed Teleco dam project in Tennessee as a result of the presence of a small species known as the snail darter. Ultimately Congress authorized the completion of the dam, but not until this major environmental precedent was set.

In the Pacific Northwest, federal hydroelectric dams have caused a serious problem, particularly in light of the endangered status of some salmon, including Snake River sockeye salmon and some chinook salmon. See Michael C. Blumm, *The Amphibious Salmon: The Evolution of Ecosystem Management in the Columbia River Basin*, 24 ECOLOGY L.Q. 653 (1997). Because of the competing interests involved and the need for cheap electricity as well as for endangered species protection, alternatives have been sought, such as literally barging or trucking salmon around obstacles. Another approach has been to increase river flow but this has the negative consequence of drawing down reservoirs and slowing electricity generation. See Michael C. Blumm & Greg D. Corbin, *Salmon and the Endangered Species Act: Lessons from the Columbia Basin*, 74 WASH. L. REV. 519 (1999). Congress has tried to balance these concerns through the Pacific Northwest Electric Power Planning Conservation Act, 16 U.S.C. §§ 839–839h (1994) as amended in 1996, 110 Stat. 2984, 3005. Under the Act, fish protection is to be considered equal in importance to hydropower operations.

3.   Small Hydropower Projects and the Public Utility Regulatory Policies Act

The 1970s were a volatile time for energy markets as prices rose, supplies contracted, and the commercial nuclear power industry collapsed. These energy disruptions of the 1970s motivated the United States to reduce dependence on foreign oil. In the electricity market, alternative sources of electricity promised to reduce electricity prices by increasing supplies, primarily from renewable sources, and stimulating competition. In 1978, Congress passed the Public Utilities Regulatory Policies Act of 1978 (PURPA) to aid, among others, small hydroelectric plant operators. PURPA section 401, 16 U.S.C.A.

§ 2701, required the Secretary of Energy to establish a program to encourage the development of small (less than 80 megawatts) hydroelectric sites, by authorizing federal loans for feasibility studies and for project costs. PURPA also required the FERC to establish a regulatory program to facilitate licensing procedures for small hydropower projects in connection with existing dams.

PURPA promotes cogeneration and small power production, including small hydropower facilities. To make investment in small power production attractive, PURPA includes statutory provisions that obligate local utilities to connect with small power producers, to furnish back-up power when necessary, and to purchase the small producer's excess electricity at the utility's "avoided cost." Thus, if the small power producer generates electricity at a rate lower than that of the local public utility, the small power producer provides a saving on electricity and has a market for the excess product. PURPA has proved highly successful in stimulating this market. When the cost of electricity from traditional large-scale electric power producers rises, alternative electricity sources such as small hydropower plants are attractive.

PURPA provides for exemptions from the FPA licensing requirement for "small conduit" (15MW) projects. The Energy Security Act, 16 U.S.C.A. § 2705(d), also provides for a 5MW exemption. The purpose of the exemption is to promote power production by reducing administrative costs for small electricity-producing projects, like small hydro facilities. Exemptions have been preferred to preliminary permits. *City of Centralia v. FERC* (9th Cir. 1986). Exemptions have been upheld without a showing of a need for hydropower. *Idaho Power Co. v. FERC* (9th Cir. 1985). However, exemptions have been restricted in order to protect the environment. *Tulalip Tribes of Washington v. FERC* (9th Cir. 1984).

4. The Electric Consumer Protection Act

In 1986, Congress passed the Electric Consumers Protection Act (ECPA), 16 U.S.C.A. § 791 et seq. ECPA amended the FPA to resolve the question of whether the preference given to municipalities and states in licensing hydroelectric facilities applied to relicensing as well as to the development of new sites. Section 7 of the act makes it clear that the preference is to be given to states and municipalities only for an "original" license and not where an expired license is up for renewal. While this section does not call for preference to an incumbent, it does state that "insignificant differences" between applicants will not result in the transfer of a license from a previous licensee to a new holder. Applications to run a preexisting facility are now to be evaluated according to whose application the FERC determines is best adapted to serve the public interest without preference for municipalities. However, there is still a disposition toward granting the previous license holder's renewal if that holder has a "record of compliance with the terms and conditions of the existing license." 16 U.S.C.A. § 808(a)(3)(A).

Open competition for hydroelectric facility licenses would be thwarted, however, if incumbent licensees were allowed to use their existing control over established electric distribution systems to gain an unfair advantage over new applicants. The ECPA contains two provisions aimed at preventing this practice.

First, under section 15(d)(1) of ECPA, the FERC may not consider an incumbent's advantage with respect to transmission facilities in determining license proposals. Second, the ECPA attempts to ensure that any new applicant who is awarded a license will have access to needed transmission facilities if the FERC determines that it is "not feasible" for the new licensee to operate the facility without obtaining transmission services from the original licensee. The Commission must attempt to have the original and the new licensee work out an agreement for use of the transmission facilities. If negotiations fail, however, the FERC will order the original licensee to file a transmission tariff, subject to a refund, to ensure that the new licensee will be able to begin operations on the date that the license is transferred. The FERC will then issue a final order, setting the tariff at a "reasonable rate," but the Commission may not order the original licensee to make substantial improvements to its transmission system, or interfere with the previous licensee's ability to service its customers.

Another new licensing criterion that the ECPA has established involves energy conservation. Under section 4(e), the Commission is to give "equal weight" to energy conservation in making licensing decisions, in order that those who receive licenses will consider energy conservation as an energy supply alternative. Section 3(b) of the ECPA also requires the FERC to consider "the electrical consumption efficiency improvement program of the applicant * * * for encouraging or assisting its customers to conserve electricity."

Public bodies, such as states and municipalities, do receive preference over private entities in the purchase of power from a federal hydroelectric facility. Construction of a federal dam allows the government to sell electric power, as authorized by a number of federal statutes. Reclamation Project Act of 1939, 43 U.S.C.A. § 485(c); the Flood Control Act of 1944, 16 U.S.C.A. § 825s. Because the cost of federal hydropower is usually well below the cost of alternative energy, competition for this energy is often intense.

This priority, mandated under the federal statutes through which the federal marketing agencies sell electricity, has been attacked in court most often by public bodies who have not received preference as purchasers of hydroelectric power, either because it was sold to a private utility or to another preference entity. Such was the case in *Metropolitan Transportation Authority v. FERC* (1986) where two state agencies, the Metropolitan Transit Authority of New York and the Vermont Department of Public Service, claimed preference status under the Niagara Redevelopment Act. The FERC's orders, which rejected preference status for both entities, was upheld by the Court of Appeals for the Second Circuit. The court stated that "for purposes of 16 U.S.C.A. § 836(b), 'public bodies' are 'publicly-owned entities capable of selling and distributing power directly to consumers of electricity at retail,' not consumers or brokers."

The ECPA also has provisions which affect PURPA. In the late 1970s and early 1980s, there was a rush in the United States to develop small hydroelectric facilities. This was caused by PURPA's extensive incentives for renewable sources, and because of favorable tax legislation. Opposition arose when the FERC decided to extend PURPA benefits to new dam or diversion projects by interpreting the "renewable sources" language in PURPA to include such new projects.

The ECPA responded to these concerns by limiting the availability of PURPA benefits involving new dams or diversions by establishing a moratorium on PURPA benefits for such projects in the future. However, to aid developers who had relied on the promise of PURPA benefits and had begun planning and developing new facilities, the ECPA established a grandfather clause, exempting most of these projects from the moratorium on PURPA benefits. Projects which fall under the grandfather clause are those which have already been approved by the Commission, as well as those for which proposals have been received by the Commission before enactment of the ECPA. Additionally, ECPA does not affect any project located at a federal dam at which nonfederal hydroelectric development is permitted.

The ECPA contains a pertinent provision relating to the enforcement of its regulations. Concerns were raised prior to its enactment that a number of hydroelectric facilities, which lay under federal jurisdiction, were operating without a license from the FERC, making it extremely difficult to monitor the safety conditions and environmental impacts of these projects. Additionally, the FERC was accused of failing to diligently monitor compliance with the terms of the licenses it had granted. In response, the ECPA states that the FERC "shall" monitor compliance with licensing and exemption requirements. The ECPA gives the FERC more authority to enforce these requirements by granting the Commission power to revoke licenses and exemptions for noncompliance with their terms, and to impose civil penalties of up to $10,000 per day of such noncompliance.

Hydroelectricity will continue to play a notable role in the country's energy supply, most importantly as a renewable resource. Nevertheless, we are unlikely to see an expansion of this resource due to the limited availability of facilities sites. Additionally, areas of future concern include increasing competition between public and private distributors for this comparatively cheap source of electricity and there will be heightened environmental concerns as existing licensees go through the relicensing process.

CHAPTER 11

ALTERNATIVE ENERGY SOURCES

In Chapter 2, we describe the dominant energy policy in the United States as large-scale, capital intensive, and largely driven by fossil fuels. Oil, natural gas, coal, nuclear power, and the electricity generated by those resources are the paradigmatic examples of the dominant policy. In this chapter, we discuss alternative energy sources and policies. We use the phrase alternative energy sources fairly broadly to encompass three distinct concepts. The most popular concept of alternative energy involves renewable energy, such as solar power and wind power. These technologies rely on costless energy sources and, it would appear, have benign environmental consequences. Therefore, as cheap and relatively environmentally benign, renewable energy sources are attractive.

The second conception of alternative energy involves conservation and energy efficiency. Conservation and energy efficiency are complementary sources of energy insofar as conservation can be simply defined as using less energy. Energy efficiency is defined as obtaining more energy from the resources that are used. Again, both conservation and energy efficiency have little or no environmental consequences except to the extent that they restrict the impacts of energy not used.

Third, the last form of alternative energy that we will discuss involves alternatives to the dominant model. To the extent that energy production can be reduced in scale, made portable, used locally, such energy sources present alternatives to the dominant model. Additionally, we discuss alternative sources for fossil fuels and fossil fuel substitutes.

We conclude by discussing alternative energy policies in general terms. At least since Thomas Malthus wrote his *Essay on Population* in 1798, the issue of population growth and its consequent potential harms to society has been with us. In his essay, Malthus argued that population growth always exceeds the growth of the means of subsistence. In brief, his argument was that population growth always tended to push beyond food supply with disastrous social consequences. The translation from population growth to energy consumption is an easy one and, as we will describe below, the idea that increasing energy consumption has disastrous consequences has had a significant impact on alternative theories of energy.

A. RENEWABLE RESOURCES

The United States consumes approximately 97 quads of energy per year of which renewable energy accounts for 5.9 quads. While 6% appears to be a respectable portion of our energy picture, most of that figure is comprised of hydroelectricity. Further, renewable energy has maintained a fairly constant portion of energy production as shown in Figure 1 below. Fifty years ago, for example, renewable resources accounted for three quads of energy and we have approximately doubled our total consumption since that time.

Figure 1 Renewable Energy Consumption

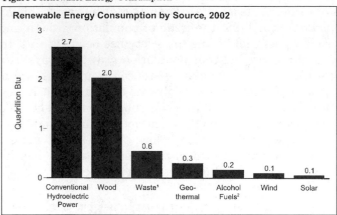

Hydroelectric power, thus plays a key role and, correspondingly, electric power generation consumes 59% of the renewable energy used each year. If we remove hydroelectricity from the picture, then energy generated from waste and geothermal constitutes most of the nonrenewable energy in the United States with a small contribution by wind and solar energy as shown as Figure 2.

Figure 2 Non-Hydroelectric Power Sources

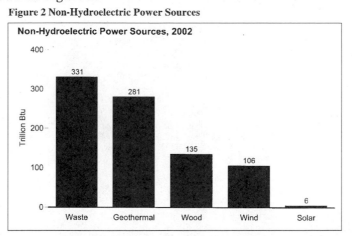

Although the country has had various conservation laws for over 100 years, it was not until the Energy Crisis of the 1970s that Congress addressed alternative energy sources. Recall that President Carter introduced a series of pieces of major legislation under the general heading of the National Energy Act of 1978. For the most part, the National Energy Act addressed traditional energy sources. President Carter followed that legislation with the Energy Security Act of 1980, Pub. L. No. 94–294, 94 Stat. 611 (1980). The Energy Security Act was comprised of several pieces of legislation, many of which will be referenced in specific subsections below. In general, the Energy Security Act addressed a wide variety of renewable and non-renewable alternative sources as a method of reducing dependence on imported oil. To no small extent, the Energy Security Act established a series of financing initiatives for developing alternative sources. Unfortunately, none of these efforts was successful either in reducing dependence on foreign oil or in notably increasing alternative sources of energy production.

If the United States is to move away from the traditional path of heavy reliance on fossil fuels and nuclear power to an alternative path of renewable resources and conservation, then government support seems necessary. Support has come from the Congress through legislation such as the Renewable Energy and Energy Efficiency Technology Competitiveness Act of 1989, 42 U.S.C.A. § 12001. The purpose of the Act is to "pursue an aggressive national program of research, development, and demonstration of renewable energy and energy efficiency technologies in order to ensure a stable and secure future energy supply." 42 U.S.C.A. § 12001(b).

Renewable energy resources are also addressed in EPAct, 42 U.S.C. § 12005. EPAct, for example, amended the Renewable Energy Act by requiring the Secretary of Energy to solicit proposals for demonstration and commercial application projects using renewable energy and energy efficiency technologies through competitive bidding processes. EPAct also encourages the export of renewable energy technologies to developing countries, and establishes a comprehensive database to provide information on energy technology needs of foreign countries with specific reference to renewable energy and energy efficiency technologies and products. EPAct also provides incentive payments to qualified renewable energy facilities which produce electricity from renewable sources, specifically solar, wind, biomass, or geothermal energy.

In short, renewable energy has maintained a modest role in our country's energy picture. According to the Energy Information Administration, "growth in renewable energy continues to be challenged by little or no development of new hydroelectric sites, a slow but lengthy decline in the use of biomass for non-electric purposes, and the high capital costs of most renewable energy production facilities, compared with fossil-fueled alternatives." Energy Information Administration, *Renewable Energy Annual 2002* ix (November 2003). Renewable energy, as is true of all alternative energy sources, must compete against the dominant model. To the extent that it replaces the dominant model, it will only do so as a matter of supply and demand. In other words, renewable energy will become a larger part of the nation's energy picture to the extent that it becomes cost-effective.

1. Solar Energy

Solar energy is principally used for water and space heating, with a growing application in the production of electricity with photovoltaic cells and large solar collectors. The largest solar collector generates 55 megawatts of electricity. A large nuclear plant, by contrast, generates over 1000 megawatts.

An early estimate anticipated that solar power would account for up to 23% of the country's energy needs by the year 2000. R. Stobaugh & D. Yergin, *Energy Future* (1979). That goal has not been met. By the early 1990s, solar power accounted for substantially less of the country's energy production than predicted. Nonetheless, solar energy is considered the premier renewable energy source. It is safe, inexhaustible, and not subject to cartelization, attributes which do not belong to oil, coal, gas, or uranium.

Solar energy is both "passive" and "active." Passive solar, also known as solar thermal, is an energy system designed with no moving parts, such as a house facing south with large double-paned windows. Passive solar energy, together with improved insulation, also incorporates the principle of conservation. Active solar energy involves mechanical moving parts, such as solar collectors that heat air or water which then moves through pipes. The air or water is then fanned or pumped through a heat exchanger in a water-filled storage tank. This hot water can be used to heat a house directly, or indirectly by pumping it through a radiator.

Sunlight can also be converted into electricity through photovoltaic conversion. Photovoltaic cells, like transmission and integrated circuits before them, are semiconductors. Sunlight generates electricity when it falls on specially treated silicon chips. These cells are used in the aerospace industry, but costs have not been reduced sufficiently to make them marketable for mass consumption. Solar Photovoltaic Energy Research, Development, and Demonstration Act of 1978, 42 U.S.C.A. § 5581; Solar Energy and Energy Conservation Act of 1980, 12 U.S.C.A. § 1451 et seq., and 42 U.S.C.A. § 6347 et. seq. The federal regulation of solar energy concentrates on stimulating the market through such devices as the promotion of small power production using solar energy, favorable tax depreciation rates and credits, and research and development. Solar Energy Research Development and Demonstration Act of 1974, 42 U.S.C.A. § 5551–66; Internal Revenue Code §§ 167, 168.

Sunlight is not susceptible to ownership like real property. Because this resource is unique, there is no comprehensive property rights regime for solar power. In order to enjoy the beneficial use of this energy source, the user must have access to sunlight and some legal protection for that access. Generally, access is secured through local or state laws, such as zoning, easements, nuisance, or prior appropriation. See *Prah v. Maretti* (1982) (construction of house created a private nuisance because it would obstruct an adjoining property owner's access to sunlight, and significantly impair the use of a solar energy system).

2. Wind Energy

The scenic windmills of Holland and those that appear on the farm landscapes of the United States harnessed the power from wind for centuries. Those windmills turned wind into mechanical energy to pump water, mill grain, and the like. Today, we look to wind to generate electricity. It has been estimated that there are sufficient wind resources in the United States to develop twice the amount of electric generating capacity as now exists in the country. A.P. Doherty, "U.S. Wind Energy Potential: The Effect of Proximity of Wind Resources to Transmission Lines," *Monthly Energy Review* vii-xiv (February 1995). However, given constraints such as economics, location, and weather variability, the actual potential capacity is considerably less. While we have been accumulating experience and technological improvements over the years, with the result that wind energy is experiencing declining costs, Union of Concerned Scientists, *Powering the Midwest: Renewable Energy for the Economy and the Environment* (1993), like all renewable resources, wind energy cannot be used widely until it becomes cost-effective.

Wind is an attractive energy source because it produces no air or water pollution and involves no toxic or hazardous waste. Consequently, wind poses minimal threats to public safety and to the environment and wind energy projects have been encouraged through the means of tax credits. EPAct 42 U.S.C. 13317. To date, California has about 95% of the operational capacity in the country. In 1994, California had 16,000 operating wind turbines which produced 3.5 billion kilowatt hours of electricity. Energy Information Administration, *Renewable Energy Annual 1995* 3 (1995).

Like other renewable resources, wind energy has grown in importance since the energy crisis of the 1970s. Initially federally funded research projects helped develop wind turbines. Private research and development has continued to develop the technology and improvements have continued to reduce the capital and operating costs. Given the relatively small size of wind turbine projects, another cost factor is remoteness from transmission lines because of the costliness of transmission line construction.

While there have been technological improvements and cost reductions for wind energy, constraints remain. The most significant constraint is the variability of wind. Recall that we cannot effectively store electricity and must then rely on a steady source of power to generate electricity. Therefore, wind driven turbines are dependent upon the nature and consistency of the wind. As a result of inconsistency in producing electricity, financing for wind projects is less attractive than for other sources of electricity generation. Similarly, the variability of wind is also affected by location in particular geographic regions and daily weather conditions. Finally, while wind power is environmentally benign, wind projects do face environmental hurdles. The building of such wind farms is problematic because many consider commercial wind farms aesthetically unpleasing. High speed wind turbine blades also can be quite noisy and, given certain wind and weather conditions, flocks of birds can be drawn into the path of the wind turbine blades.

The role of the federal government in wind programs has largely been financial. In the 1970s the government began funding projects and those funds peaked at $60 million in 1980. During the 1980s, however, those resources declined to less than $10 million per year in 1988 through 1990. In the 1990s funding increased to a level of $45 million in 1995. It declined to about $40 million thereafter. Energy Information Agency, *Renewable Energy Annual 1996* 42 (1996). Consistent with solar energy tax credits, the Energy Policy Act of 1992 also provided tax incentives for wind energy. In addition to financial incentives, the federal government provides technical assistance through the Department of Energy's Wind Energy Program which, together with industry, supports the development and testing of wind turbine technology. The purpose of this program is to decrease costs through increased operating efficiency. In 1994, a joint industry and government organization called the National Wind Coordinating Committee (NWCC) was formed. The purpose of the NWCC was to develop a commercial market for wind power by identifying key issues and by incorporating the views of industry as well as environmentalists in developing this renewable resource.

3. Biomass and Alcohol Fuels

These two sources are discussed together because they are the subject of Title II of the Energy Security Act of 1980, which is known as the Biomass Energy and Alcohol Fuels Act of 1980, 42 U.S.C.A. § 8801 et seq. The Solar Energy Research, Development and Demonstration Act of 1974, 42 U.S.C.A. § 5551, authorizes and funds research into the field of biomass conversion. The Resource Conservation and Recovery Act of 1976 creates a joint federal-state program to study the energy potential of solid wastes. 42 U.S.C.A. § 6901 et seq.

"Biomass" has been broadly defined as "any organic matter which is available on a renewable basis, including agricultural crops and agricultural wastes and residues, wood and wood wastes and residues, animal wastes, municipal wastes, and aquatic plants." 42 U.S.C.A. § 8802. Biomass is converted to methane gas through the decomposition of organic matter. The energy derived from biomass is originally solar energy stored in organic matter through the process of photosynthesis. This energy can be reclaimed from the harvesting of live plants or from wastes.

Biomass comes from several possible sources including animal manure, landfills which are garbage depositories, coal which can be converted into gas, biomass which comes from aquatic sources, crop residue, peat, sewage, sludge, and ethanol which is produced from feed stalks such as corn. For the most part, biomass is converted into methane gas. It can also be converted into liquid fuel ethanol used in the transportation industry.

The Department of Energy's Office of Energy Efficiency and Renewable Energy oversees several biomass research programs and created the Office of the Biomass Program. The purpose of the Office is to engage in the development of biofuels, biopower, and bioproducts on a sustainable basis under the assumption that biomass can contribute to domestic energy supply, provide for a cleaner environment, and stimulate economic growth particularly in rural communities.

Key research and development initiatives of the Office of the Biomass Program include thermochemical conversion and bioconversion. Thermochemical conversion creates synthetic gas for heat, power, and other purposes. Bioconversion transforms biomass into useful fuels and chemicals. In addition, the Program looks at refineries and the development of bio-based products such as engine oils and solvents, plastics and enzymes. Research is also being conducted to develop small electric generators from the 1 kilowatt to the 5 megawatt range.

While the application of biomass for products and transportation fuels has been developing for years, biomass is also being developed for power generation. It is the hope that biomass and other renewables have essentially benign environmental consequences thus reducing carbon dioxide emissions.

The Alcohol Fuels Act provided hundreds of millions of dollars of appropriations to the Secretary of Energy and the Secretary of Agriculture to carry out energy production from biomass energy sources to produce gasohol and ethanol. Through various financial devices such as insured loans, loan guarantees, and price guarantees, the federal government helped research and development in this area.

4. Geothermal

Geothermal energy is generated by the heat from the earth's interior. This heat can be used to turn turbines to generate electricity. It is a relatively safe and clean fuel. The environmental repercussions in developing this resource include noise, odors, thermal pollution, the discharge of dissolved materials into surface or ground waters, and subsidence. The relative environmental safety and cleanliness of this resource stem from the fact that these hazards occur principally at the site rather than throughout the fuel cycle, as is the case with coal or oil.

Most geothermal heat resides in the earth's molten core and mantle below the earth's crust at depths incapable of being tapped by drilling. However, there are locations around the globe, called "hot spots," where the earth's protective crust is sufficiently shallow to permit human access to geothermal heat. In certain places, there are hot springs or geysers (like Old Faithful in Yellowstone National Park) where geothermal energy has broken the earth's surface. In the United States, as much as 1.3 million acres of land, including Alaska and Hawaii, have potential for power production from geothermal energy. Most of the potential domestic geothermal sites are located in the western United States, the most productive of which are in the Geysers region of California.

In 1960, the Pacific Gas and Electric Company became the first American utility to generate electricity from geothermal steam in the Geysers region. In 1986, the Geysers region generated 10.3 billion kilowatt hours of electricity, and at a lower cost than fossil fuel generation in the same area. Electricity generated from geothermal sources peaked in 1987 at

11 billion kilowatt hours. Geothermal steam has high economic value. In *Grace Geothermal v. Northern Cal. Power Agency* (N.D. Cal. 1985), one prospective purchaser offered $145 million for an interest in a federal geothermal leasehold.

Geothermal energy comes from two sources. Electricity can be produced from hot dry rock under the earth's surface by locating the hot rocks, pumping water into and out of the area, and thus creating steam to turn a turbine to generate electricity. Research into this technology is being performed by the Hot Dry Rock Program of the Geothermal Division of the Department of Energy. According to the last Energy Information Agency report, this technology remains uneconomical. Although energy funding has stopped in the United States, research continues in Japan and France. Energy Information Agency, *Renewable Energy Annual 1996* (1997).

The other way that geothermal energy can be extracted is directly for heating and for heat pumps. This direct use can be used for district heating or heat pumps. District heating involves delivery of heat to end users after passing fluid through a heat exchanger. District heating is an open loop system and the fluid can be delivered or not to the end user, but in either case, it is reinjected under the ground or disposed of on the surface. Geothermal heat pumps have been efficient technology for home cooling and heating and operate similar to a home boiler or refrigerator insofar as they form a closed loop system.

There are several active geothermal projects in the United States, including plants in Nevada, Hawaii, and California that range from 13 to 33 megawatts. Perhaps the most significant recent event in the United States was the start-up of a 40 megawatt plant in the Salton Sea.

Geothermal energy is generally seen as environmentally friendly. This energy source has a minimal negative impact on the environment insofar as it does not release carbon dioxide or nitrous oxide into the atmosphere. While geothermal power plants do emit sulfur, they do so at a fraction of the sulfur emissions from fossil fuel alternatives. Geothermal plants require relatively little land, and adjoining lands can be used with little to no interference. The most significant impact, however, is the destruction of rare geyser activity as a result of changing water levels in a particular area.

The Energy Security Act addressed the field of geothermal development with the enactment of the Geothermal Energy Act of 1980, 30 U.S.C.A. § 1501. The Act is designed to promote this resource by overcoming economic and institutional barriers. Loans will be made in connection with the Geothermal Energy Research, Development, and Demonstration Act of 1974, 30 U.S.C.A. § 1101, to assist in the exploration of geothermal reservoirs. The Act also provides for a study of the feasibility of establishing a reservoir insurance program, and for a study of financial incentives for the development of geothermal resources for nonelectric applications.

One state and federal law problem with geothermal resources has been to determine whether they belong to the owner of the underlying "mineral" estate or to the surface estate owner. Geothermal resources have been held to be the property of the mineral estate rather than the property of the surface owner. *Geothermal Kinetics, Inc. v. Union Oil Co.* (Cal.App. 1977). The geothermal owner may enter the surface estate and build an electrical generating plant, even when the surface owner objects. *Occidental Geothermal, Inc. v. Simmons* (N.D. Cal.1982).

The United States owns a significant amount of land where geothermal resources are located. Congress early adopted a policy of leasing geothermal resources on federal lands pursuant to the Geothermal Steam Act of 1970, 30 U.S.C.A. § 1001, *Crownite Corp. v. Watt* (9th Cir. 1985); *Getty Oil Co. v. Andrus* (9th Cir. 1979). The Ninth Circuit has held that the federal government reserved the rights to the geothermal resources covered by the Stock–Raising Homestead Act of 1961. *United States v. Union Oil Co.* (9th Cir. 1977).

B.   CONSERVATION AND ENERGY EFFICIENCY

1.   Conservation

Another "alternative fuel source" is conservation. Energy conservation has two meanings. First, energy is conserved simply by consuming less. Second, energy is conserved as energy production and use become more efficient. Conservation through greater efficiency can take place on a number of fronts. Retrofitting of buildings and appliances or producing more fuel efficient or alternative fuel cars can conserve energy. Tax credits and deductions can be used to encourage installation of conservation measures. Taxes can also be used to increase the cost of energy, thus reducing demand and use. The decontrol of fuel prices in a time of shortage will also bring about conservation by causing prices to rise and demand to fall. The government can directly curtail supplies, and thus force conservation. A crude example of such curtailment is lower speed limits.

Three federal statutes enacted during the energy "crisis" days of the 1970s promote conservation. The Energy Policy and Conservation Act, 42 U.S.C.A. § 6201, includes such measures as appliance and car efficiency standards, industrial conservation targets, federal conservation efforts, and grants for state conservation programs. The Energy Conservation and Production Act, 42 U.S.C.A. § 6801, establishes an office for energy information and analysis, and proposes energy conservation standards for new buildings.

Perhaps the most sweeping conservation act is the National Energy Conservation Policy Act (NECPA), 42 U.S.C.A. § 8201. Title II of the Act addresses residential energy conservation. Under the Act, the Secretary of Energy is directed to establish procedures for the creation and implementation of residential energy conservation plans by state utility regulatory authorities. The Secretary is authorized to implement and enforce a federal plan in the event of inadequate state action. Specifically addressing residences, for example, the Act has allowed an increase in the eligible income level for weatherization grants as well as established a financing program for the installation of weatherization materials.

Title III of the Act addresses energy conservation in schools, hospitals, and buildings owned by local governments. The Secretary is authorized to make grants to states to conduct energy audits in such facilities as well as to finance conservation projects. Title IV of the Act provides civil penalties for violations of fuel economy standards, requires fuel efficiency disclosure for certain vehicles and requires an Environmental Protection Agency report on the accuracy of fuel economy estimates for new automobiles. Title IV also directs the Secretary to establish energy efficiency standards for specific household appliances and certain classes of industrial equipment.

Title V of the Act addresses federal energy initiatives and amends the Energy Policy and Conservation Act. The Secretary of Energy is directed to establish a program to demonstrate solar heating and cooling technology in federal buildings as well as to set criteria for evaluating federal agency proposals regarding such demonstration programs. Title V also declares it to be the policy of the United States that the federal government have the responsibility to promote the use of energy conservation, solar heating and cooling, and other renewable energy sources in federal buildings. The Secretary is likewise directed to establish energy performance targets for federal buildings. The Act also establishes a photovoltaic energy commercialization program for federal facilities.

Finally, Title VI of the Act expands the already existing industrial energy reporting system to reach other industries identified by the Secretary as major energy consuming industries or industries with a need for at least one trillion BTU's of energy per year. The Act also requires utilities to adopt a comprehensive conservation program. Each utility must inform its residential customers who own or occupy a residential building about suggested conservation measures, the savings in energy costs that are likely to result, a list of suppliers and lenders for energy savings installations, and suggestions regarding energy conservation techniques.

2. Energy Efficiency

The Department of Energy views energy efficiency as a vital component of the nation's energy strategy. In an effort to promote that strategy, the DOE is engaged in measuring efficiency through its Office of Energy Markets and End Use. The DOE uses the concept of "energy intensity" to describe the amount of energy actually used or consumed relative to the amount demanded. Energy Information Agency, *Measuring Energy Efficiency in the United States' Economy: A Beginning* (October 1995).

In the residential sector, it was found that, while people were purchasing more electric appliances, frequently those appliances used less energy than older models. See National Appliance Energy Conservation Act of 1987, 42 U.S.C. § 6201. The amount of energy consumed in the residential sector is greatly affected both by location and by weather, which make data sometimes difficult to accumulate. With roughly 90 million households in the United States, over the last twenty years, energy consumption has remained relatively stable even though the number of homes and the population has been growing steadily.

In the commercial sector, we have experienced some changes due to reactions to the energy supply disruptions in the 1970s. As a result of those disruptions, commercial buildings were being designed for particular climates with better insulation, more efficient space heating, lighting, and air conditioning. Nevertheless, there has been a generally steady increase in energy consumption since that time. During the period that the DOE measured energy intensity, it found that during periods of economic growth, energy efficiency decreased and during periods of economic recession or recovery, energy efficiency increased. In short, the gains and losses in energy efficiency in the commercial sector have been roughly off-setting.

In the transportation sector, energy consumption continues to grow. In an attempt to achieve energy efficiencies, Congress passed the Energy Policy and Conservation Act of 1975, Pub. L. No. 94–163, which established corporate average fuel economy (CAFE) standards for automakers. These standards have been subject to controversy ever since their enactment. The current controversy involves whether some trucks and popular models of passenger vehicles such as sports utility vehicles, should be subject to higher CAFE standards than currently apply.

In the industrial sector we have begun to consume less energy recently as a result of a decrease in manufacturing activity. Like the commercial sector, depending upon particular energy users, there have been gains noted as well as losses registered in energy efficiency. In short, measuring energy efficiency and the gathering of sufficient data and information by DOE is just beginning; therefore reliable analysis and prediction are difficult.

C. ALTERNATIVES TO TRADITIONAL ENERGY SOURCES

Earlier we mentioned two alternatives to traditional energy sources. One is an alternative to large-scale power production and the other is fossil fuel alternatives to coal, oil, and natural gas, which we discuss immediately below.

1. Distributed Generation

As the electric industry continues along the path of deregulation, one impediment to complete deregulation involves the transmission segment as discussed in Chapter 8. To date, large-scale power facilities can generate electricity at a more efficient rate and the inability to store the product diminishes the possibility of more localized distribution. As a response to both constraints is the concept of distributed generation, which constitute smaller electric generators and generators that are closer to the load. In this way, reliance on the existing transmission network can be reduced and the cost of transmission can be lowered. Distributed generation involves new technologies for generating mostly under 50 megawatts, including photovoltaics, microturbines, fuel cells, as well as others, which can reduce the scale of the production as well as provide for the storage of the product in various ways. Distributed generation is also seen as a way of moving electricity toward a more competitive marketplace. Both industry and government projections indicate an increasing use of these technologies.

Distributed generation technology can be used to achieve several purposes, including providing energy to consumers; meeting peak demand requirements; maintaining additional reserve capacity; contributing to power reliability; and serving as back-up and stand-by service. Perhaps not so ironically, the whole idea of distributed generation was exactly the idea that Edison tried to displace with the first central power station in New York City. The concept of the central power station was antithetical to the then prevalent isolated plants (forerunners of distributed generation).

Given the variety of services that can be supplied by distributed generation providers, the market will grow competitive as consumers can pick and choose which of the DG services they will purchase. We also hope that distributed generation can have positive environmental effects as well as achieve increased energy efficiencies.

2.   Synthetic Fuels

The Energy Security Act of 1980 established the United States Synfuels Corporation to stimulate the commercialization of synthetic oil and gas. According to the Act, a "synthetic fuel" is defined as "any solid, liquid, or gas which can be used as a substitute for petroleum or natural gas and which is produced by chemical or physical transformation of domestic sources of coal, shale, tar sands, and water." 42 U.S.C.A. § 8702. Synthetic fuels development was to be accomplished through federal subsidy of private efforts to extract liquids and gas from coal, oil shale, and tar sands. Federal subsidies took the form of loans, loan guarantees, price guarantees, purchase agreements, joint ventures, and, as a last resort, direct ownership by the federal government. The original goals of the Synfuels Corporation were to subsidize production of 500,000 barrels a day of synfuels by 1987, and 2,000,000 barrels a day by 1992. These goals were never met.

Basically, synfuels are oil replacements which result from processing oil shale and tar sands into liquid, and from the gasification of coal. Because of the great abundance of oil shale, tar sands, and coal, and because technologies exist for their transformation, synfuels are scientifically and technologically promising energy sources. However, synfuels are not commercially feasible. They are more expensive than conventional fuels. Environmental problems also surround synfuels' processes, not the least of which is the possibility of climatic change due to the release of massive amounts of carbon dioxide into the atmosphere from the burning of carbon-based fuels.

The most advanced synthetic fuels technology is coal gasification. In this process, coal is heated together with steam in a "gasifier." The gasifier causes some of the hydrogen in the steam to join with the carbon in the coal to form methane, the primary ingredient of natural gas. Coal gasification has certain environmental and distributional advantages. Gasification of coal removes harmful sulfur, particulates, and heavy metals to produce a clean burning gas. In addition, there already exists a network of natural gas pipelines to transport the gas to end-users.

Coal can also be converted to oil through a process of liquefaction. Liquefaction was used extensively by Germany during World War II. Millions of barrels of oil a year were produced directly from coal in Germany during the war years by using inexpensive, disposable catalysts. Other liquefaction methods first convert coal to gas and then convert the gas to oil. The DOE has experimented with several coal-to-oil technologies.

Oil shale is sedimentary rock containing an organic rock-like material called kerogen. The kerogen may be processed by heating it into shale oil, a form of crude oil. The United States has an abundance of oil shale. Known reserves amount to about 600 billion barrels of oil and possible reserves may exceed two trillion barrels of oil. The most extensive and highest grade of oil shale deposits in the United States are located in the Rocky Mountain States of Colorado, Utah, and Wyoming. In this region, oil shale is contained in three basins, the Piceance Basin, the Green River Basin, and Uinta Basin. The Piceance Basin in northwestern Colorado has the largest deposits of high-grade oil shale, estimated at 1.3 trillion barrels of oil (more than the amount of oil underlying Saudi Arabia.)

Oil may be extracted from oil shale either by conventional mining and surface processing (surface retorting), or by the use of water to extract the oil from the shale while it is still in the ground (in situ processing). The major problems associated with recovery of oil from shale are water availability and pollution. Shale oil development on a scale of 1 million barrels of oil a day is estimated to require between 121,000 to 189,000 acre-feet of water per year. Oil shale also produces waste water which is high in salt content. In addition, spent shale must be disposed of, and the retorting process produces emissions which causes air quality to deteriorate.

Tar sands are deposits bearing hydrocarbons that are not capable of production using ordinary oil wells because of the high viscosity of the tar hydrocarbons. Tar sands include oil sands, bitumen sands, and rocks that bear oil or bitumen. In North America, the richest known tar sands deposits are in Utah (up to 30 billion barrels or more) and near Alberta, Canada (up to 250 billion barrels). Most tar sands are not near the surface and thus may not be strip mined. However, once-recovered, extraction of the hydrocarbon from tar sands is much more efficient and consumes less energy than the extraction of kerogen from oil shale. There are no commercial tar sands operations in the United States. Even if developed, the impact of tar sands on the total domestic energy supply picture is thought to be limited.

While synfuels are scientifically and technically feasible, synfuel projects are not economically competitive with conventional oil and natural gas resources. Since 1984 until recently, the United States enjoyed a glut of oil and a "bubble" of natural gas. With so much supply, the price of oil and gas was low, and there was little pressure to develop synfuels. Not surprisingly, the federal government removed itself almost completely from synfuels development. The Synfuels Corporation was funded initially at $24 billion dollars. In the early 1980s, the Corporation's budget was slashed to $8 billion, of which $5.7 billion was required to meet the substantive commitments already undertaken by the Corporation. On December 12, 1985, the Synfuels Corporation was dissolved.

D. ALTERNATIVE ENERGY POLICIES

Discussion of alternative energy policies can trace its recent history to the environmental movement beginning in the 1960s. Books such as Aldo Leopold, *A Sand County Almanac* (1949) and Rachel Carson, *Silent Spring* (1962) became popular and brought awareness to threats posed by man to nature. An influential empirical study by a group of scientists and economists called the Club of Rome, *The Limits to Growth* (1972) raised the alarm about the irreversible consequences of continued resource consumption. Such publications fueled the environmental movement and also influenced a movement toward alternative energy policies.

Alternative energy policy can be discerned as having three periods. In the late 1960s and early 1970s, the environmental movement provided the impetus for energy policies sensitive to clean air and water, particularly for cleaner burning coal and for the promotion of renewable resources. The energy "crisis" of the mid–1970s moved alternative policies in two directions. First, the crisis demonstrated that conservation could play an important role in energy planning. Second, renewable alternatives to limited supplies of oil and natural gas were sought. The final period is just beginning. Events of the late 1980s, especially with the publicity surrounding global warming, reinvigorated the earlier discussion about renewable resources and conservation. Today, the effort is being made to wed environmental and energy policies in a complementary fashion under the rubric of sustainable development.

The dominant model of United States energy policy relies on the hard path of large-scale, capital intensive high-technologies. President Carter's Energy Security Act of 1980 evinced a government commitment to experiment with, and fund, research and development of alternative fuels, and a willingness to try alternative policies. As things turned out, this effort was sustained neither by economic markets nor by political preferences. Instead, since the late 1970s and early 1980s, support has diminished and we find ourselves fairly well settled into conventional policies.

We can point, however, to a significant policy development. Until the mid–1980s, energy laws and policies and environmental laws and policies were largely distinct areas. Since then, environmental laws and policies have taken into consideration their costs and benefits and are increasingly tested against market-based standards. Energy laws and policies, likewise, pay increasing attention to their environmental consequences.

The emergence of environmental law throughout the 1970s, together with the energy crisis of that period brought to our awareness a basic conflict at the heart of both policies. The conflict was perhaps best described in Amory Lovins' book, *Soft Energy Paths: Toward a Durable Peace* (1979), which contrasted a soft path of renewable, energy-efficient, small scale alternative resources with the traditional hard path of capital-intensive, large scale, nuclear and conventional fossil fuels. Lovins argued that soft paths were not only environmentally sensitive, but made sound economic sense and that the country should no longer entertain the belief that there was a direct relation between energy growth and economic growth.

The controversy regarding an energy-GNP link is not inconsequential and the belief in a direct link is very powerful. Robert Stobaugh & Daniel Yergin, *Energy Future* (1979); Julian L. Simon & Herman Kahn, *The Resourceful Earth: A Response to Global 2000* (1984). The discussion of the energy-GNP link has two dimensions. First, those who prefer energy alternatives argue that there is no direct connection between more energy consumption and a better economy and feel a concern that prices will rise to unacceptable levels if we continue to rely on traditional fuels. Second, for those who prefer markets, the linkage is real but because resources are plentiful, prices will not rise to unacceptable levels.

After the energy crisis, energy policymakers began to talk with environmentalists about the harmful consequences of energy exploration and production. At the same time, environmentalists became aware of certain market realities, that is, that consumers would use conventional resources as long as conventional resources were cheaper than alternatives. In addition, environmental policymakers realized that there is a significant role to be played by the market in curbing pollution, promoting conservation, and promoting the use of alternative resources. Policymakers then went on to advocate the use of market-based incentives, for example, emissions trading, to further environmental goals.

During this time, international environmentalism became a more significant field for policymakers. International environmentalists had to confront an extremely difficult dilemma, however. It is one thing to argue that developed countries should impose strict environmental standards. It is quite another thing to try to force developing countries to adopt strict (i.e., costly) environmental standards which may retard their economic growth. From this conflict between the need for developing countries to sustain economic growth, and the need to recognize the harmful consequences of energy production, the concept of sustainable development was born.

1. Energy Futures

To a certain extent, the environmental movement can claim priority in our nation's attention coming full-blown as it did on the effective date of the National Environmental Policy Act of January 1, 1970. Ten years later, after the energy crisis of the 1970s and the crisis of Three Mile Island, "energy futures" study began to appear. Publications such as *Resources for the Future, Energy: The Next Twenty Years* (1979), Robert Stobaugh & Daniel Yergin, *Energy Future: Report of the Energy Project at the Harvard Business School* (1979), and Sam H. Schurr, *Energy in America's Future: The Choices Before Us* (1979) began to look at the nation's energy supply problems and propose future scenarios. The concerns of those studies were less about environmental consequences than about the effect that depleting resources would have on the economy. These studies addressed the concern that the country was running out of energy, and markets were inadequately responsive to our needs for a reliable supply of energy. Of course, they were also concerned about the country's dependence on foreign oil which, as we have learned, has not abated. For the most part, the studies argued that neither the country nor the world was running out of energy and that adequate supplies existed, although it should be expected that prices would rise—but not drastically.

A review of energy futures reports raises the question whether or not the country should or can, in fact, develop a comprehensive and coordinated energy policy and concludes that the chance of such an effort's succeeding is for several reasons minimal. Paul L. Joskow, *Energy Policies and Their Consequences After Twenty-Five Years*, 24 ENERGY JOURNAL 17 (2003). Joskow argues that a comprehensive policy is unlikely because there has never been sustained national leadership to develop a long-term energy program. Joskow then argues that the one clear way to reduce demand is to allow prices to rise but that that idea has been politically unacceptable. Consequently, government regulations continue in an effort to keep prices "reasonable." Finally, he recognizes how politically contentious energy debates are, as we have seen most recently with the failure of the Energy Security Act of 2003.

Energy future studies overpredicted the amount of energy consumption and overpredicted the increase in energy prices. Nevertheless, their basic premises, with the exception of reducing dependence on foreign oil, seem to be relatively accurate. There are adequate supplies of energy, the market mechanisms are effective ways to control supply and demand, and alternative markets should be developed.

For the most part, the studies just mentioned rely on conventional fuels and sources of supply. To the extent that their predictions about the future were off, they were not off by much, and, as noted, the country has maintained the status quo. Other energy futures have also been discussed. Policy analyses such as *The Limits to Growth*, Bill McKibben, *The End of Nature* (1989), and Amory B. Lovins, *Soft Energy Paths: Toward a Durable Peace* (1977) argue for changes in consumption behavior, for increased environmental protection, and for more aggressive use of alternative energy conservation measures. Such studies argue that human activity has irreversibly and negatively altered the environment in the case of *The Limits to Growth* and *The End of Nature* and that energy savings abound through conservation in the case of *Soft Energy Paths*. To some extent, this is an extreme picture which argues that the very health of the planet depends upon radical change.

These two sets of studies about our energy future present opposite poles and present a choice between the traditional path and a radically new one. One example of an attempt to mediate between the continuation of the accustomed national energy policy and the "end of nature" scenario is attempted by the Natural Resources Defense Council in *A Responsible Energy Policy for the 21st Century* (March 2001). The NRDC policy takes account of the economic realities of energy as well as the needs of the environment. Recognizing that the energy industry plays an important role in the economy and that energy policy must continue to provide affordable energy services, the NRDC proposal addresses industrial innovation as well as environmental protection as a way of thinking about the future. The report also pays attention to the increasing difficulty and cost of extracting and producing additional resources. The report also argues for a reduction in dependence on oil and coal as well as an increase in energy efficiency and technological improvements and investments. For example, the report cites that between 1975 and 2001, manufacturers developed energy efficient refrigerators that consumed only 75% of the electric power used by the ones built before 1975. The NRDC says that 60,000 megawatts of electricity are saved, as well as reducing the corresponding amount of power plant emissions. The report goes on to say that the cost of building 60,000 megawatts of power plants would have been $50 billion compared with the industry's investment of less than one billion dollars to produce the more efficient refrigerators. Similarly, CAFE standards have had a positive effect on reducing gasoline consumption and the report indicates that those standards should be increased to promote even further conservation. The report provides recommendations for oil, electricity, and natural gas as well and develops a moderate plan for an energy future.

Regardless of the energy future that we choose, greater awareness of global climactic and environmental changes, changes in domestic and world markets, disparate use and distribution of energy, and wealth among the countries of the world challenge policymakers to reject business as usual and attend to the future. Energy policymakers must anticipate the long-term social costs associated with large-scale projects, even as they set policy for short- and medium-term energy needs. Likewise, environmental policymakers must factor into their more ambitious programs the short- and medium-term energy needs of active and productive national economies.

2. An Alternative Energy Policy: The Sustainable Development Model

Over the last decade and one half an emerging alternative energy policy has developed called "sustainable development." "Sustainable development" is defined as a policy or program that "meets the needs of the present without compromising the ability of future generations to meet their own needs." World Commission on Environment and Development, *Our Common Future* 8 (1987). Sustainable development is driven by two concerns. First, energy production and environmental protection should work together through the common language that sustainable development provides. Second, this common language should facilitate cooperation among developed and developing countries. Thus, the model requires energy and environmental policymakers to look to safety, intergenerational effects, democratic political participation, and environmental care, as much as to efficiency, productivity, and wealth creation.

Does the choice of a new energy/environmental vision necessitate a change in life style? This is the important cultural question. It is the cultural question that makes decision makers hesitate before they adopt alternatives to the dominant model. The dominant vision promises wealth creation, economic efficiency, and energy production for a healthy society. The alternative vision promises an equitable distribution of goods, environmental protection, and ecological sensitivity. The sustainable development vision promises a melding of all of these.

Today "sustainability" is part of the rhetoric of United States domestic energy policy. In 1991, the Bush Administration published a *National Energy Strategy* which begins: "The National Energy Strategy lays the foundation for a more efficient, less vulnerable, and environmentally sustainable energy future." Likewise, President Clinton has addressed sustainable development as has President George W. Bush (see respectively President's Council on Sustainable Development, Sustainable America: A New Consensus for the Future (1996); National Energy Policy Development Group, National Energy Plan (May 2001)). Nevertheless, the country has yet to deliver the idea of bring to actuality the rhetoric of sustainability in real day-to-day policies except in a few cases. The country has exercised caution on expanding oil exploration and production in environmentally sensitive areas. The Clean Air Act amendments also address greenhouse gases. The Endangered Species Act was reenacted, conservation measures promoted, and renewables supported with research and development as examples of an environmentally sensitive energy policy.

The Iraqi invasion of Kuwait on August 2, 1990, the 1991 War in the Gulf, and to some extent the current war in Iraq, raise serious concerns about the country's energy security. Once again, reminiscent of the mid–1970s, energy policymakers called for energy policy planning, a strategy for reducing dependence on foreign oil, possibly greater use of nuclear power, increased conservation, and increased domestic oil exploration. Although the oil shortfall caused by the Iraqi invasion of Kuwait was made up, the hypersensitive geopolitics of the Middle East oil supply, and the ease with which disruptions can occur, tend to destabilize energy planning. In a period of such destabilization, the likely course is to follow familiar paths. In other words and unfortunately, future energy policies seem more likely to resemble traditional fossil fuel policies than alternative policies such as the sustainable development model. The first decades of the 21st century will be important for energy law and policy planning as the dominant model confronts global challenges.

E. CONCLUSION

The key to understanding the political economy of energy is recognizing the symbiotic relationship between government and industry, which is manifest by four characteristics. First, in some segments of the industry energy resources are complementary, so the regulation or promotion of one does not necessarily adversely affect the other. Oil and electricity, for example, divide the energy pie into two more or less equal shares. Electricity does not occupy much of the transportation sector, and oil is an uneconomic means of producing electricity. Therefore, federal energy policy can support both oil and electricity production. Second, other energy resources are susceptible to inter-fuel competition. A federal policy that promotes the use of coal to generate electricity simultaneously discourages the use of nuclear power for the same purpose, thus promoting competition. Third, industry and government depend on each other for the distribution and allocation of economic benefits and burdens. The federal government, for example, controls most of the new oil reserves but depends on private industry for their development. Finally, both business and government are stimulated to act by market disequilibria. Oil price controls were responses to the embargoes, and increased exploration for natural gas was the reaction to a loosening of federally established prices. This interplay between government and industry has created the dominant policy model described above.

Domestic energy policy from the late nineteenth century to the present is based on the fundamental assumption that a link exists between the level of energy production and the gross domestic product. As more energy is produced, prices will remain stable or relatively low and the GDP will grow. Implicit in this simple formula is the thesis that the general welfare increases in direct proportion to the GDP. Energy policy continues to rely on this fundamental assumption and reiterates its faith in the market.

As a consequence, domestic energy policy favors large-scale, high-technology, capital-intensive, integrated, and centralized producers of energy from fossil fuels. These archetype energy firms are favored over alternatives such as small solar or wind firms because energy policymakers believe that the larger firms can continue to realize economies of scale. Policymakers gamble that greater energy efficiencies can be achieved by archetype firms, rather than by alternative firms, through technological innovation, discovery of new reserves, and discovery of new energy sources. Put another way, as long as energy production, consumption, and prices remain stable, the embedded policy will continue. Thus, the dominant energy policy has the following general goals:

(1) to assure abundant supplies;

(2) to maintain reasonable prices;

(3) to limit the market power of archetype firms;

(4) to promote inter- and intrafuel competition;

(5) to support a limited number of conventional fuels (oil, natural gas, coal, hydropower, and nuclear power); and,

(6) to allow energy decisionmaking and policymaking to develop within an active federal-state regulatory system.

This policy, developed over the last 100 years, has served the country well by providing long periods of reliable energy supply and respectable degrees of economic stability. In light of this historical intransigence, we can project this policy into the future.

We have yet to resolve a fundamental conflict between energy policy and environmental policy. Energy policy, regardless of its awareness of its negative environmental consequences, is firmly based on the idea that economic development and growth is of central importance to the country. Environmental policy, regardless of its accommodation to market-based regulations, is firmly based on the idea that resources protection is fundamental to human happiness.

Both attitudes, of course, are correct. It may very well be the case that both attitudes are reconcilable as our earlier discussion of the optimal level of pollution demonstrates. Nevertheless, the discussion of optimal pollution was about a model, not about reality. The problem remains for policymakers to develop market-based regulations that incorporate environmental and other social costs in energy prices. In other words, applying the model is extremely difficult because it is extremely difficult (we hesitate to say impossible) to quantify the benefits of environmental policy. Thus, the failure to "internalize the externalities" results in economic gain at the cost of environmental degradation.

INDEX

References are to Pages

385

†